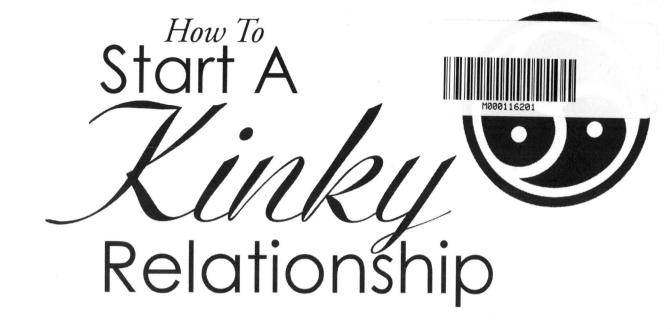

How To
Start A
Kinky
Relationship

*The definitive
guide to starting and
sustaining a healthy, loving,
satisfying alternative relationship.*

James Amoureux

How To Start A Kinky Relationship
By James Amoureux
Copyright © 2011 James Amoureux, The TantraLogic Group

ISBN: 0-61545-855-6
ISBN-13: 978-0-61545-855-7

Legal Disclaimer:
The content of this book shall in no way be construed as legal advice. All concepts, suggestions, examples, and guidelines provided herein are for informational purposes only. Anyone with specific legal questions is advised to consult an appropriate professional familiar with the laws in your area.

Special thanks to (in alphabetical order): Add, Ben, Carly, Chuck, Clarisse, David, Derek, Eric, Eyb, The Falcon, Franklin, Jason, Kirill, Kitten, Nadia, Nemp, The Next Generation Chicago, Phil, President Kennedy, and Suzy.

www.tantralogic.com

To all the people who made this book possible. Especially the freaky ones.

Contents

About The Author

James Amoureux is the founder of The TantraLogic Group, a sex education and relationship coaching service dedicated to freeing men and women to experience more fulfilling love lives. He is a professional psychologist with a background in social psychology and human development. His expertise in meditation, altered mental states, and mind-body connectedness has allowed him to experience and share the core elements of Tantric sexuality and spiritual practices.

Having discovered the joys of bondage when he stumbled upon his uncle's girlie magazines at age ten, James had his first serious kinky relationship when he was seventeen and has incorporated various aspects of role play, bondage, domination, and submission into his sexual repertoire for over twenty years.

James has personally worked with hundreds of people to uncover the most important and rewarding elements of their sexuality. His diverse experience affords him a unique perspective on how sexuality, social anxiety, societal norms, and kink come together in a relationship—and how they foster (or stifle) the loving, healthy, productive communication that leads to great sex and deep intimacy.

Introduction

This book is for the kink-curious novice as well as the seasoned bondage master and long time S&M submissive. People who never had the pleasure of a kinky relationship will find all the tools they need to get the ball rolling. People who have been kinky in the past but "just fell into it" will have a systematic approach to starting and growing their next relationship. People who already self-identify as *kinky* or *queer* or *pervert* will find plenty of insights that will improve their overall communication and sexual relationships.

This book delves into the mindset, activities, and communication styles that make kinky relationships great. It shows you how to get comfortable with kink, find partners, screen them for compatibility, communicate your desires, and grow your relationship. It does not detail rope bondage techniques, how to become a leather-studded sex machine, or how to use the Force to lure unsuspecting Jedi to *the Kinky side*. Rather it will help you understand your own personal preferences and how to find a compatible partner to play with.

The focus of this book is on relationships, not landing kinky quickies with your online hook up. Still, casual encounters follow the same principles: know what you want, be congruent, define your relationship terms, get enthusiastic consent, and take responsibility for your actions. Then you can keep yourself busy having the most amazing, wild, mind-blowing sex the world has ever known.

Enjoy your love life, may it be a kinky and wild ride.

James Amoureux
The TantraLogic Group

How To Use This Workbook

First and foremost this is a workbook and not some abstract tome or theoretical treatment of human sexuality (and sure as hell not the final word on kinky sex). Generalizing about human beings is inexact, rife with contradictions and counter-examples. Perfect generality is generally perfectly useless so instead you are asked to use the discussions and examples to guide your investigation of your own and your partner's sexual tastes.

Chapter Sections

Each chapter in this workbook presents a concept relating to kink, sexuality, and relationships. Keywords and definitions are shown in **bold.** Technical terms are defined when they are first used or are found within the glossaries at the end of the workbook (see below).

Personal Examples

Throughout the workbook you will see personal examples and sidebar anecdotes demarcated by a pair of handcuffs. These sidebars serve to illustrate the concepts being discussed from the author's admittedly hetero-euro-andro-uppermiddle-classico-anthropomorpo-control-freako perspective. But if you use your imagination and change around select pronouns, you'll be able to see yourself in a few similar situations.

Devil's Advocate

A *Devil's Advocate* is a person who takes a skeptical stance. They argue a case from the opposite perspective, challenge the evidence, and press for proof. The questions asked by a devil's advocate promote a richer and more complete understanding of the topic being discussed. Near the end of each chapter a *Devil's Advocate* question and answer section recaps the main ideas and offers a slightly different take on the material being considered. If you have concerns or reservations as you read, see if the question and answer format of the *Devil's Advocate* section clears them up.

Think For Yourself

You gain the most benefit from this workbook if you *critically engage* the material and challenge yourself to apply what you read. Because a step-by-step treatment can't possibly account for the variety of personal preferences everyone has and because your own preferences are unique to you, answer the *Think For Yourself* questions at the end of each chapter so you gain a deeper insight into your own sexuality. Don't just leave them jumbled in your head—actually write your thoughts down! If you don't want your partner or your roommate to pry, write your answers on a separate sheet of paper.

Glossary of BDSM/Polyamory Terms

The Glossary of BDSM Terms and Glossary of Polyamory Terms serves as a supplement to add depth to the concepts discussed in the chapters. Readers who are more experienced with kink and fetish activities will be able to read the chapters without being slowed down by excessive terminology, whereas readers new to kink and fetish activities are advised to skim the glossary to acquaint themselves with many of the concepts and terms being discussed.

Appendix Worksheets

The appendix consists of tools and worksheets of worksheets that allow you to discuss and plan your sexual activities with your partner. Once you have completed the workbook the appendix will come in handy as you maintain and grow your relationship with your kinky partner.

- **Appendix 1: Ideal Partner Profile** is a tool to allow you to clarify just what you want from your kinky partner.
- **Appendix 2: BDSM Worksheet** is comprehensive checklist of things you might want to try that involve bondage and discipline.
- **Appendix 3: Role Play Worksheet** is similar but focuses on the setting and the psychology of role playing.
- **Appendix 4: Spanking Partner Worksheet** is for you truly sick bastards to decide between an open hand or a tennis racket.
- **Appendix 5: Humiliation Activities Worksheet** will help you to turn your sub into a groveling mess.
- **Appendix 6: Fetish Consent Worksheet** is meant to facilitate communication regarding fetish activities between a top (master) and a bottom (slave).

Why Do It Kinky?

What attracts people to kinky sex? Surely it must involve childhood trauma and Internet pornography... Seriously, critical thinking is always encouraged but this one is pretty self-evident: *People are into kink because they like it.*

Like other sexual activity, kink is tied to arousal, excitement, stimulation, and physical gratification. Some people are simply "born kinky" while others discover their kinky side in the course of their sexual development while playing cowboys and Indians with the neighbor kids. You might be a happily married empty nester before you realize you simply love bedtime floggings and leather corsets. Kinky tastes are widespread, natural, and normal. (*Normal* is defined more precisely in the next chapter.)

But kink is far different from instant gratification or wanton hedonism. Kinky sex play involves interpersonal power dynamics, primal human emotions, self-knowledge, and intimacy. Here are some reasons people commonly give for their preference for kinky sex. See if any of these reasons resonate with you.

Pleasure

Pleasure has to be the most common, most compelling, and most important reason people give for their kinky inclinations. There are typically strong psycho-sexual rewards that are specific to kinky sex acts. These pleasures often (but not always) arise from childhood experiences or previous relationships where kinky sex elements were associated with anticipation, stimulation, and orgasm. A lot of people find they express their sexuality better if they incorporate a kinky ingredient than if they restrict themselves to more traditional or conventional **vanilla sex.** The satiation of deep psychological drives and emotional needs provides a wellspring of pleasures from all variety of things kinky.

Counterintuitive though it may seem, *pleasurable* does not necessarily mean *pleasant*. A very unpleasant experience can produce intense pleasure from the anticipation, actual sensory stimulation, and satisfaction of having had an encounter with your partner. A great deal of kinky sex involves taking pleasure in some form of pain. Thrill-seekers don't jump from airplanes or ride roller coasters for the safe and serene pleasantness of the experience. So too, a kinky person can derive immense pleasure in physical pain, psychological control, self-sacrifice, and discipline.

This kind of pleasure seeking comes with the same proviso as anything sexual in nature: if you don't like what you're doing, *stop it.* Your body communicates to your mind through your physical state, and your intuition is pretty darn good. If something feels fundamentally wrong (i.e., it feels like you're being stabbed but you're not actually being stabbed), it's probably causing damage to your physical health or emotional welfare. It's up to you to determine how tolerant you are of things you don't like. In my case, I've learned to *like* the feeling of being socially uncomfortable. I make a game of meeting strangers, provoking heated debate, and discussing taboo subjects because it helps me grow as a person. Just as hitting the gym hurts while your muscles tear (I'm no masochist so I don't *like* pain for its own sake), if you're going to be fit you have to *endure* the unpleasantness of pain to achieve satisfying results.

Exposing yourself to challenges can give you the pleasure of knowing yourself better. Sounds like a path to spiritual awakening, doesn't it? Well guess what…

Personal Discovery

Talk with people who lead kinky lifestyles for a while and you'll hear that kink enables a kind of personal growth and development. Moving beyond your conventional assumptions about sex requires an understanding of what it means to be a thinking animal. It involves coming to terms with your own instincts and your cultural programming, wrestling with your biases, reconsidering your basic values, and dealing with all the crazy shit that found its way into your head.

 Give Anything A Try Once

One college girlfriend was wild. She was a stimulation junkie with pierced eyebrows and purple hair who was down to try anything. Bondage started as a mutual curiosity and blossomed into a sexual pattern for us. Sex on the coffee table, in the dining room, in library stairwells, "surprise sex" after work, and usually with some rope or restraint. She also practiced tying me, using toys, and giving blow jobs. As long as it doesn't violate your core being, discovering your sexual self means just about anything goes.

TIP: *When rope is not available a cheap Ace bandage allows for awesome improvised restraints.*

Kink runs counter to cultural norms in a way that can help you better understand yourself and the society you are part of. A friend once told me, "My family was so uptight, this kind of thing would have *never* have even crossed anyone's mind!" Traditional families tend to come across like some halcyon *Leave It To Beaver* dystopia. In reality, titillating sexual imagery went through mom's head and dad's head, grandma's and grandpa's too. But if you're from a family that repressed all things sexual (like mine), it probably never crossed your mind that you could ever *talk* about sex, much less that you could hogtie your partner to the bedpost.

I was raised Catholic with all the unfortunate guilt and shame you'd hope to find in a dysfunctional household. Catholics (both practicing and lapsed) are some of the kinkiest people out there, having been indoctrinated into a worldview in which the human being is fallen, flawed, and evil. The nuns made it clear to me that my hard-on during geometry class arose (get it?) from original sin on my soul. Repression of all forms of unmarried, non-reproductive sexuality can provoke fetishization intensified by the sheer taboo of sex. I for one love a school girl's short plaid skirt, although I prefer it on my stripper girlfriend rather than an actual schoolgirl. Fifteen gets you twenty in most states.

Whatever the religious or personal reasons, that repression and suppression of basic sexual curiosity (though the social emotions like embarrassment and shame) cut short a healthy, non-traditional exploration of sex. Avoiding a topic like sex in polite conversation makes it taboo, and denying sexual urges instills in us a fear of violating such taboos. Some taboos originate from the biological aversion to inbreeding (think about going through your great aunt's underwear drawer—*eww*), but most merely punish sexual expression that is not socially sanctioned. Kink can arise as a *reaction* to that repression.

Sexual Expression

In a healthy relationship, kink can be incorporated naturally into the expression of sexual desire. What can appear abusive to an outsider is actually an extremely arousing performance for those involved, provided the act is undertaken with **informed consent**. This means partners give consent with a full awareness of the consequences of their actions (i.e., there's no *gotcha* twist like at the end of a *Twilight Zone* episode once you're in bed). Violence, aggression, and control can then stimulate sexual arousal rather than inflict harm on others.

Often this sexual arousal is intensified in virtue of kinky situations, objects, or anticipated rewards. While human sexual behavior is difficult to divide into clear and distinct nature and nurture components, animal researchers have conducted *birds-and-bees* research on, appropriately enough, birds. Specifically they studied Japanese quail. Scientists conditioned the quail to associate the sight of a stuffed toy dog (how erotic) with a chance to copulate. Guess what? After five days of reinforcement, the mere sight of that stuffed Fido got the little buggers horny. While people are far more complex it should come as no surprise if you get warm fuzzies from an angora sweater that reminds you of the one your busty young aunt wore when she lavished attention on you at your tenth birthday party. This also explains how people fetishize such things as leather chaps or silk stalking. If you regard high heels as sexy and reinforce that notion in your own fantasy fulfillment by wearing heels in bed, it won't take long for them to become a kind of erotic trigger.

Intense sexual activity can provide an expressive escape from the tension of everyday, self-conscious, hyper-attentive waking state (sometimes called the **ego state** by consciousness researchers). Movies, drugs, alcohol, and thrill-seeking activities change the chemistry of the brain. They literally alter the brain's state. So sex can induce various **altered states**. For some people, the fantasy- and taboo-laden elements of kinky sex can induce a greater chemical rush than vanilla sex. Unconventional sex can help a person get in touch with their sex drive, embracing the basic biological impulse that gets suppressed, sterilized, and civilized in everyday life.

It's informative to note that in Freud's conception of the mind, a person's biological sexual and aggressive drives were pitted against their own rational mind. The resulting tension between animalistic instincts and rational behavior was thought to produce anxiety, which gets resolved through an explosive cathartic release. While the scientific evidence discredits his ideas of how the brain works, his intuition about human behavior was fairly sound. It's quite common that sex and aggression commingle in a person's aroused **fantasy state,** even though literally acting out many of the fantasies that arise in one's mind is unsafe and impractical. The excitement of unsafe, irresponsible behavior, regardless of its feasibility, is terrifically (and terrifyingly) exciting stuff. Kink allows sex and aggression to find an outlet in a safe and constructive setting.

For example, fantasies about (and taboos against) rape, the essence of violation in the form of nonconsensual sex, provide the foundation for the **ravishment** role play, the *consensual* simulation of the act of being taken by force which can produce intense sexual excitement. Prohibitions against violating another's will are the foundation of ethics and law—yet that very violation is the stuff of bodice-ripper novels and hardcore pornography. Ravishment and role playing can fuel intense passion and intimacy when toyed with in a responsible way.

Sensory Stimulation

Kinky romps are predominantly thought of as foreplay between partners leading to sex, but for a surprisingly large number of kink scenesters genital sex is totally incidental and unnecessary.

This fact shocked me during my first visit to a dungeon. People kept referring to their maybe-sex-maybe-not companions as **play partners**, and repeatedly asked questions like, "How do you like to play?" In that setting it was simple to ask matter-of-factly, "I'm curious about you, are you a top or bottom? Are you here for education or stimulation? You okay with penetration?" The casualness of this sexual negotiation belies the essence of the issue: that actual sex is *optional* and that a lot of people get off from the intense mental and physical experience.

There are plenty of kinky people who separate arousal and orgasm. **Erotic play** allows just such a separation. Kissing and petting and making out on the couch can be extremely pleasant even if it doesn't result in orgasm. It induces excitement, teases, titillates just like a little dirty talk on the phone. By some measures, men think about sex every 52 seconds. Erotic play without release is yet another chance to experience that kind of sexual arousal.

Sharp sensory stimuli (e.g., spanking, biting, whipping) releases endorphins and induces dopamine flow in the brain, transforming the physical pain into a tool for inducing an altered state. Depending on the severity this is called **impact play** and can range from light spankings to canings and beatings. Often it's not that being slapped "feels good" like a massage feels good—it just *feels*. Pure physical stimulation can be pleasant even if not pleasing. Much like it hurts good when you eat spicy food, listen to sad songs or watch a tragic film, so too for some people those painful acts can hurt so good.

It's insightful to note that memories of both pleasing and painful experiences are dependent on the *intensity* and *duration* of the experience. In retrospect we tend to recall the intensity more vividly than the duration. One study on memory and happiness showed that people tend to enjoy a one-week tropical vacation just as much as a two-week vacation if there are no truly distinct or novel experiences during the second week. More of the same does not increase enjoyment because in retrospect we simply don't recall duration all that well. For a lot of kinky people the act of having the senses spiked is far more exhilarating than a night of gentle lovemaking by candle light. (Your kinky partner might in fact prefer some **wax play** and have those candles drizzled on their bare skin. That's hot...literally.)

Enjoying painful experiences has less to do with the pain itself and more to do with the **meta-sensation** or *appreciating the intensity* of the sensation. Rough rope. Cold metal chains. Smooth, tight leather. The impact of an open hand. Knowing that your partner's *intent* is sexual lends an erotic depth to the raw sensory dimension of your encounter.

Mental Experience

It often comes as a surprise to people who haven't experienced the kinky **headspace** firsthand that a remarkable amount of the appeal of kinky sex is mental in nature. When I started talking about kink with others and they described this thrilling mental state that did not involve orgasm, I thought they were nuts. I was more interested in the tight little wet space between the legs than some peculiar mental space between the ears.

Yet people regularly experience a sense of euphoria, well-being, excitement, and "flow" while performing kinky sex acts, whether in anticipation of the planned kink event (the pleasure coming from a kind of preconsumption of the experience); during the kinky experience itself (when **dominating** another person, thus asserting your will over someone; or **submitting** and yielding to another's will); or after the fact while relishing the experience. In fact, dominants routinely lose track of time as they focus intensely on the task at hand of applying rope to or spanking their partner. When I top I find myself contemplating in the back of my mind the stimulus-response experience of my partner. When I tickle here, slap there, stroke that, what kinds of feelings or reactions can I produce? I become extremely alert and detail-oriented, like a craftsman practicing his art. By contrast, submissives commonly experience something called **subspace**, a state of peace and serenity and introspection that's similar to meditation.

Outside the bedroom, kinky partners may establish rules and protocols based on the will of the dominant and the obedience of the submissive. Challenges to these rules and protocols results in discipline which can be punitive or stimulating, depending on the kind of consequences and the temperament of the playmates involved. The dominant partner may order the submissive to end each sentence with "Sir" or "Madam" as a signal of deference and obedience. Failure to use the proper salutation carries the penalty of punishment, in which case the whole arrangement serves as an eroticized power trip by creating a hyper-awareness of the sexual relationship between the dominant and the submissive.

The degree to which sex is a mental and chemical experience is often overlooked. Sex produces complex chemical reactions in the brain and throughout the body. Sex releases dopamine and serotonin, two pleasure-oriented neurotransmitters, as your body's "reward" for mating. The hormone oxytocin, sometimes called the "love hormone" or the "cuddle hormone," is involved in childbirth and breastfeeding and may contribute to pair bonding following orgasm. All these chemical reactions are bound up with the reward-seeking instincts of people which served us well when certain resources were scarce (like sugar and fat were in early man's hunting and gathering diet). Today our unchecked urges can do us more harm than good.

While sex and love cannot be reduced to mere chemicals, the *interpretive context* that we apply to our sensual experiences is what makes them so potent. In other words, it should come as no surprise that so much of the pleasure of kinky sex, like sex in general, is really all in your head.

Acceptance And Belonging

Some people are drawn to the **fetish community** precisely for the sense of community it fosters. Some come to it even though their sexuality which would otherwise be vanilla, but because of their social or political interests they affiliate with kinky people yet don't have any serious interest in kinky sex itself. Goths, metalheads, and punks have appropriated kink and fetish trappings as much to delineate their own community in contrast with the mainstream as to express any actual kinky inclinations. The fetish community provides such a strong support network that people often turn to one another for friendship and a sense of belonging even if their specific interest in kinky sex acts is low.

Sometimes people take to kinky sex to compensate for a personal feeling of unattractiveness. They believe that a willingness to do anything will make them more attractive to prospective partners, reasoning, "I may not be a ten, but at least 6+kinky=9." When those people find what they like about themselves and learn to share it with others, they often have very satisfying physical encounters.

I have a friend who had been a submissive into light bondage and costume play but was not particularly hardcore. She married a fantastic vanilla partner and left the kink scene almost entirely. Still, every year she comes to the same convention and meets with the same group of regulars and checks out the play space. It's exciting, stimulating, and familiar for her. They accept her there.

Some people are drawn to the fetish community primarily because it's underground and hardcore. They belong to an exclusive group of sexual deviants. Others like me feel kink is common and healthy and the only reason it's underground is that education and public conversation are lacking. For us, acceptance and belonging are derived from a satisfying relationship.

And certainly there are abuse victims, neglected children, overweight folks, social outcasts, and other "injured misfits" who take to the fetish community to repair emotional damage, just as you find emotionally damaged people in every part of society. Kink doesn't draw any more nutcases and weirdos than your neighborhood supermarket, although the vivid depictions of "the sexually molested hooker who became a dominatrix and wound up with an axe murderer" that *Lifetime TV* broadcasts to pay its bills might tell us otherwise.

Don't be surprised if you meet people who are unusually open about their sexuality in the community, though. They're used to being accepted "as is." You'll learn more about the nonjudgmental, non-defensive mindset that's prevalent in the fetish community in the chapter *The Kinky Mindset.*

Novelty

For some of us the thrill of kinky sexuality is in the novelty of the experience, whether it's splitting new bamboo, or visiting your friendly neighborhood dungeon for the first time, or playing with a new partner's toy box. The sheer sense of sexual excitement and possibilities that a new partner unleashes, the **new relationship energy**, can drive steamy sexual exploration together.

Modern technological advances have made us more aware than ever of the variety of sexual possibilities we have available. Where obscure lithographs of the Kama Sutra and short stag films were once scarce and forbidden, people who grew up in the 1970s during the era of adult theaters and risqué magazines through the 1980s with the VCR (not to mention the Internet) witnessed an explosion of kinky movies and videos. This proliferation of easy-to-copy titillating porn imagery exposed people to a vast range of unconventional sexual behavior involving **bondage, power exchange, humiliation**, and the like. First exposure can be darkly appealing or completely appalling, but usually very provocative.

That said, porn is entertaining but not all that educational. The stuff you see in movies is a slickly produced fiction (okay, most porn is sloppy and rushed) caked in makeup and smothered in cringe-inducing dialog. Still, porn introduces us to sexual potentials. As curious people examine their tastes for aggressive sex, navigating the boundaries of consent, control, and force, they can experience the thrill of discovery and a newfound awareness of how unforeseen sexual possibilities can guide their own romantic exploration.

After one very long relationship came to an end I was looking for someone to play with, someone who would challenge me and move me out of what I considered a romantic rut. One evening I was out with friends and I started talking to a stunning girl who had a wonderfully playful "I don't give a fuck" attitude. I teased her and had fun with her friends. She worked hard to get my attention by being pushy and interrupting me when I spoke. I stopped her, looked her square in the eye and with deadpan seriousness delivered a classic pick-up artist's line, "I don't know who your boyfriend is, but he's *not* spanking you enough!" "You have no idea!" she snarled back with a smile. "I do. Shame, I don't think you're kinky enough for me..." She quickly qualified herself, "Oh, honey, I don't waste my time with a man who can't take charge!"

The relationship we forged had us testing each others' **limits**, sharing our likes and dislikes, pushing each others' buttons, and having great sex. It truly recharged my batteries.

Maybe at this stage you're just kink-curious. Maybe you find fishnet stockings, leather jackets, and handcuffs totally arouse you. Whatever your motive, remember this basic principle: *Do it kinky because you like it.*

Devil's Advocate

> A *devil's advocate* is a person who takes a skeptical stance. They argue a case from the opposite perspective, challenge the evidence, and press for proof. The questions asked by a devil's advocate promote a richer and more complete understanding of the topic being discussed.

What if I feel dirty or guilty or shameful about my kinky urges?

It helps to recognize that sexual thoughts and fantasies are a normal, natural, and healthy aspect of being human. Our minds fantasize, as much as anything, simply because they can. Think how your brain was optimized to help you (or your ancestors at any rate) scheme, plan, and strategize to find food and to mate more effectively. Today, when you're not struggling to survive because you're killing time texting in a taxicab, you still scheme, plan, and strategize about food and sex. Things go into our heads—movies, magazine photos, romance novels, beer ads—and kick around in there. I hate to break it to you, but in this regard you're not that special. Kinky fantasies are widespread. Paying attention to those fantasies can be a healthy means to understand your own unconscious thoughts, feelings, and desires.

Now having a fantasy and acting on it are very different things. If you feel shame or guilt, that suggests there's a conflict between your *expected* behavior (either the behavior you expect of yourself, or the behavior you think others expect of you) and *actual* behavior. If your fantasy is incompatible or incongruent with something you've been taught (like *thou shalt not covet thy neighbor's smokin' hot wife*) then it's going to be hard for you to live with yourself after getting a hard-on in the company of said pretty neighbor. Guilt can be a fairly potent prescription against perfectly normal mental activity.

This is sick! No one should be doing it!

There are a lot of people who believe this and that's fine by me. My agenda is not to persuade people who do not want to learn about kinky relationships that they should get into one, or even that they should like the fact that I'm going to have one. I'm an educator, not an advocate so you can try to silence me if that makes you feel better. But that won't make anyone's fetish go away. My interest is in helping people who want to get into kinky relationships do so with less stress and less frustration, in a more healthy and constructive manner.

Talking about this is really hot, but I don't think I'm ready to act out.

Talking, researching, educating yourself—that's the best place to start. And that may be where it ends for you. Even if you don't act out, kinky fantasies can be used as dirty talk in foreplay, to improve communication between sex partners, and to share fantasies with your lover. There are plenty of people who get their motors running by talking dirty and yet when it comes time to screw they like the familiarity of the missionary position. If your needs are satisfied that way more power to you. When you're ready for it, kink will be ready and waiting for you.

You say kinky people love novelty. How do I know I won't become a sex addict if I try this? How do I know this won't escalate out of control?

It may be tempting to think that sexual experimentation is a slippery slope, and once you've opened the Pandora's Box of kink you'll be seduced into a world of drugs and Satanic sex and axe murders. This lascivious association between kink and criminality is unfounded, but stems from the confusion between the intentional expressions of *healthy* non-standard behavior and compulsive lack of control in *destructive* non-standard behavior.

The next chapter discusses how preferences vary greatly among perfectly normal people. For now it's enough to realize that if you try something you don't like you can just give it up. The idea that things might escalate out of control has nothing to do with kinky sex but instead has to do with an individual's general addictive tendencies. If you're not sure that you can handle experimenting with your sexuality, it's best you find a therapist who can help you identify a plan of action based on the specific circumstances of your situation.

Interestingly, most of the sadistic and dominant people I know are control freaks who exhibit a high degree of self control. I for one am one happy little sex addict and have been perfectly content in self-imposed celibacy for months at a time. I wouldn't be worried that just because you're kinky somehow your sexual urges will spiral out of control. I'd be more worried that unhealthy suppression could boil over and cause much worse damage to yourself and to others than a little leather gear and some role playing.

Think For Yourself

Answer the *Think For Yourself* questions at the end of each chapter so you gain a deeper insight into your own sexual preferences. Don't just think about your answers, but actually write them down.

1. What turns you on about kink? What turns you off?

2. What kinky things have you already tried?

3. What kinky things do you want to try with your super awesome smoking hot new partner?

What *Exactly* Is Kink?

When you think "kinky" what comes to mind? Whips? Leather? Naughty nurses shoving thermometers up your ass? You must be one sick individual. Psychiatrists once meant that literally.

The word **kinky** (Dutch, "twisted rope") has been used to mean "odd" since the 1800s and to describe "eccentric" people and behavior since the 1900s. It came to mean "sexually perverted" in the 1960s and the term has stuck for people who engage in unconventional sexual behaviors.

Kink covers a lot of ground and may get used to label just about any sexual practice that diverges from the traditional or conventional conceptions of appropriate sexual behavior. So when someone says, "I'm kinky," what exactly does that mean?

Is Everyone Kinky?

Precise measures of "typical" sexual behavior across a large population are hard to come by. Human sexuality researchers like Alfred Kinsey and Edward Laumann have investigated this question with impressive results, but when the Center for Disease Control collects data on human sexual behavior it has yet to add the question "What's the kinkiest thing you've ever done?" to its surveys.

It would not be pure conjecture to suggest that everyone exhibits some degree of kink in their sex life if kink is taken to include any sexual practice that differs in some way from the average, the conventional, or the prevailing norm. As a matter of simple arithmetic, the number of people who can express their sexuality in *precisely* the exact same average manner in every regard all the time becomes vanishingly small. Who do you know has precisely the average number of lifetime sexual partners (about seven, according to the Kinsey Institute), precisely the average number of orgasms per month (about eight), only in precisely the average position every time (who knows…probably missionary)?

By definition that person is having average sex. Sounds very…well, very *average*.

In *any* large group of people, you'll find variety and individual differences. There will be members of that population that diverge from the god-awful boringness of just being average. We label *certain* expressions of these sexual differences "kink."

On the other hand, the degree of kink or the factors that sexually excite any given person will depend on that person. Certainly not everyone in the world is a latent leather fetishist and your typical rope bondage dominant is absolutely not itching to be tied up. It makes sense that sexual tastes can range from unusual but tame to hardcore and extreme, since the word "kinky" is mostly used to establish contrast with traditional vanilla heterosexual missionary position sexual intercourse. Sexologists refer to vanilla sex and the associated cultural value system as **heteronormative** (*hetero:* short for "heterosexual" + *normative:* "should, ought").

Rather than dwell on the prevalence of kink in the general population, you will want to focus on the essence of the matter for a kinky relationship. What do *you* like and what will your *partner* like? What will allow you to play *together?*

Philias And Fetishes

If we take *kinky* sex to mean "a non-vanilla sex act performed by consenting adults," the clauses about consent and adulthood are in there to distinguish kink from mere abuse. Kinks that involve other people in consenting relationships can be perfectly healthy, whereas most urges that require non-consensual participation are identified as disorders or classified as sex crimes.

Kink itself was once regarded as a psychological sickness—a perversion of the mind. As scientific thought supplanted religious moralizing in Europe during the Enlightenment and onward, the focus shifted from punishing *sinful* behavior to curing *problematic* mental states. In the twentieth century psychologists "problematized" the human condition in a compulsive classification scheme, culminating with the Diagnostic and Statistical Manual of Mental Disorders (DSM). For a long time, non-heteronormative sexual expression, from homosexuality to enjoying needle pricks, was classified as a disorder regardless of the psychological or emotional damage the patient or the partner actually experienced. Even quite happy, harmless perverts were thought to be afflicted with mental problems.

This belief is far less prevalent today, and the use of the word **perversion** (Latin *perversus:* "subvert, overturn, to face the wrong direction") has been replaced in psychological settings by the diagnostic term **paraphilia** (Greek παρά *[para]:* "adjacent, amiss" + φιλία *[philia]:* "love, arousal"). Paraphilias describe all variety of unconventional sexual arousal, including extreme cases of **fetishization** where the object of arousal becomes so essential that physical gratification is impossible without it. Paraphilias include: *coprophilia* (feces), *acrotomophilia* (amputees), *frotteurism* (rubbing against someone), *biastophilia* (assault and rape), *raptophilia* (rape, actually committed), *vorarephilia* (being eaten whole), *zoophilia* (animals), *pedophilia* (children), *necrophilia* (corpses). Some list, huh?

Object fetishism (arousal from inanimate objects) and *partialism* (arousal from nonsexual body parts, like ears or feet) can bring a seductive and titillating dimension to consensual relationships. *Exhibitionism* (showing your naked body to others) and *voyeurism* (watching others) are healthy kinks when everyone involved consents to the act, like when your girlfriend arranges to have you watch her through the bathroom window when she showers. But showing your penis to a complete stranger will put you behind bars. The focus of kink in a relationship is on the partner-to-partner interaction, arousal, and stimulation. Anything that is consensual and does not spill over to unsuspecting or unwilling public is up for consideration.

Masculine-Feminine Polarity

The **masculine polarity** reflects both the biologically expressed and culturally reinforced masculine qualities of strength, aggression, assertiveness, and stillness. We can credit natural selection for making human males larger, stronger, more aggressive, more dominating, and more visually or spatially oriented on average. After all men had to hunt in packs and fight off lions before we took to living in downtown soft loft. (You know we haven't always lived in cities, don't you? We're maladapted to modern life. We suffer from environmental tox-

 Bring It Up

During a busy period in my life I was looking for a casual playmate but nothing serious. I didn't care if it was kinky or not, I just wanted someone for stress release. I met a fantastic stacked woman and we had really solid vanilla sex. One night the pillow talk was sweet but a little boring so I leaned over and said, "I'd like to just tie you to the headboard and fuck you senseless!"

Her eyes grew wide. "Oh, god yes!" she said breathily. We got aroused all over again. From then on her sex was at my service.

ins, information overload, and overstimulation but that's another story.) Considering how little value males add to the biological gestation of a child it makes sense that nature allowed us to be stronger to ward off threats and scavenge for food while competing for mating privileges with healthy females.

Masculine energy is concerned with domination and control. In the hunter-gatherer archetype, the primitive male exerts control over the environment with his spear in hand and his fellow tribesmen following his lead to take down big game. This aggressive, dominating energy translates into mild dominance even in a vanilla relationship.

The **feminine polarity** complements the masculine polarity, yielding and submitting to the masculine energy. The feminine is concerned with goodness, vibrancy, and life. The archetypical primitive female rears the young to keep the species populated, tends the land, and maintains social order while the males make very important stabbing tools from desert rocks and things. This division of domestic labor is played out in cultural archetypes throughout the world. It is a template for Judeo-Christian marriages, Muslim polygamist harems, the Eastern notion of yin and yang, and Tantric sexual rituals.

Feminine energy is concerned with expressiveness and understanding. The females of early societies needed to depend on good neighbor relations and more empathetic communication to function in clans and depend on one another for the care and feeding of offspring. Whether or not child rearing is "women's work" is debatable; either way, women bear the greater cost of reproduction in terms of gestation and delivery. The development of social cohesion practices to help share the work load makes evolutionary sense.

The exertion masculine of power and feminine reception of power is a basic social pattern in human mating. Whether it is built into the species or is simply an artifact from all known cultures is uncertain. Anthropologist Margaret Mead claimed to have located both perfectly egalitarian and female-dominated cultures, although the empirical data in support of her findings are sketchy at best. What is universal is the **sexual dimorphism** (Greek *di*: "two" + *morphē*: "form") that makes males physically stronger, more muscular, and heavier than females provides a basis for the directional flow of energy.

Every individual expresses a range of both masculine and feminine qualities. For a male to draw upon feminine energy is not the least "unmanly" when it is done with an intention of goodness balanced with strength. The yab-yum (Tibetan

ཡབ་ཡུམ: "father-mother") symbols common in tantric Buddhism represent complementary dark masculine and light feminine energies in creative sexual union. The yin-yang (Chinese 阴 [yin]: "feminine; moon" + 阳 [yang]: "masculine; sun") symbol represents the balance of masculine and feminine elements synthesized into the whole being. Artists, musicians, dancers, and entertainers draw upon the creative feminine energy (yin) to express themselves and perform, while audiences draw upon the masculine strength (yang) of observation and stillness. Either aspect of a person may be suppressed, but masculine and feminine are not at odds in the whole person. Expressing either does not compromise one's sexuality.

Rather than inevitably creating a **value hierarchy** (a decidedly contemporary notion if you imagine the *survival value* of a tribe of men with no women to bear offspring—or vice versa), the masculine-feminine polarities define the *direction of energy flow* (or intentionality, will, conscious action) and its reception. Energy flows *from* the masculine and *to* the feminine. These polarities simply acknowledge and respect central sex-based differences. When this energy flow is construed as justification for a value hierarchy, patriarchal social systems have emerged. Male dominated cultures devalue women but there is nothing intrinsic to the masculine-feminine polarity that necessitates devaluing either sex.

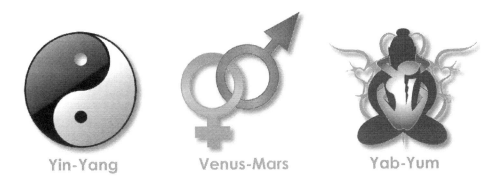

Yin-Yang   Venus-Mars   Yab-Yum

Symbols of Masculine-Feminine Polarity

When a **dominance hierarchy** establishes itself, masculine strength dominates feminine acceptance. This is true in family (my grandma was a domineering matriarch who embodied substantial masculine energy), at work among boss and coworkers, among friends, and in sexual relationships. Pecking orders are a consequence of social organization. It's not so much that they *devalue* members lower in on the totem pole; they simply give structure to power in groups. Dominance hierarchies in one form or another are inescapable. Even the most alpha male has a boss. CEOs report to boards and customers allow the small business owner to eat. And when the motorcycle renegade who reports to no one breaks the law, the state takes control of his life.

The masculine-feminine archetype is a prominent factor in sexuality in general and in kink in particular. At its core, kink is about reconsidering and ultimately transgressing the traditional model of masculine-feminine polarity. The traditional archetype is codified and reinforced in high culture, religion, and everyday conventions in a way that tacitly defines social mores and cultural taboos. Those taboos revolve around an unspoken reinforcement of the qualities of masculine domination-feminine reception. In recognizing these polarities, the kink experience goes further to *manipulate* and *challenge* these archetypes. Kink transgresses taboos consciously and intentionally. Whereas "vanilla" sexuality reinforces to the masculine-feminine template, kink deliberately toys with conventional notions of sexual polarity.

MASCULINE	FEMININE
Strength	Goodness
Aggression	Receptivity
Death	Life
Destruction	Creation
Darkness	Light

Contrasting Masculine and Feminine Qualities

If you happen to be a cultural critic who regards gender roles as socially constructed stereotypes, that's lovely. Just keep in mind that they're very *useful* stereotypes when applied to erotic **power exchange**. Furthermore, individuals are not eternally bound to the roles they play. Kinky sex practices regularly mock, contravene, or simply ignore male and female gender roles while the masculine and feminine energy are consciously adopted by partners who negotiate a new sexual dynamic.

Consider the following ways of varying the masculine-feminine polarity.

- **Intensification.** The relationship is taken to an extreme, as in a master-slave arrangement where mild domination is replaced with total power exchange, subjugation, or ownership. The receptive slave accepts the subordinate role out of devotion to the master and acts to satisfy the dominant's desires.

- **Inversion.** The female dominates the male. Some executives or men in positions of power and control will hire a dominatrix (a **pro-domme,** professional dominant, or a **service top,** a person who **tops** another for the pleasure of the **bottom** rather than to gratify themself). Yielding control can relieve a person of the pressure of continual responsibility and produce soaring levels of excitement.

- **Expansion.** Instead of a simple polarity, multiple partners are involved. The masculine-feminine polarity remains intact but may consist of a polyamorous group marriage, swingers swapping partners, or a master with multiple slaves. Energy still flows from masculine to feminine. In all likelihood such an arrangement is comprised of one masculine and many feminine, for the simple reason that multiple masculine forces directing energy will tend to conflict with and contradict one another. Hierarchies of the form one master/many slaves are one-to-many relations because matrix relationships (e.g., multiple bosses) are hard to keep under control.

- **Object Fetishization.** Some physical object becomes part of the sexual experience. Objects can include clothing, sex toys, bondage gear, and other items that are used to create arousal and stimulation. In a relationship, object fetishization can involve degradation, humiliation, or objectifying another person. An "owner" may make their "pet" service them when they let them out of their cage.

- **Role Playing.** Taking on a role can involve playing with traditional roles or intensifying roles that involve inherent power hierarchies and latent sexual taboos such as secretary and boss, student and teacher, banker and borrower, and so on. Roles can even be extreme and aversive, like parent and child or brother and sister. Role playing frees each participant to explore an alternate consciousness, to "get into the role" and shift some of the responsibility for experiencing the scenario off themselves and onto the role. ("What? I was just playing along!") Institutionalized taboos can be violated when these assumed roles and latent power structures foster a deviation from normality as pure play encourages mocking, toying with, and disregarding them.

Deviance Defined

To build intuition about how kink arises in the population it helps to get a better sense of normal populations and the sociological and mathematical definitions of "deviance."

The word **deviant** (Latin *de:* "away" + *via:* "path, way") is a pejorative label for an individual who violates social norms, protocols, or expectations. The term was originally used by sociologist Émile Durkheim who observed that perfectly normal societies exhibit some amount of deviant behavior, ranging from simple criminality to subculture formation (be it street gangs or Masonic brotherhoods) to founding fathers who break with colonial rule and start revolutions.

"Deviance" intuitively connotes something bad, broken, or reprehensible. It is loaded with moral overtones. Yet Durkheim's concept of deviance was more a description of how a population expresses predictable *variation* than a condemnation of how individual members of the population were *bad* people for being different. It applies to rare brilliance and starving artists as well as it applies to criminal behavior. The rock-and-roll gangs of 1950s England were a deviant subculture that went on to produce the British invasion. Not all deviations are socially destructive or morally wrong. In this sense, deviance is not about denying the prevailing norms or conventions but instead providing alternatives to the *status quo*.

To appreciate how **perfectly normal** societies can survive and even *thrive* with so many unusual or uncommon denizens—people that deviate from average, or defy socially promoted norms—it helps to understand the meaning of the words "normal" and "deviation" in a statistical context. Consider height. The typical American adult male is 5 feet 9 inches tall according to the Center for Disease Control. That means the *average* height of an American male is 5'9". But that does not mean some random guy on the street stands 5'9". Rather, the *standard deviation* of the adult male population is 3.3 inches. That means that sixty-eight percent of American adult males stand between just under 5'6" (5'9" minus 3.3 inches) and just over 6'0" (5'9" plus 3.3 inches).

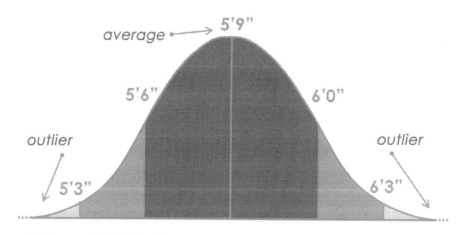

A Normal Distribution: Height of American Adult Males

In fact a population of individuals is called **normal** *precisely* when its members express some characteristic (like height) in terms of a *normal* or a bell-shaped curve. American males are normal with respect to height because they conform to a normal distribution. Some people are really short like Dr. Evil's clone, Mini-Me. Some people are extra tall (I'm a lanky 6'3"). But basketball teams are *not* normal. They are composed of **outliers,** those extremely deviant members of the population that are way above or way below average. Very tall and short people are outliers and relatively rare compared with the rest of the population. The fact that they occur infrequently scarcely makes them "abnormal" in the sense that they're defective or problematic. On the contrary, in a normal population these very tall and very short outliers *must* exist. They show up because of the healthy variety of heights that occur naturally in the population.

The average of a large population is sometimes called the *expected value*. The confusion arises when one suggests that the expected value of a normal population should be applied for *each specimen* in the population. For example, I expect a random American male to stand 5'9" on average, but when I expect *every* male I encounter to stand 5'9" I have simply failed to recognize that there is variation in the population. I can condemn this variation and say that God or nature or common sense tells me that short people are abhorrent and must be eliminated. This only serves to reveal my ignorance and intolerance of variation in large populations. Perhaps my sense of self is shaky and I need others to "be like me" in order not to feel my identity is threatened. Whatever the reason, populations exhibit variety with or without my approval.

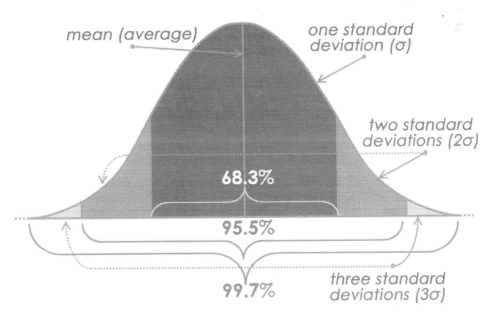

A Normal Population Distribution

The standard deviation is a technical measurement that quantifies the difference from the average. One standard deviation captures just over sixty-eight percent of the variation (e.g., the range of height differences); two standard deviations capture over ninety-five percent of variation. Deviation is not *perversion*, but a description of *variety* in a normal population. Now not every variable in a population is distributed along a normal curve. Biological sex is not "averaged" across a range of values but rather polarized into male and female. (For the sake of accuracy, biological sex is not strictly either/or. An **intersexed** individual has neither fully male nor female genitals but genitals somewhere in between, and a **hermaphrodite** has both. Neither of these cases are unnatural, just quite rare. The next chapter examines sex and identity and orientation in greater detail.)

The characteristic "enjoys being spanked" may or may not be distributed normally on a *yes–mostly–sort of–not really–no* continuum in the American population. My point is simply that just because you see variation that is not socially sanctioned (like kink, homosexuality, or other alternative sexual practices), it does not follow that the variation is "abnormal." It certainly may not be widely discussed, culturally reinforced, or historically endorsed. It may be the object of contempt and ridicule by mainstream culture. And just to be clear, at one point so were women, black people, aboriginals, Eskimos, men who didn't own land, fatties, dyslexics, the Irish (seriously, who can stand the Irish?), the elderly, Jews, skinny people, the Japanese, the Germans, the Russians, the Poles, the North Koreans, the Iraqis, the Kurds, politicians, bankers, lawyers, businessmen, and the Irish. Did I mention those filthy fucking Irish?

The word "normal" gets used very loosely in everyday speech. "You know, the stuff everyone agrees on. What everyone else does. You know—normal." I do know. They are widespread templates and archetypes. The myths and traditions. The stories that predate scientific research and diversity training and Tolerance 101 during freshman orientation. The beliefs and biases and assumptions that have accumulated over thousands of years of human history pass for normal.

- *You better be a manly man or a girly girl and you're fucked up if you're not.* Untrue, but regularly assumed.
- *There's this telepathic zombie astronaut Jew who will keep you alive forever if you eat his skin and never masturbate.* Absurd and disturbing, but widely accepted.
- *Girls are fragile flowers and if you play rough you'll break 'em.* Scary for boys and sad for girls, but commonly taken as truth.

All perfectly normal.

Or if you allow your mind to open up, you see that "common sense" normalcy is very **biased**. Normal populations require the expression of healthy variation (with some uncommon traits showing up, and some very rare outliers that make average look bizarre), but social institutions propagate *conforming* stories that are meant to portray "what everybody else does," regardless of any actual empirical evidence. Normal means "a population distribution that has the property of fitting a normal (bell-shaped) curve." The moralistic and judgmental connotation of normal means, "the way I (or my God) wants things to be for everyone around these parts." Once we appreciate that normality and deviation are statistical descriptions of members of any population, with judgmental and pejorative interpretations having been added over time, a lot of light can be shed on the prevalence of kink and its consequences.

When we say "normal" in everyday speech, we mean to covey the nuance of being mainstream, conventional, or average. We're trying to indicate "accepted by the general public as socially appropriate." By this criteria it was once "normal" in America to burn witches, intern Japanese, and closet homosexuals. It wasn't necessarily common or widespread. It wasn't right. It was, however, *socially accepted.* "Normal" doesn't mean it's more prevalent than alternatives, and it certainly doesn't mean it's more healthy. Kink, however underground and forbidden, is as normal as a glass of wine with a meal during the Prohibition era.

The job of a social activist, by the way, is to change what is socially accepted. You and I don't need to be social activists to enjoy a kinky relationship. The beauty of a private experience is that it can remain *private*. I don't mean sex should be made some dirty little secret, but there's no harm in allowing what happens behind closed doors some room to retain its mystery and romance (after you're done reading this explicit tome, of course).

The realization that being a healthy deviant is not a malfunction, not a sickness, and not a problem to fix brings a certain kind of relief. You may not be atrociously average but by George, you deviant, you're perfectly normal.

Kink And Emotional Health

So the essential issue is whether your deviation is *healthy*. All deviation is not healthy, just as all deviation is not kink. If a deviant sets out to harm the social structure, the social structure (consciously or otherwise) defends itself. As social structures evolve, healthy variation in the population creates new strains of social behavior that become codified into subcultures. Just as the brotherhood of police officers forms a subculture within American culture at large, with its own standards of professional conduct and expected behavior (think the *Thin Blue Line*), so the kinky subculture has developed certain norms and expectations regarding health, consent, and respect that we touch on in the next chapter.

The *ars erotica* ("erotic art") described by philosopher Michel Foucault is about a personal experience of sexuality and sexual pleasure. Victorian mores and twentieth century moralizing may have stifled the openness to sexual investigation that prevailed during the Age of Enlightenment, turning *ars erotica* into *scientia sexualis* ("a science of sexuality"). Now researchers seek to conduct experiments and analyze sex in clinical manner, much as I'm analyzing kink. They turn a subjective, emotional experience into a program in the mechanics of locating the G-spot (named after gynecologist Ernst Gräfenberg if you're wondering) and measuring epidemiology rates of viral infection. But in *ars erotica* the act of two or three or four coming together is not analyzed or described but merely experienced. Sexuality did not fall under the jurisdiction of mental health professionals.

An unspoken understanding, preverbal in its awareness, enabled partners to share in a sense of unity and community. A sense of *we* arose directly from the experience itself, as in "We have *experienced this* together." Think about how you bond with someone you travel with. Think of how much you enjoy your recreational activity partners and compare that with your work colleagues who you may spend upwards of eight hours a day around. Work colleagues who are nice enough but somehow not "real" friends. You work together but you don't share anything deep with them. Unity and connection follow from engaging in a kinky encounter.

Kinky feelings and actions can contribute profoundly to a healthy personal identity. Sex is a private and intimate matter, part of your personal history and your physiological response process. Kink creates a kind of in-group where we can derive pleasure from a sense of belonging. Think of how you feel when someone offends a member of your family or a friend. Most people feel they have been *personally* slighted. To a lesser degree, age, race, sex, and geography are dimensions of who we are. Pejorative phrases like "stupid Polack" and "filthy old man" both come across as epithets. Our values and interests (i.e., our politics) and our sex practices are much the same, subject to identity-based attacking and defensiveness.

The downside of *identifying* with sexual preferences is that it places stress on people of a certain temperament when those preferences are not generally accepted. More than a matter of expecting simple tolerance, sexual behaviors can come to predominantly define a person (overriding the common sociological **master statuses** like age, gender, and race). If you come out and reveal how different you are, and demand that everyone accept your difference, you've placed quite a demand on everyone else. Everyone else may find it in them to meet your demands. Or, more likely, they might not.

So the early psychologists got it wrong. Kink in and of itself is not a sickness any more than vanilla sex is always perfectly healthy. Kink is part of the *ars erotica*. It is not a degenerative condition and not something to "fix." Totally kinky people are often otherwise pretty average. Kinky sexual expression is uncorrelated to issues of deviance like criminal behavior or antisocial tendencies. There is no indication that lack of empathy or other psychological "perversions" correlate to kinky behavior and no basis to attribute mental deficiency or psychopathology to kinky behavior, despite the DSM's long and illustrious history of making sex unnecessarily scary.

Of course social science is inseparable from the society that utilizes it. In this sense the science of mental health reinforces preexisting codes of moral conduct. Social psychology demonstrates that as social beings we actually carry around imaginary people in our heads—a "generalized other" that forms the conscience and helps us empathize. These imagined people provide the basis of a super-ego or conscience that stops us from lying and cheating, and when they are not functioning properly we can become schizophrenic or sociopathic. It is not hard to see how moral social codes have fused with the business of practicing medicine on the mind.

The pejorative connotation of the word "perversion" is an immediate consequence of the social urge for order and conformity. Just as deviants deviate from prevailing norms much to the chagrin of the people in power, so perverts pervert the prevailing norms, subversively replacing them with their own norms and behaviors much to the chagrin of many of the same people in power.

Being different is difficult. Sorry about that. I'll make some calls and see who I can talk to about getting that all fixed. Don't wait up for me, though. You get busy being kinky and I'll catch up.

What Is Not Kink?

Claiming jurisdiction over what constitutes "kinky sex" and what does not is an ongoing process. Supporters would tend to say that any healthy expression of sexuality that is not vanilla is kinky. Detractors would attribute things that the kink community would typically not include such as incest and bestiality.

Recall the working definition of kink as "a non-vanilla sex act performed by consenting adults." That includes certain things classified as paraphilias but it's not a catch-all term for every sex act imaginable. Not all paraphilias are kinks, and certainly not all kinks are paraphilias. With inadequate care, otherwise harmless kinks can "spill over" as the kink is acted out in public and witnessed by passersby. Public humiliation, exhibitionism, and lifestyle servitude run this risk. A useful guideline is that if something is illegal (like public nudity) it's probably best to keep it private. Or if you can handle the pressure, turn it into a cause others can champion and fight for your right to be a public pervert.

The underlying concern in this regard is the physical safety of the participants and passersby. Kinky sex can appear abusive to an outside observer. The easiest way to disentangle kink from abuse is to recall the principle of informed consent. As long as the participants agree to the act and both fully appreciate the consequences of their actions (no surprises or *gotchas*) then the act is not abuse. It may be illegal, it may be immoral, but it is not abuse. The term "consenting adults" captures this ethic neatly.

Consider the widely reported rape fantasy again. *Ravishment* involves overpowering the partner, using force, meeting resistance and yielding to a lover. Consent is given, even if the "contractual terms" are not established in complete detail. When consent is absent, the subjective nature of assumptions and expectations expect produces the he-said/she-said issues that arise in differing accounts from different perspectives in a physical encounter. Rape defiles and harms the victim. Ravishment excites and unites partners, bringing them closer through the consensual exchange of power and control.

Rather than settle the issue, I raise these points of ambiguity to establish the context for the concerns that come up when starting a kinky relationship.

By the way, I have yet to meet any long-standing member of the kink community who advocates deception, harm, or inclusion of unwilling participants in anything sexual. Kinky people tend to complement their vivid imaginations with a keen ability to distinguish fantasy from reality. There seems to be continual disagreements about what passes as kinky dogma, as you would expect with *any* community that is in the midst of establishing its own boundaries while remaining inclusive to dissenting views. "Live and let live" means that kinksters play kinky and let vanilla people remain vanilla.

Devil's Advocate

I don't care what you say! I know normal when I see it.

I'm sure you do. You would also know normal when you saw it if you were a man who lived during the Roman Empire and regularly engaged in *pederasty* (that's man-boy sex to you and me). You would know normal if you happened to be the third wife in a middle-Eastern harem born during the seventh century.

To say that you know normal is to say that you are, like I am, and he and she and all of us are, a product of your own time and your own culture. To think otherwise is an arrogant display of egotism that I must strongly encourage for the sake of laughs. Keep up the remarkable work.

Hey, my definition of kink differs from yours.

Frankly, different definitions don't much matter unless you try to date me. My purpose here is practical. How do a few people come together to explore and express their alternative sexual interests to foster a safe and healthy relationship? If you have a definition you prefer that helps you meet other people, use it with your partner. I won't sue.

What if people don't approve of my kinks?

What people? Random strangers on the street? Or grandma from beyond the grave? Maybe the jurists on the court of public opinion? Really the only people who need to approve of our private sex acts are the adults consenting to those acts. Later when we discuss the kinky mindset we will examine how to let go of the need to judge others in large part by letting go of the fear of being judged yourself. For now, public opinion matters less than your degree of self-awareness and your own attitude toward kink.

The space between kinky and abusive is unfortunately a bit gray (and exciting for a lot of people to play in). Is it abuse if you beat a submissive partner black and blue as long as they consent to it? In my opinion people who have mastered the kinky mindset and want a relationship—as opposed to a punching bag—clearly separate *hurt* and *harm.* Controlled hurting can be a lot of fun. Inflicting harm is for brutish cowards. And when I hear of a self-mutilating masochist consenting to have a sadist beat them, I personally find that gray area not all that enticing to play in regardless of whether or not others approve.

What about homosexual, transgender, or multiple partner relationships?

Even non-heterosexual and multiple partner arrangements typically involve a power exchange dynamic where a masculine and a feminine energy emerges (remember masculine and feminine do not necessarily mean male and female). Despite the post-feminist postmodern revisionist egalitarian "all people are identical" agenda, a lot of people get off on power asymmetry. A lot of women like men to take control of them. Plenty of men like women to take control of them. A lot of men like men to…you get the idea. Power exchange happens whether straight or gay or somewhere in between. People are not perfectly equal all the time. Deal with it.

If you want to learn more about multiple partners, read through the **Glossary Of Polyamory Terms. Polyamory** (Greek *poly:* "multiple" + Latin *amour:* "love"). is the act of loving multiple people, sometimes with multiple couples paired up and sometimes collectively loving an entire group. Polyamory differs from swinging and open relationships where sex with other people is allowed. In polyamorous relationships the feelings of love and commitment are long-term and enduring. They're just not exclusive.

Is a kinky person sick? Don't they also want to have sex with horses and molest children?

This is slippery slope reasoning that somehow says *any* deviation from average must be an *extreme* deviation. This denies the normal distribution and assumes a simple bifurcation and that all deviation is some sort of abomination. As a fun exercise, make a mental note the next time you hear about a sadomasochistic sex crime of some kind in the news. This will provide a vivid example for detractors of an inevitable criminal link to kink. Then start counting how many vanilla sex crimes you hear about. How many murders that are in no way sex related. How many simple assaults have to do with jealousy and alcohol not rope bondage. The proportion will convince you that kink is hardly a significant factor in criminality.

Kinksters and fetishists would see fit to reappropriate the term *pervert* like *nigger* was reappropriated by the black community and *dyke* by the lesbian community. In the natural course of natural and healthy sexual development you are allowed to consider new things and experiment with sex in a way you're not used to so you can decide what you will incorporate into your sexual repertoire. You don't *have* to try everything, but you *get* to. You are allowed to be a pervert. You won't suddenly want to fuck horses.

What if my kink involves illegal or immoral acts?

I'm not one to claim that all laws are fair or reasonable and certainly there are evolving standards of decency within the judicial system. I personally believe that if you do something without another person's consent you have inflicted harm and you deserve punishment according to the law.

Recognize that if you break the law and you get caught, you'll be held accountable and face the consequences even if you or I believe that law is wrong. Among consenting adults, if it doesn't break the law or inflict harm on someone it would seem anything goes. The age of consent in America is eighteen in most municipalities. That's a great age. To me any younger is just not worth a visit from the FBI.

As for immoral acts, I can't imagine any value to a moral code beyond something like "Don't do *to* others what they don't want done to them." That is, don't violate my *personhood*. But a morality that asserts "Don't do *around* others what they don't want done around them" (i.e., don't violate my *sensibilities*) is simply rendered irrelevant if you act under your own will (*thelema*).

Am I sick or broken for being into this stuff?

Yep. Sorry.

Think For Yourself

1. What does *kinky* mean for you? What does *kinky* exclude for you?

2. Do you consider yourself tolerant of other people's kinks? Why or why not?

3. Are you open to trying your partner's kinks? Do you have things that are off limits and can you explain them?

Essential Kink: BDSM

You probably noticed that the masculine-feminine archetype does not require that the masculine energy originate from a male nor the feminine from a female. Well the gay community noticed this interesting fact and in the 1970s the gay leather S&M subculture emerged. Butch doms recruited boy subs to play with, expressing a clear masculine-feminine polarity in same-sex pairings.

S&M is often associated with gay culture (think *Village People*), but this branding is an historical artifact. The gay rights movement in New York and San Francisco brought gay men out of the closet and once they were out the leather fetishists who were also gay figured, "Meh, I'll out myself about this little part of my sexuality, too." At the time a lot more straight people were playing in dungeons and meeting in homes across the country, but unlike the newly-outed gays, straights were too chickenshit to take to the streets and fight for their right to whip each other's asses. The gay community led the BDSM charge.

What Is BDSM?

In the mid-1990s people finally discovered a practical use for the Internet: trading kinky sex recipes online. The letters **B-D-S-M** form a conjunctive acronym that gained popularity as Usenet emerged on the Internet as a catch-all term to express different aspects of kink sex and power exchange.

B&D: *Bondage and discipline.* **Bondage** means tying, strapping, restraining, or otherwise restricting someone's movements so they can be *physically* controlled. In the West, bondage is usually of two forms: cuffs (e.g., leather straps, handcuffs, medical restraints) and functional rope (i.e., "damsels in distress" tied to the train tracks). In the East, especially Japan, bondage is often elaborate and decorative, usually done with hemp or jute rope and called *shibari* (Japanese 縛り [shiba]: "tie" + ri: copula) or *kinbaku* (Japanese 緊縛 [kin]: "tight" + [baku]: "bind") or *nawashi* (Japanese 縄師 [nawa]: "rope" + [shi]: "craftsman") or simply "Japanese rope bondage."

Discipline emerges from physical consequences to violating rules. The **top** is the one who exerts control (binds or disciplines) and the **bottom** receives control (is bound or disciplined). Thus restraining or binding can be coupled with spanking, slapping, and whipping although in its more severe forms discipline bleeds over (pardon the pun) into sadism and masochism.

D/s: *Domination and submission.* (Note the lowercase "s" to emphasize subordinate status of the submissive.) Domination is generally about exerting *psychological* or *social* control over a **submissive** who accepts the **dominant's** power. Domination and submission activities often elaborate on conventional power relationships such as

- Boss/employee
- Teacher/student
- Husband/wife
- Doctor/patient
- Nanny/infant
- Owner/pet
- Master/slave

Does this give you some ideas for kinky role playing to act out? D/s is hardly an institution of privilege analogous to male-dominant society, but rather a relationship-specific pairing of the dominant partner's will *(thelema)* over the submissive's. The focus of D/s is on interpersonal power dynamics in a relational setting, whether temporary or long-lasting.

Contrast this with the subjugation of women that feminists rightly object to. The trouble that postmodern feminism introduced by equating a class *(womyn)* with each member of the class *(Andrea)* was that it denied individual class members the autonomy to opt into power structures, knowingly and with consent, that were deemed too repressive to the class as a whole. Thus Andrea came to represent all womyn, and Andrea's individual actions were evaluated not in terms of what is best for Andrea, but what is best for womyn. Andrea wasn't allowed to enjoy porn because porn degraded each and every womyn. This is a fine schema for exposing the institutions of power to scrutiny, but it fails to meet the essential feminist goal of freeing Andrea to choose.

Instead of being beholden to the patriarchal power structure, Andrea became beholden to womyn's agenda and was still not liberated. Oops.

S&M: *Sadism and masochism.* **Sadists** (named after the *Marquis de Sade,* a distinguished French aristocrat and pervert) derive pleasure from inflicting pain on others. **Masochists** (named after *Leopold von Sacher-Masoch,* a distinguished Austrian novelist and pervert) derive pleasure from receiving pain from others or inflicting pain on themselves. Pain can range from mild pinching and clothespin play to Inquisition-style rack induced confessionals. So relationship between sadism and masochism is complementary, not symmetric. For a long time, psychiatrists diagnosed sadism and masochism as clinical disorders since they seem to be associated with injuring oneself or others. Freud himself wrote extensively about sadomasochism and prescribed psychoanalytic treatments.

Of course, psychiatrists had no particular agenda to distinguish **hurt** (i.e., temporary, controlled pain) from **harm** (i.e., unhealthy, damaging, or destructive as indicated by the pain involved) and saw sadomasochistic activity as a cry for help rather than an expression of sexual pleasure. The S&M community as a whole didn't distinguish hurt from harm until about the late 1980s, so it would be misinformed to fault the psychiatrists' effort to prevent personal injury.

Be careful not to confuse a *tolerance* for pain with the *desire* to experience pain. When describing self-discipline I compare the hard work of character development with hitting the gym in that you can't put on muscle if you don't learn to bear the pain of exercise. But I exercise not because I like pain; rather that pain is the *cost* you have to bear for the result you want. I want a healthy physique more than I want to avoid the stress and sweat of lifting weights. That does not make me a masochist. On the contrary, I'm a sissy when it comes to pain. If fitness came in a little blue pill I'd be the first in line.

The BDSM Triskelion Symbol (sort of)

The *triskelion* (Greek τρι [tri]: "three" + σκέλος [skelos]: "legs") icon, similar to the ring described in Pauline Réage's sadomasochistic novel *Story of O*, has come to be a symbol of BDSM affiliation. The symbol is defined precisely so as to avoid confusion with more general symbols. Quagmyr, the symbol's designer, describes its intent on the website http://emblemproject.sagcs.net as follows.

> *The three divisions represent the various threesomes of BDSM. First of all, the three divisions of BDSM itself: B&D, D&S, and S&M. Secondly, the three-way creed of BDSM behavior: Safe, Sane, and Consensual. Thirdly, the three divisions of our community: Tops, Bottoms, and Switches.*

> *It is this third symbolism that gives meaning to the holes in each unit. Since BDSM is at the very least a play style and at its greatest a love style, the holes represent the incompleteness of any individual within the BDSM context. However "together" and "whole" individuals may be, there remains a void within them that can only be filled by a complimentary other. BDSM cannot be done alone.*

> *The resemblance to a three-way variation on the Yin-Yang symbol is not accidental. As the curved outline of Yin and Yang represent the hazy border between where one ends and the other begins, so do the curved borders here represent the indistinct divisions between B&D, D&S, and S&M.*

> *The metal and metallic color of the medallion represents the chains or irons of BDSM servitude/ownership. The three inner fields are black, representing a celebration of the controlled dark side of BDSM sexuality.*

> *The curved lines themselves can be seen as a stylized depiction of a lash as it swings, or even an arm in motion to deliver an erotic spanking. The all-embracing circle, of course, represents the overlying unity of it all and the oneness of a community that protects its own.*

Roles In Power Exchange

Power is a trip. It can make you strong or leave you vulnerable. But too often we think we *have* or *don't have* power when in fact we usually *direct* and *manipulate* the power that is granted to us through social situations, roles, and scripts.

Imagine for a moment that you're on vacation walking down the street of a big city minding your own business. You pass people along the way, some of whom notice you but most merely go about their business. *You* know that you're "just you," but there's no way for *them* to know much of anything at all about you.

You haven't revealed information about yourself that someone else could pick up on.

Now imagine the same walk down the same street, only this time you're wearing a police officer's uniform. Something changes. People notice you and become self-conscious. Sensing authority they defer to you, quickly moving out of your way and averting eye contact. This might even go to your head as you slow your pace and adopt a swagger, relishing your newfound power. *You* know that you're still just you but there's no way for *them* to know much about you. To them you're a cop. The uniform has cast you into a well-defined *role*.

If you're prepared to handle the stress of this role you'll thrive. Good cops are the ones who use their position of power in the name of public service and protection. If you're not prepared—well, the power has that tendency to corrupt. There is profound experimental evidence that role play alone facilitates psychological power and control. In 1971, psychologist Philip Zimbardo conducted the *Stanford Prison Experiment*. In this experiment, 24 healthy middle-class students were split into two groups: half were designated guards, with uniforms and night sticks; and half were designated prisoners, with ill-fitting smocks. They were locked in the basement of a lecture hall at Stanford university with the stipulation that the guards were not to physically injure the prisoners, but they could exert psychological control over their schedule, verbally abuse them, belittle them, etc. The mock prison was to be run for two weeks.

The experiment had to be terminated after six days because the prisoners began having nervous breakdowns and rioting. The guards grew belligerent and sadistic. In the course of the experiment, both guards and prisoners internalized their roles. They acted "as expected." They followed the **social scripts** that they believed governed how prisoners and guards ought to behave.

Role play in power exchange functions similarly but with a keen awareness of the well-being of each partner. Masculine and feminine **roles** (or **schemas**) are adopted by kinky partners who are aware of the game they're playing and consent to participate, all the while recognizing that it's the combination of role and actor that makes the scene come together. Role play need not deteriorate like the Stanford experiment, which was designed to replicate an adversarial and hostile relationship. Yet just like the experiment, sexual roles can provoke *emotional responses* that when used responsibly in erotic play become exceptionally stimulating.

	(B/D) Physical control	(D/s) Psychological control	(S/M) Pain
Masculine (exerts or gives)	*Top*	*Dominant*	*Sadist*
Feminine (yields or receives)	*Bottom*	*Submissive*	*Masochist*

BDSM Power Roles

For people with no experience in theater, the idea that *acting* and *role playing* and *scripting* extends to everyday life can seem a little absurd. You're you, after all; you're not *acting* like a character called "you." But think about how you might act a certain way in the company of your coworkers and yet differently when at your parents' for Sunday dinner. You're casual and loose when you're with old friends and reverent in church (or synagogue or temple or your Celtic tree worship drum circle). In fact you, as a human animal, are the best imitator of behavior this planet has ever seen. You learn how to behave—we call this process **socialization** (or **indoctrination**) when we unconsciously adopt customs from our native cultural, and **acculturation** when we borrow customs from other cultures. Why is it strange to think you take on a learned role and act it out during sex? And that you could even consciously choose from multiple roles?

Ah, right. Sex is who you are. *It's one thing to be on your best behavior at a job interview, but sex isn't like that!* So do you also think porn stars are showing their most authentic side on screen and that women never fake orgasms to boost their lovers' egos? Instead of equating your sexual behavior with your identity, it might help to clarify "I am" and "I do."

Personally I like to tie up women and usually do this as foreplay leading up to sex. That means I top. Not, "I am a top," because I am who I am and qualifiers like "top" don't do much good to elaborate my sense of identity. I've also bottomed, dominated, submitted, and engaged in sadism and masochism. But I don't feel "I am a bottom," or "I am a dom," etc. These labels come in handy as I determine what I like and they help me to communicate my preferences with others including my partner, but in and of themselves they are irrelevant to my sexual self-identification. I am not my role.

The reason I prefer to top is simply that it gets me hard. When I've bottomed my dick has gone limp and I've enjoyed no mental engagement, so I've found it's not for me. I hate pain so I don't like masochism, and I can be a *service sadist* if my partner likes pain— provided it's not too severe, there's no blood, and we get around to tying her to something at some point.

Switches, or in gay jargon **versatiles**, understand this ability to take on roles perfectly well. Depending on the day, the scene, the partner, and the direction of the wind they will top their partner or bottom for their partner. Find out if your partner is a top, a bottom, or a switch. Two dominants will fight for power and if they do manage to have sex, it's a safe bet that one of them won't get off.

Who's The Boss?

I had an affair with a professional dominatrix. She was sexy, savvy and smart and made a nice living tying up and humiliating men. As we got to discussing sex I found she wanted to try something different: she wanted to be the bottom. I stepped up to be her "service top"—almost. I did a chest harness with a breast tie. She felt compelled to correct my rope work, telling me what to do and how to do it (*topping from the bottom* in BDSM-speak). So I dug into my role.

"Don't like it? What you gonna do about it?" I proceeded to tickle and tease, spank and stroke, mindful of the fact that this was her first time bound and in the control of another person. I wouldn't have held it against her if she used the safe word to call it off. She never did.

Perhaps ironically, bottoms usually find that giving up power is *empowering,* in the sense that they have to locate some *source of power within themselves* (whether it's psychological, physical, psychic, spiritual or otherwise) in order that it be yielded. There are certainly submissives that are meek and weak, just as there are timid and shy **clueless horny dominant wannabes (CHDWs)**. But this indicates more about personality and temperament of the bottom than it has to do with the role of bottom itself.

Expansive or polyamorous relationships (i.e., multiple-partners) are usually formed as **triads** or **vee** (V-shaped) arrangements. It's most common to have one top and multiple bottoms but that's not required. Japanese *bukkake* videos feature multiple men masturbating onto a woman. It's not that she's submissive *per se* but she's bottoming and receiving from multiple ejaculators.

Sex, Identity And Orientation

Pansexual (Greek *pan:* "all" + *sexual*) means "without regard to sex," or inclusive of homosexual, bisexual, transgender, and nonsexual individuals. When used to describe a person the term usually means sexual interest in men, women and intersexed individuals; straight, gay, and bisexual; and gender matched or transgendered. When used to describe clubs and social groups it means "not discriminatory based on sex or sexual identity." A very inclusive term, indeed.

Straight folks who are not used to keeping company with homosexuals are often uncomfortable in their first leather outing. If you're heterosexual the whole leather scene can seem "a little gay." This should not be a surprise if you know some history. The path of acceptance and free expression was paved by the gay community in the wake of the civil rights movement. The pansexual nature of BDSM does not mean BDSM enthusiasts are predominantly gay, but the queer-friendly vibe of most tolerant events means there's often a significant homosexual contingent at kink and leather events.

If you're a straight male who grew up in America all this talk about homosexuality, transgenderism, and so on may be threatening or downright revolting. But if you're going to spend any time in the kinky community as you get your relationship started, you're bound to encounter a pansexual group and that group will have its share of proud queers and drag queens. If it troubles you, try to clarify for yourself the difference between homosexual and **homosocial** sentiments. Homosociality involves same-sex friendships, interaction, and bonding and has nothing to do with sexual orientation. Just because you like a guy's bondage style or admire his ripped physique does not mean you subconsciously want to fuck him.

Guys liking guys is usually more a case of burgeoning **bromance** than latent attraction. Also, gayness is not contagious. Hanging with queers will not make you queer, but it may infect you with sharp wit and a sense of fashion. And frankly, dude, if you're going to learn how to be comfortable in your own skin despite having sexual preferences that society frowns on, there isn't much better a lesson than to chat with a few gay folks about their coming out stories.

The masculine-feminine polarity is so pronounced that it can be confusing how sexual variation expresses itself in the population at large so it is useful to have a basic knowledge of the combination of sexual identities and orientations you're likely to encounter.

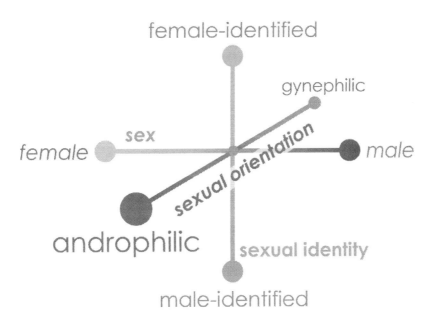

female-identified

gynephilic

sex

female · · · · · male

sexual orientation

androphilic

sexual identity

male-identified

Sex-Identity-Orientation Matrix

Sex. Sex is the biological reproductive configuration of the person, distinguished as male or female. But be careful since approximately one percent of the population consists of *intersexed* individuals who are neither strictly male nor female, and there are ultra-rare *hermaphrodites* who have complete elements of both sex organs. Sex is not normally distributed like height but polarized into binary forms male and female, simply because humans reproduce sexually so the polarity keeps the species going. But nature has variation, and there is a continuum in animal physiology (anyone who has grown up on a farm knows intersexed animals are uncommon but not that odd). For about a century an intersexed individual was surgically assigned a specific sex during infancy, usually by simply lopping off the offending penis-related parts. Sorry about that, guys.

In Other Words: You can usually split people into the "has penis" group or the "has vagina" group, but sometimes it's a mess down there. And a whole lot of people don't identify as their naughty bits at all. Really. Call someone a dick or a cunt and see what kind of response you get.

Sexual Identity. Sexual identity describes how a person perceives his or her own sexuality. An individual's brain structure and chemistry is a major factor in determining their sexual identity, while individual identity is constructed from personal history and social factors. People who are *cissexual* (Latin *cis:* "on the same side" + *sexual*) identify with their birth sex. People who are *transsexual* desire to be or have already become the sex opposite their birth sex. (This is tricky because after sex reassignment surgery, a *transsexual* female is indeed a female but not a *cissexual* female.) People who are *transgender* may desire to be or to behave like the sex opposite their birth sex. For example cross-dressers are considered transgender but not transsexual.

In Other Words: Most boys like being boys and most girls like being girls, but sometimes not so much. Let folks be who they are. And just because it looks like a girl, talks like a girl, smells like a girl, and kisses like a girl, that don't mean it's a girl. Trust me on this one.

Sexual Orientation. Sexual orientation identifies the kind of people someone finds sexually attractive. This can mean heterosexual, homosexual, bisexual, asexual, or egosexual (you self-loving narcissist, you). At the same time a person may have a pansexual orientation and be attracted to people regardless of sex, meaning a prospective mate is attractive whether male or female, pre-op transsexuals or transgender XY females. To deal with relational terms like *hetero-* and *homo-*, sexologists (yes there is such a thing) have defined the terms *androphylic* (likes guys), *gynephilic* (likes girls), *bisexual* (likes guys and girls), or *pansexual* (likes 'em all).

In Other Words: If you like them like that, and they like you like that, well then that's that.

At some point you will probably find yourself saying, "Hold on, I'm into that but I'm not that extreme! And that's just sick. I'm not into leather and I don't need to have threesomes to get off" This is because your mind is busy at work trying to detect patterns of norms, protocols, and conventions for these pansexual groups. We seek **social reference points** so we know what constitutes "acceptable" behavior, because ten thousand years ago to be cast out of your clan meant the end of you. Literally. Ostracism meant you would starve to death. Banishment meant you would wander forever outside your homeland, always an outsider.

It is fairly typical in kinky relationships to include some kind of power and control play. Holding someone down and having your way with them can be done in a perfectly healthy, nurturing relationship. An appreciation of the different types of control and pain that people enjoy along with a working knowledge of identity and orientation factors can help you set expectations so your relationship can indeed remain healthy.

Types Of Control

Since the different varieties of BDSM overlap, a mutually exclusive and exhaustive classification system is not very useful. Instead an overview of different types of control allows you to express your wants and needs (and *meh's* and *do-not-want's*) more clearly with your partner.

Physical Control. Bondage is the most obvious form of physical control because it restrains the bottom, thus limiting their physical freedom. Of course, physical control is not only about restraining limbs. It can involve confinement, such as keeping someone prisoner in a dungeon or locking a person on a human-size birdcage. It can involve physically overpowering someone without restraints and instead pinning them down with your forearms or using your body weight to keep them off balance. It may involve having a third person stand guard at the doorway in case the bottom flees.

The essence of physical control is that the bottom is not necessarily playing along with the scenario. He or she can resist. The bottom may struggle against restraints, or try to flee the cage, or fight back in a simulated abduction all as part of the escapist arousal process that lends to the sensation of being overpowered by a stronger force—but not necessarily outsmarted by a superior intellect.

Restraint has been shown to induce a mental and physical state of peace, relaxation, and bliss in the bottom; to send them into subspace. Subspace is an altered state. It's a perfectly natural and normal altered state, like sleep or a runner's high, but an altered state nonetheless. Imagine the spine tingle you get from a well-told story, the pleasing frubble during a good night drinking, or sense of euphoria during a chemical high. Altered mental states are potent and enticing to your neurochemistry. Being drunk or on drugs induces chemical and physiological changes within your brain, liberating us from our stone-sober, hyper-attentive ego state. Ask a sub to describe the feeling of being controlled by someone else. They'll usually say, "It's like going to my happy place."

I once met a young rope fetishist who was a well-known top, highly analytical and articulate about his own experience. He explained things this way.

I love to bottom. I feel at home in rope. The feeling I get, it's ensconcement, like being hugged, cocooned, even cradled in rope. I bottomed for Sir Moon who moved out of the state and so I sought a new top but could not find someone even close to the same skill level. Sloppy rope just sucks. Moon's technical precision is unmatched. Nothing produced the same satisfying sensations. So I decided to start topping. If I couldn't experience the sensation for myself, I would capture it empathetically by giving it to others. I would do it right.

By the way, people who identify as top or bottom but who never experience things from the other side are missing out on a remarkably enlightening perspective. I top. I am in my glory when I'm tying a woman I'm attracted to and have a deep emotional connection with. But it's extraordinarily difficult to "feel" things from a point of view other than your own, even if you have an incredible imagination and tons of empathy. For the purpose of *education* (as opposed to *stimulation*) I've bottomed, and there are practical and ineffable aspects that cannot be observed from the perspective of the top. The sensory elements, the touch, the presence. To describe it destroys it because words give an artificial sense of specificity, as though the whole episode were a mechanical process rather than a subtle experience. Words fail.

In fact that's an important truth. The BDSM experience cannot be transmitted to someone who has not experienced it firsthand merely by watching others or simply with a description. Despite the fact that I use writing as one medium to convey ideas, even the best writing only conveys gross concepts, makes metaphorical connections, and illustrates logical points. Experience *alone* captures essence. Words cannot do justice to the actual sensations, the feelings, and the nuance of a kinky experience. And thank goodness for that.

Psychological Control. In contrast to physical control, psychological control is about the submissive yielding to the dominant, whether fully and without hesitation or as a spritely minx who pokes, prods, and cajoles the dominant into action.

Psychological *resistance play* involves a submissive who tacitly agrees to the dominant's desires, but in the spirit of play seeks loopholes, denies her own malicious intentions, and provokes an incident to create erotic drama. Often in resistance play the submissive challenges and thwarts the dominant, apparently out of disrespect or irreverence, only to find the dominant's reprisals used to reestablish the default power dynamic. Bottoms who engage in resistance play are referred to as **brats**, **sprites**, or **smart ass masochists (SAMs)**.

Psychological *acquiescence* incorporates the active search for discipline, structure, and servitude. Once the templates of traditional relationship structures have been destroyed in a fit of sexual ecstasy, it is not uncommon to meticulously restore order from the new wide-openness, to reassert boundaries, principles, and expectations under the guidance of the dominant. Thus the submissive fully and unhesitatingly accepts the dominant's directions. This does not mean the submissive asks no questions; rather, questions are used to *clarify* the intentions and *anticipate* the likely desires of the dominant. Questioning is generally not intended to confront or debate the will of the dominant as in resistance play.

In some sense, the distinction between resistance play and acquiescence illustrates the degree to which the roles are taken seriously. That is, the relationship may involve a serious commitment by both partners, yet the type of psychological control may be accepted lightly or with great solemnity. Psychological control relationships can be made formal and may incorporate servitude contracts, specific rules, and explicit consequences such as physical punishment, humiliation, or the removal of privileges.

To an outsider the behavior in a control relationship may appear abusive. But for the participants there is an incredible amount of physical and mental satisfaction. These controlling elements create

What A Predicament

When I do resistance play I like to set up predicaments where my bottom has to make choices. But the choices involve trade-offs and dilemmas, little *gotchas* that make the game more fun and challenging.

I have one playmate who loves to instigate. "You're free to slap me at any time," I tell her. "If you do, I'll crop your ass red." "Okay but I don't want to be tied up today!" she responds. "No problem. You can tell me you don't want to be tied up by slapping me," I say. "But, then you'll tie me up AND crop me," she notes with a sigh.

Damned if you do and damned if you don't.

structure and order, like a puzzle to be solved. Rules and consequences encourage strategic thinking much like chess and other games of strategy sharpen the mind. The thrill for the top or dominant is to establish the rules of the game, to define the structure and take control. The thrill for the bottom or submissive is to play within or violate the rules, to explore the structure, to vie for or yield control.

A piece of advice to dom(me)s: *don't make rules you won't enforce.* Even though my inner sensitive new-age guy tempts me to say, "Hey little buddy, it's okay. Anything goes! You do what works for you and I'll do what works for me and the world will be rainbows and unicorns!" I can tell you from experience that there's nothing more frustrating for a submissive than a dominant who doesn't keep his word. It destroys trust, creates confusion about true expectations, and sours the relationship.

Distinguish rules from guidelines if you must. But enforce your rules.

Types Of Pain

For most people, pain simply induces a flight reaction. *Ow!* sends a clear message to the brain to avoid the source of pain as quickly as possible. Learning to master the initial reaction to pain, the flight reaction, so you can *respond* to the physiological stimulus as a *sensation* rather than a *threat* is central to sadomasochistic pain play. Pain play varies in its severity, from mild bottom spanking to nipple clamps and clothespins on the genitals; from teasing a submissive with the point of a knife (careful not to break the skin), to labial piercing, cutting, and scarring.

The crazy torture devices of the inquisition and the execution of witches in Salem show how sadistic people can become in their will to dominate and control others. This seems to be the popular notion of how kink works (coupled with the scene at Zed's pawn shop in *Pulp Fiction*). But the fact is I don't know of a single kinkster who is out to impale anyone in a medieval confession chair, and I certainly know of no volunteers. I'm sure it has crossed some minds, but safe and sane prevail.

In fact I've found most sadists to be power mad sissies who whine and bawl if they stub their toe. But you don't have to endure pain in order to inflict it with erotic potency.

Physical Pain. Physical pain can serve as sheer erotic arousal (or meta-sensation). Hyper-focus on the body and skin combined with the anticipation of the next sensation produces endorphins, distorts the perception of time, and allows the masochist to enter their happy place. While whipping, slapping, and **blood play** may seem like extreme lengths to go for gratification, consider the fact that the modern forms of boxing, wrestling, and mixed martial arts have been mainstream recreational activities for decades. Gymnasts, body builders, and long distance runners derive immense satisfaction from stressing and straining their bodies, only to experience the reward of better fitness once they've allowed them to repair. And they don't even get to orgasm at the end of a workout.

Some people love blood play with knives, needles, piercings, and so on. In its extreme form, *picquerism* involves sticking or stabbing a victim and arousal can go so far as attraction to amputees *(acrotomophilia)*, body modification, self-mutilation, and dismemberment.

One night I witnessed a scene between "The Preacher" and "the sinner." I made the following notes in my journal.

By 2AM there was an hour left to play. The stage was set: a petite, busty young woman ("the sinner") chained in 4'x4' cage, hands cuffed above her head and legs spread wide. Naked but for leather boots, gloves, and extensive tattooing. A plastic tarp covered the floor, hinting at the fun in store. A dom ("The Preacher") entered the scene, swabbing alcohol on her labia as she writhed and bit her lip. Removing the sterile needle from its plastic wrap he asked (more like demanded), "Ready?" "Mmmmm," she replied. Demonstrating great experience he swiftly and firmly pushed the first needle through her labia. "Ohhhhh!" came the loud breathy moan, the sudden pain dulled by what I expect was a massive endorphin rush. After inspecting his handiwork he opened the next needle. And so it went, alternating left and right, until she had nine needles. "Fuck you! Oh my God! Stop! Fucker!" she shouted as she struggled, all part of the prearranged scene. Having moved closer for a better look by this point I noticed her forearm tattoo which read: "Do Not Be Gentle." When the needle rites were finished she slumped, as if any will to resist had left her body.

The next day I ran into the sinner during lunch. "Shit I saw you in the dungeon last night. That was quite a scene. How you feeling?" "Great!" she said, bright eyed and smiling. "Really? Any lingering pain?" I asked. "Pain?" she said, looking half confused. "No." She could tell I wasn't in the know. "Oh, yeah that doesn't last. After like an hour I don't feel it anymore." "Really?!" I said incredulous. "Yeah, nothing," she said gently stroking her crotch, "but boy was it fun!"

Despite my shock this was all highly informative. The Preacher had taken safety precautions to avoid serious injury but his aim was to hurt. He enjoyed inflicting pain. He was careful to avoid any harm (i.e., long-term damage, impairment, or disfigurement). He was sadistic yet not malicious. The lesson to be learned is that to the right person, pain can be fun.

Psychological Pain. For many of us emotional pain is much more intense than physical injury. Personal history and temperament determine much of what hurts us, and quite a few masochists seek humiliation, degradation, and insults almost as therapy for their psycho-sexual emotional situation. Sometimes stimulation triggers associative memories such as when someone enjoys being scolded and threatened because their mother who loved them very much always scolded and threatened them. It's a comforting and reassuring brand of pain.

In other cases, the mere attention of another person can fill an anxious void that is made all the more intense when it's pointedly directed at your shortcomings. If someone tells you what a stupid bitch you are and then fucks you senseless, you may savor the intensity all the while plotting your revenge when the bastard finishes his attack and lets his guard down.

Control in the context of power exchange determines whether the painful experience is erotic. As one masochist put it to me, "I like it all: pinching, impact, humiliation. But if I slam my fingers on the car door, it hurts in a not-so-good way. And if you call me a stupid dick on the street, well that's just mean." All pain hurts, but not all pain is erotic.

Realize that unless your partner is malicious or self-destructive, they won't usually hurt you out of sheer cruelty or spite. People generally hurt one another when they *don't know* what to expect, and they fill in the gaps with gloriously impossible fantasies—only to blame the other person when reality sets in. The kinky version of controlled pain is different from accidentally "hurting someone's feelings." The more you learn to communicate and negotiate (as detailed in the chapter *Negotiate A "Scene")*, the better you'll avoid hurting your partner in this manner.

As with control, hurt can be either physical and psychological. If you genuinely care about someone and you make yourself vulnerable to them emotionally, at some point or another you are going to hurt one another. The more openness and intimacy you share with someone, the more your expectations will grow. Relationships are built on a shared history and expectations about the future. Disappointment is simply the failure of someone to live up to expectations. Should your expectations become unrealistic and not be fulfilled by your partner, painful disappointment follows. This is probably not the kind of pain you're looking for and it can be handled better with clear expectations and ongoing communication.

Aftercare

Before I got involved with the fetish community my notion of aggressive sex was that it ended with something like aftercare. The tone was different. My fantasies tended to involve ravishment and resistance, but after all the violent sex the object of my desire would have fallen in love with me (or at least with my awesome sex instrument), and we would stroke and cuddle one another in an effort to ward off post-coital *tristesse*. When my ravishment fantasies found their outlet with women I was already in love with, the value of "aftercare" became obvious.

Aftercare is the soothing, comfort, and reassurance that follows an intense encounter, especially one that involves resistance and physical aggression. For most people aftercare includes cuddling, petting, and pillow talk; for some it means being left alone to recoup and reflect. This gradual transition to normalcy after the sexual performance helps the bottom through what can be a startlingly empty feeling. Think of a time when you finished some exhausting undertaking, like cleaning up your place after a holiday party or your last few nights in an empty house before a cross-country move. A moment's pause and the high-stimulus individual begins to ask, "Okay, what now? What next?" Aftercare fills the craving for closeness and fullness, the absence of which can produce a very unsettled feeling.

I had one happily hyperactive girlfriend whose attention span would go to zero whenever we had sex. Aftercare involved a few minutes cuddling followed by one of two things, either going out to party or going straight to sleep. Finishing before midnight guaranteed her restlessness would get the better of her and cause us trouble falling asleep. "Okay, what do you want to do now?!" she'd ask. "Umm, take off my condom…"

Devil's Advocate

⟿ What if my dom(me) is not forceful enough?

I get this question from women a lot. Dominant does not necessarily mean sadistic so it's reasonable that your top may have mixed feelings about inflicting pain on you. For example I'm happy to spank and pinch and pull a woman's hair, but electrodes and blood play are not my thing (even if they're hers). If your dom(me) is not instinctively vicious or hasn't calibrated your pain threshold, talk about it. Describe what you like so you can both get off.

As a sub, it's your responsibility to learn what satisfies you and seek a dom(me) who's a good fit for you. If your partner has potential you can suggest you attend a regional fetish conference or a local dungeon workshop together. Rope craft and topping are skills that can be learned. People can take lessons and train with experienced kink educators. This is a great investment of time and money if it improves both of your sex lives.

As a practical matter you can use a **go word** (like "green") that acts like a complement to a safe ("stop") word. Just like the thrill comes in saying "no" even though you don't mean "no," a go word can be used to say "harder" without actually saying "harder," i.e., without topping from the bottom. It gives the top the green light to let loose — the bottom can handle it.

In the end though, if he or she can't deliver what you like you'll want to consider finding a new top to play with.

⟿ What if my partner is not doing what I like?

Clearly your partner is an asshole. After all, he or she has read your mind, determined exactly what you want, and intentionally denied it to you. The nerve!

Look, most of time if someone you care about is not giving you what you want it's because they don't know or don't quite realize that you want it. The fact that you smile whenever you look at the candles on the kitchen table does not flawlessly communicate the message, "Drip hot wax on my chest babe, I love it!"

I know that talking about sex is scary and self-disclosing. You make yourself vulnerable when you share predilections with another person. But sharing yourself is the whole point of an intimate relationship. You share your time, your experiences, and your physical space so suck it up and bring it up.

If we start with light bondage play will things get too rough?

This is a great question that has to do with human psychology and is not restricted to kink. What would you do if your partner had an addiction to gambling, or alcohol, or drugs? Mild recreation can escalate depending on the person, the situation, and the activity. But just because it can escalate does not mean it will.

Discuss this concern with your partner. Learn about past addictions or problems. When people learn to be comfortable in their own skin they regularly become reflective, self-critical, and self-aware enough that they can sense their own compulsive tendencies coming on. If you're nineteen and you don't know if things will escalate then the short answer is that they might. A safe and supportive outlet to explore this aspect of your sexual curiosity will be healthier in the long run than denying it until you're forty to suddenly one day quit your job and leave your family to become a filthy spanking slut.

But what if I actually hurt someone because I lose self-control?

People with some experience in the BDSM community tend to control themselves better. In bed I get extremely aroused playing with my partner but don't rush penetration. My arousal comes from control, from her arousal, and from intensifying and prolonging the experience. I don't feel an urgent need to release. As a dominant I like to remain in control of the environment, the scene, and myself for a good chunk of time.

If you're on the verge of losing self control, repressing or denying your kinky tastes will not help. Avoiding sex entirely can help, which is why cloisters, off-site treatment, and interventions can help "cure" people. Out of sight, out of mind is a useful coping mechanism. But denying or repressing your physical urges will not help if you ever find yourself exposed again.

If you're afraid of a little pain, distinguish hurt from harm. If I accidentally elbow a girl in the nose, that hurts but it's an accident—it happens. If I start slapping her around without negotiating and keep it up after she says the safe word, that's harm—it's malicious. Expect a little hurt but avoid doing harm.

Think For Yourself

1. What specific elements of BDSM excite you?

2. Do you identify sexually as more *masculine* or as more *feminine*, re-gardless of your biological sex? What aspects do you identify with?

3. What, if anything, do you enjoy about each of the following?

   - *Psychological* control

   - *Psychological* pain

   - *Physical* control

   - *Physical*   pain

The Kinky Mindset

There's something funny about being kinky. Literally—kinky sex is playful. Think of the words people use: play space, play party, role play, play partner (or playmate), sex toys, toying with taboos.

The ability to play requires a certain level of comfort in your own skin, levity, and humor. While kink is not necessarily silly, it does tap into playful pleasures, mood alteration, and deeper emotional experiences.

If you've ever been around children you know that boys and girls instinctively play fight, just like kittens and puppies. Playing helps us develop coordination skills and mental resourcefulness. There is no reason this playfulness must end with sex. In fact the best sexual experiences (even those with "dark" themes) are fun and playful in tone.

While every individual is unique, there are patterns, themes, and norms in the fetish community that continually arise and collectively help shape what can be thought of as a *kinky mindset*: a way of considering yourself and others that is fairly serious but enables kink's playfulness to come through.

Congruent

One of the most attractive qualities a person can possess is *congruence*—knowing who you are and what matters to you, having your own personal "code" and acting according to it. A person who has no code or is simply faking it reveals a major Achilles heel. The more you can learn to be entirely

Test The Waters

Women like to test men to see what they're made of. In general, if a guy backs down she knows she can push him around so she takes charge. If he refuses to take her shit and she likes him, she often grants him control. An ex-girlfriend and I were on our first date when she said a few snotty things to test me.

"Damn, you're mouthy," I told her with a smirk. "Yeah, whaddya gonna do about it?" she baited. "Teach you a lesson...trust me," I answered knowing what was in store. Our night ended with her handcuffed in my bed.

congruent—to completely own your intentions so you ultimately lose the need to defend them—the more you will attract quality people into your life for relationships. Whether you're a "kinky person" or not you find there's no need to deny your sexual proclivities.

Kink may be a passing curiosity that you experiment with and use to spice up your sexual relationships. On the other hand it may be identity-based, an intrinsic aspect of your personhood. In this regard congruence means self-acceptance. It means owning your sexual interests, kinks and all.

In social settings I act under my own intentions for my own amusement and rarely do things to win the approval of others. I've been lucky enough to have had some amazing, mind-blowing carnal experiences so I don't really have to worry about what people think of me since my validation stems from living a storied life. The scorn of strangers is irrelevant. At times this comes across as aloof and arrogant, derogatory terms for unconcerned and self-confident. Now, I'm quite conscious of how I present myself to others. I've been a performer and public speaker for over a decade and I teach classes in body language. I'm tall, I look like a scruffy biker type (this week), and I can seem intimidating to strangers. Being a shade pushy and borderline confrontational has become a central feature of my personality.

I've experimented with alternatives, just to see what would happen. When I go out of my way to be accommodating, or friendly, or "nice," I literally confuse people. It doesn't match how I look, how I carry myself, or how I am. It is not the least bit congruent with me.

The biblical concept of **thelema** (Greek θέλημα [thelema]: "desire, will") captures this idea nicely. Each person has urges, wishes, and wants. To pursue them with complete clarity of purpose and complete dedication is to be congruent. To repress or deny your own will is to be artificial. To declare artificial intentions and operate with a hidden agenda is fraudulent. I'm not saying *you* should act like a dickhead because *I* act like a dickhead. That would be stupid. If you borrow a persona that doesn't fit then you can't help but worry about being "outed" as a phony. Instead, move through the world in a way that is congruent with *your* core personal values, or your *thelema*. (Occultist Aleister Crowley used the idea of *thelema* in his writings but I'm not specifically referring to his philosophy here.)

A handy way to decide if something is congruent with you is to use the *New York Times* test. Suppose something you do gets splashed across the front page of the

New York Times (you might relate better to the idea of a permanent and public *Facebook* feed). Could you live with yourself? Or would the shame, guilt, embarrassment, or threat of job termination be too much to bear? For instance, suppose you meet someone and have crazy dungeon monkey sex that's so amazing the neighbors call the cops and it leaks to the press. Can you live with that? Or are you terrified of people knowing you have sensual appetites like every other person on the planet? It's hard to be congruent when you live in fear of being revealed as something you are ashamed of. Or go ahead and deny your desires while you suffer silently in fear if you have some kind of martyr complex, you sick masochistic fuck.

The *New York Times* test will not instantly correct your beliefs of make your behavior authentic. But if you try it, after a year or so you'll find you simply quit doing things you can't live with and instead focus your energy on things you really want. You don't actually have to live your life like an open book and blog it every time you get laid. But the guilt, shame, and anxiety that arise from your decisions disappears.

I can tell you that women instinctively sense if a man is insecure and "fronting," and it can spoil things in the bedroom. Initiating something kinky and then freaking out when it becomes too real because the sounds and smells and hair and sweat are not what you imagined reveals inexperience and a lack of self-control. At the same time, there's no harm in taking things slow and starting a relationship with a kink-curious partner (or a seasoned veteran) to learn the ropes. Own up to your current skill level. That's authentic. You're sure to find a willing counterpart to play with openly and honestly.

As with most tops I don't want my bottom to do anything only for my benefit. I want an enthusiastic partner. If you don't like what you're doing, stop it. Disingenuous self-sacrifice and accommodation are just turn offs. I want a bottom that loves being topped. That's hot.

Nonjudgmental

Tolerance starts where agreement ends. Being nonjudgmental is not about *denying* your own judgment, feelings, and opinions but instead it's about framing your experience in slightly more useful terms. Rather than evaluating something as good or bad, right or wrong, like or dislike, you ask the question, "Does this get the job done as intended?" You accept that another person has legitimate interests of their own and resist the urge to pit your tastes against their will.

It's hard to be congruent when you're different and yet deny others the privilege of being different in their own way. Once you give up your urge to judge others your ability to tolerate differences of opinion—and the bearers of so many stupid, childish, disgusting opinions—rises dramatically. After all, what benefit would there be if everyone thought the same? Is my goal to rid the world of uninformed ideas one heated debate at a time? Provided their point of view does not threaten my life or my limbs, I feel no urge to argue matters of taste and I certainly have no need to critique opinions merely because we disagree. And attacks *ad hominem* are for junior high debate teams.

For example, if you love to be spanked and I absolutely detest spankings, being judgmental prompts me to opine, "Damn that's gross. You should knock that off." Being nonjudgmental leads me to say, "You want to be spanked? Do you like an open hand, or a brush or paddle?" I remain curious despite my initial aversive reaction.

This should not be taken to mean that you become uncritical or completely unthinking and permissive. Quite the opposite. By asking, "Is this good *for this purpose?*" you simply entertain and consider ideas you may disagree with. Thinking can't hurt you and if something works better for you, steal that better idea. If you object you can disagree with the result *on principle,* not because you don't like the means. For example, if someone makes the argument that somehow I must endorse pedophilia because I'm nonjudgmental I reply, "I don't care if someone is turned on by kids. That's not my business. But actually having sex requires informed consent and children can't give it. Pedophilic behavior is a great way to violate one of the basic principles of the fetish community." Not all paraphilias are kink and not anything goes, but sexual activity is evaluated in terms of its consequences not my sense of "ickiness." (Or *squick,* a negative visceral but subjective response to something, as in: *Blood play squicks me.*)

For example, I have a boatload of opinions, some well-reasoned and insightful and others useless bullshit that somehow made its way into my skull. You'll hear me say, "I like that," "How does that work?" or "What evidence do you have for that belief?" Rarely will I say, "You should do this," or "You better not do that." When pressed for advice I give it, after talking extensively with a person to understand their intentions. And I do my best to provide reasons and evidence to support my recommendations.

It's tricky to describe this nonjudgmental, evidence-based, tolerant attitude precisely. It's even more difficult to install such an attitude in the population at large. So accept that it's rare and enjoy it when you find it in others. The advantage of being nonjudgmental is that you can fake being a regular judgmental fool when it suits your purpose. Judgmental fools can't fake tolerance. They're stuck. You respect that people have a right to exist. You allow differences to coexist. Those judgmental fools get their underwear in a bunch when people don't accommodate their anal retentive desire for order. Let them medicate their hemorrhoids while you enjoy the world for the incredibly kinky sexual playground that it is.

Taking a nonjudgmental attitude becomes easier when you recognize that differences need not necessarily be a source of conflict. Liking apples does not require me to suddenly become militantly anti-oranges, even though sometimes people manufacture false opposites in an effort to curry political favor. When I tell people I like rope I often get, "What do you got against leather?" Like I'm out to take away other people's shackles. There's evidence that people didn't think in mutually exclusive terms so routinely until a few thousand years ago, where we got into "one true" thinking like the One True God and whatnot. You can't worship Allah and Aphrodite. Both send you to heaven but one also condemns you to hell.

So note your opinions and let them guide your congruent behavior. Stay curious, accepting, and open-minded. And don't inflict your opinions on others.

Non-Defensive

Being non-defensive is a consequence of being nonjudgmental and having something you stand for. Rather than defending yourself against whatever onslaught of attacks, mockery, and ridicule that come from simply being different, your energy is directed toward enjoying your little slice of deviance. You *presuppose* the right to exist and learn how to express your kink in a healthy way. The world doesn't need to make special accommodations for you.

I once met an ordained rabbi and observant Jew at a leather fetish convention. He was a master who gave spankings. I asked him how he reconciled his religious calling with his fetish. "I act as God commands." "Yeah, but doesn't this violate some ethical stance toward sex?" I asked. "I see," he replied. "Let me clarify. This is an expression of my love of God and my love of the slave. Who am I to reject that which God has given the both of us?"

If I would have attacked him and condemned his behavior I get the feeling he would simply answer, "You're entitled to your opinion. I could be wrong. Find what works for you." He had no need to persuade me to agree, he was happy just to share a perspective I could weigh and consider.

Non-defensive does not mean that you fail to advocate for your rights or refuse to demand consideration for your beliefs. On the contrary, the nonjudgmental perspective accepts that you will always meet opposition regarding matters of opinion. That's part of life. You anticipate the opposition and establish the *frame of reference* for the dialog you engage in. You avoid being baited into a defensive posture because you tolerate disagreements and even open hostility toward you opinion. You don't take it personally.

Neither does it mean that you remain silent on matters of fact. People of reason may have differences of opinion but facts are not matters of taste. They are empirical. Your goal in any given conversation is to educate and describe yourself rather than advocate your views and defend yourself. You share a perspective with no need for agreement. If this doesn't sound easy it's because it sure as hell ain't.

One of the best ways to lose the urge to defend your sexual preferences is not to attack the sexual preferences of others. "Love your enemy" is not meant to be some kind of paradoxical mindfuck. It's a description of what happens when you let go of your own judgmental tendencies. With no need to argue or persuade or

Top This!

Just because someone wants a strong top does not mean they are shrinking violets. I've met countless strong women who are looking for even stronger men to take charge, and this can scare off your Average power-averse Joe. In one encounter I literally wrestled a woman to the ground and held her down as the moment escalated to sex, all the while laughing and teasing and biting and fighting. This is such an ambiguous scenario—*Is it going to happen or not? Is this consensual or forced?*—that the thrill comes from sheer violation of norms, formalities, and expectations about "appropriate" behavior.

set the record straight, conversations mature into an empathetic investigations of other people rather than some contest in which each person tries to install their will in the fabric of the other person's being. I *love* having enemies. I feel fortunate to have brighter minds than mine disagree with me. And I love to push foolish folks out of their comfort zones.

Moreover, once you're busy having amazingly satisfying sex, defending yourself feels like such a waste of time. It seems utterly irrelevant whether or not others validate your beliefs. Your direct and immediate personal experiences guide your decisions. Others are under no obligation to approve, or for that matter even understand. It helps if your partner plays along, but that's about all the agreement that counts.

Being non-defensive allows you to share your innermost self in a relationship. The more your self-discovery leads to greater self-awareness and self-acceptance, the less difficulty you have communicating your likes and dislikes in a matter-of-fact way that is free from qualifications or apologies. This gives your partner something of you to experience, an unguarded sliver of your character. When you find a partner who is also non-defensive and you open up to one another, you elevate and support each other in a way that's remarkably liberating.

Safe And Respectful

Kinky people often know their own limits and boundaries and they respect the limits and boundaries of others. Hey, if you're deal is knives and fire that's cool but I won't have that in my life. Playing with that boundary safely, getting to that edge, is part of the game. You can go to the brink and if you establish the terms you can do so safely and without much unintentional terror. (Although controlled terror as part of **fear play** is another story.)

Safety is a central consideration in the fetish community although there's plenty of debate about precisely what it means to be "safe." It's standard practice among rope bondage enthusiasts to keep EMT shears handy in case of any problem with the tie. The goal is to suspend your bondage partner from the ceiling not to terminate their life. Furthermore a lot of training in bondage physiology involves avoiding nerve damage and bending joints so they don't snap. Likewise, masters tend to keep around extra keys for handcuffs to free their slaves from shackles if something goes wrong.

A word to the wise: *replaceable*. Toys are. People aren't. Cut your fancy leather swing to shreds if it's choking your playmate.

A **safe word** allows for meta-communication that lets the intensity of play continue while the bottom expresses concerns to the top. Safe words can be any phrase not spontaneously uttered during sex ("stop" is a poor safe word during ravishment play). *Yellow* is often used for "slow down, this doesn't feel right" and *red* for "stop right now." Being able to call *cut* on the scene allows the bottom to let go and truly experience the moment, knowing that it's possible to snap out of it if they have to. These words are easy to remember and I don't know about you but I've never had a girl shout, "Oh God you're so red!" If you don't like these words come up with your own, like "banana," or "Hello Kitty."

Many Buddhists adhere to the principle of **ahimsa** (Sanskrit अहिंसा *[a]*: "no" + *[hiṃsā]*: "violence") meaning "do no harm." This philosophy asserts that living beings are to be revered and respected, even if individual specimens of humanity are difficult to like. Taken to the extreme, *ahimsa* suggests treating insects and animals in the same class as people. It's more commonly understood to provide due consideration for the core dignity and welfare of other living beings.

Ahimsa really governs the way kinky people play together. If at my core I respect my partner, I'm happy to humiliate and degrade her if we both get our rocks off. As the top, I'm ready to give as much pain and take as much control as the bottom can handle. But if I feel I'm harming the bottom (doing significant physical or psychological damage), or if the bottom feels harmed, the play eases up or stops. Thus the brilliance of safe words and scene negotiation. Play rough if you like it, but don't break your playthings.

For a long time the fetish community has used the phrase **Safe, Sane, and Consensual (SSC)** to capture this notion of safety and respect. But safe can seem boring to people who get a thrill from high-risk **edge play,** such as breath control, blood play, and fire play. The totally unsafe, completely insane thrill of letting someone nearly suffocate you (who knows what they're doing, of course) is better designated with the phrase **Risk-Aware Consensual Kink (RACK).** Both are common shibboleths in fetish circles and distinguish kink from abuse. The more anal retentive members of the community engage in the verbal equivalent of scat play, slinging epithets and debating the merits of one versus the other. The more pragmatic among us benefit from both and negotiate consensual scenes from the principle of *ahimsa.*

Realize that your personal safety is first and foremost your responsibility. The excitement—and the corresponding risk—in power exchange arises from crossing personal boundaries when toying with conventional and "safe" situations. Trust your instincts. Learn to anticipate your need for safety and demand it from your partner. If someone makes you feel unsafe, send them back to the woodshed to learn some fundamental fetish skills at a class or from a qualified sex educator.

Discreet

You might ask, "If kink is so healthy, why the instinctive urge to maintain discretion and preserve anonymity?"

Being congruent does not mean tweeting a message from your cell phone the moment you penetrate something. It's not about being an open book. Whereas the *New York Times* test allows you to say: *I can live with myself if I'm ever outed,* the principle of discretion adds the notion: *At the same time I'd prefer to keep my private life private.*

Think of it like the Las Vegas effect. If you know that whatever happens in Vegas stays in Vegas you'll be able to open up, experiment, and experience sex without an unwarranted fear of hostility or scrutiny. Strictly speaking, you incur no *reputational cost* due to your sexual appetites. Reputations are funny in that we have surprisingly little control over our own. Your reputation is *about* you rather than *created* by you. Intuitively we protect our reputations from damage because earning a bad rap when you live in a tribe of a hundred other people gets you ostracized and you'll starve. So much of the tension of being different stems from the obsessive desire to preserve one's public reputation, thus keeping two sets of books: the public face and the private self. Respecting one another's natural need for privacy allows partners to open up to each other more fully.

As a side note, the **reputation management** instincts we harbor (e.g., being self-conscious, worrying what others think of us, guarding our intimate thoughts, or avoiding taboo subjects) are by and large obsolete. In the majority of modern social settings the scrutiny of others can do you no damage. Sure, you don't want your boss to think you're an incompetent ass and fire you. But strangers in a restaurant, passengers on a train, people on the street—what are they going to do to hurt you? Call you names? Point their fingers? As long as they don't stab you or kick your dog you'll be just fine.

Being **outed** (i.e., having people find out that I take my sex with a side of kink) does not bother me because I'm interested in examining my own sexuality and sharing it for the benefit of others. It can be awkward to come to terms with the fact that we were born into a species that has reproduced itself prolifically. I find nothing awkward or shameful in the fact that my sexual drives and desires deviate from the norm since I don't aspire to have an average sex life anyway. So I'm free to act without anxiety or fear because I've internalized this nonjudgmental attitude along with a permissive, progressive belief system. I love people who would see me condemned for my deviant behavior. I encourage their reaction, their resistance, their disapprobation. The battlefield of public opinion is irrelevant when you accept responsibility for your own views, especially those that differ from prevailing mores. By educating I hope to raise awareness among people who are receptive, to reduce the fear and frustration that stifles sexuality so that in seven generations everyone can get their freak on.

Discretion comes naturally if you have little desire to chastise or punish what can be a flawed psychosexual world. People have different attitudes and to explore them is part of how society grows. Imagine for a moment that we did not have incredibly strong sex drives. Imagine we did not feel the urge to reproduce ourselves. Well, the planet would continue to have buildings and computers but there wouldn't be people for long. And those buildings and computers would not last. Being sexual and being alive are fundamentally linked.

During your own sensual explorations discretion will serve you well. Explorers are eager to investigate things and entertain possibilities without necessarily committing themselves to some agenda. They have not signed up for the responsibility of complete membership or *identification* with the kink community they're experimenting in. Explorers reserve the right to back out later, because they're just trying it on to see if the like it or not. They go out of their way to avoid guilt by association.

In other words if I tie up a girl and flog her ass only to find it's not for me, I don't think I want people to say, "Oh he's that sicko pervert who beats up girls." Especially if later on I myself think such people are sicko perverts. To be identified with this group would cause me internal tension as I wrestle with my own self-image. The realization that I *have done* what I *condemn* would induce a **cognitive dissonance**, the unpleasant sensation of having conflicting and contradictory ideas kicking around one's head. This is more likely to produce neurotic trauma than it is to induce enlightenment.

For the record, I don't consider myself to "be kinky." If it helps you to regard me as "a kinky person" that's fine but that's now how I regard myself. As I've said, sex is something I do, and my sexual preferences are something I express. I *am* a sexual being, in as far as *I am a being* who was born sexual and male, but my sexual practices are *activities* and I do not construct my own *identity* from sexual behavior. This mild case of depersonalization allows me to avoid the temptation to defend my behavior from those who disagree with it.

I'm secure in the knowledge that I do as I will but not at the expense of others—I avoid harm. There's a huge amount of sexual variety in our species, so learning what turns me on and turns me way off is not a big deal. It's personal in that it pertains to me, but everybody goes through it so it's not all that unique. And there are plenty of perverts who make you and me look like Mother Theresa by comparison, so there you have it.

If this all seems like common sense advice along the lines of "Be honest with yourself and others," I think it is. But it's honesty for practical reasons not moralistic ones. Lying takes effort, increases your anxiety of being "found out," and damages trust. If you want to trick someone into sex, lie. There's not much someone like me can do about it anyway. My experience is that honest, trusting kink is simply better for everyone involved. It fosters healthy, happy, and productive sexual relationships.

Doesn't that sound better than trick-fucking someone for laughs? It does to me.

Devil's Advocate

WTF? It sounds like kinky people are stuffy, politically correct, self-righteous saints!

Once you've accepted yourself and learn to accept others as they are, you free yourself to be more open and irreverent and light hearted. If politically correct means *inclusive* that's probably right. Instead of attacking folks and passing judgment on others like some kind of over zealot crusader, I find that I playfully tease and mock and make fun of my partner and community members in a way that is congruent with my biting and sarcastic nature. This just happens without a lot of the anxiety brought on by continually worrying what people think.

Maybe I'm too dumb to think the melodrama of being sexual is serious business, but it's all just a little absurd when you think about it. You can be tense about it if you like. When you're done with that I'll be over here giving multiple orgasms to the hot chicks.

You say all these things about the kinky mindset. Are you trying to tell me how I should think?

No, but it's tough to describe how a lot of people operate without tacking on, "And so should you!" Fundamentally you should do what works for you even if you disagree with me. The reason I describe congruence, nonjudgmental, safety, and respect is that these beliefs tend to free people and open them to sexual adventure. If you want to call leather fetishists sick fucks and you're willing to get permanently banned from whatever dungeon you're playing in, knock yourself out.

It's funny, when you put a group of people together (even sexual deviants) you find that norms emerge. The norms in the kink community have been pretty well established around the themes of mutual consent and risk management. Note that tolerating all this perversion does not imply advocating or even liking it, merely accepting some given behavior as someone's choice. I personally find blood play revolting, but if someone else gets a kick out of it I'm perfectly happy to accept the fact they like it and can do what they want with a willing partner. Over there. Way, way the hell over there.

⎯↪ It's really hard to feel nonjudgmental and non-defensive.
Tell me about it. With repeated exposure to things that put you off and a huge dose of self-awareness and self-acceptance it gets easier. I've worked with and interviewed literally hundreds of people regarding this way of experiencing the world and virtually everyone I know takes anywhere from months to years to let go of the instinct to critique, attack, and belittle things they don't agree with.

I'm not sure how to create a liberal utopia where nobody judges anybody, but I do know from personal experience that if you work on yourself you can dramatically reduce this tendency. It's difficult but not impossible. Don't let perfection be a prerequisite for you starting down the path. Really, life is so much better on this side.

⎯↪ Does everyone in the kinky community think like this?
Yes. We took a poll and found out that the kink community is a monolith that shares one brain and one agenda which is to recruit hot young pony slaves to go to the fridge and bring their masters cold beer. Didn't you get the memo? I suspect the reason this tolerance mindset is so widespread is that on the whole the kink and BDSM worlds have matured from an "advocacy at any cost" countercultural fringe group to a self-reflective and self-correcting support community. It's common to see queer queens and ultra-macho straight doms share rope techniques at nationwide bondage conferences. In an effort to learn from each other and share experiences, prejudices and biases simply interfere. When you have a common cause, especially a shared mission, differences are easier to set aside.

The fetish community doesn't seem hell-bent on public acceptance either. There's no protesting in the streets for equal rights, shouting "Rethink! Try kink! Get bruised with us!" As it has evolved, the community has grown constructively critical and I get the sense the fetish world is more secure in its own skin. There are twelve step programs to cope with sex and drug addiction conducted at nationwide sex expos alongside the dildo and corset vendors. Kink itself isn't a problem and healthy happiness is a central goal. Nonjudgmental, non-defensive, and discreet come together in a powerful way to help the sick people heal and healthy people grow. Sounds positively good for you, yes?

What about the hypermasculine dom(me)s who control every aspect of their submissive? They seem belligerent and not like you describe.

There's a difference between this overall kinky mindset and the specific agreement people make as part of an erotic power exchange. In this scenario public rough play and humiliation are probably arousing for both partners. The sub knowingly and willingly submits to the dom(me), or else it's unlawful detainment and will land someone in jail. If that's what everyone has agreed to, cool. If you over-identify with the sub and feel threatened by *their* erotic power exchange, that's your hang up.

Most relationship-bound fetish play does not spill over into everyday settings or involve random strangers. Think about this—if the dominant person were to be the same hypermasculine control freak and run into someone like me do you think he or she would be in a position to push me around give me orders? They can try, but they're probably sensible enough to realize they might lose a tooth if they do. Most masters have learned to calibrate their behavior because not everyone submits to them, nor should they.

The *de rigueur* approach to domination and submission can be confusing for newbies. Not every sub submits to any arbitrary dom(me), and not every dom(me) dominates any arbitrary sub. If everyone did this, the D/s relationship would be nothing special. There may be sexual tension and attraction between people who aren't already paired up, but actual domination and submission is negotiated. It's a defining element of the relationship.

Think For Yourself

1. What aspects of a kinky mindset do you already possess?

2. What aspects of a kinky mindset do you want to work on?

3. What aspects of a kinky mindset will you look for in a partner?

Meet Kinky People

Everything discussed up to this point has been designed to prepare you to play nice and rough with your kinky partner. Now it's time to meet some people to play with. If you're going to meet kinky people, first things first you've got to get out and meet people. Meeting kinky people means, first and foremost, meeting people you like. Then you gotta find that *kink connection*.

It can be tempting to cut to the chase and search for a kinky partner while avoiding vanilla social settings altogether. That can work. But my experience in the dating scene has shown me that people who are open to kink are far more common than you might imagine.

It's Okay To Look

A lot of anxiety stems from fear of judgment from others—fear a person will shun, criticize, disapprove of you or ruin your good name so others shun, criticize, or disapprove of you. Of course the disapproval of a random stranger doesn't matter; if someone you meet in a bar thinks you're a pervert, you won't get fired. But if your boss were to find out that you're kinky you may reasonably fear losing your job. Imagine a world in which everyone simply accepted the normal distribution of sexual preferences as fact and did not punish "outliers" as deviant perverts. For some this is heaven. For others, this is simply what the fetish community offers.

We may not talk about kinks, fetishes, and sexual urges because we consider it impolite—but we damn sure *think* about it. People often support ideas *they think* people believe in an effort to please the group, even though everyone *secretly* believes the idea to be stupid. This is illustrated in the story of the **Abilene paradox**. A family is enjoying the shade during a hot summer afternoon in Coleman, TX when Father, hoping to please Mother, says, "Maybe we should go to Abilene for dinner." Abilene is fifty miles away. Mother hopes to please Father and says, "Yes, it's been a long time since we've gone." Both secretly think the drive will be hot and tedious and the food subpar, but hoping to please the parents everyone goes along.

Not surprisingly, the drive is hot and tedious and the food is subpar. Upon returning home when Daughter says insincerely, "That was a great trip, wasn't it?" Mother replies, "No, not really. It was hot and uncomfortable. I just went to please Father." Father responds, "Really? I only went along with it because everyone else wanted to go!" As everyone says they would have preferred to stay home, they look at one another puzzled that they just wasted the afternoon on a trip no one wanted to take.

The phenomenon of **pluralistic ignorance** sheds light on the situation. Pluralistic ignorance occurs where a majority of people *privately* reject a norm but *publicly* espouse it, because they incorrectly assume the majority of people accept it. This can arise due to lack of data, misinformation, or projecting one's own fears on others. The apparent vanilla norm is something like, "Thou shalt not be kinky, you weird perv." But a whole lot of people who might publicly deny it have freaky fantasies they'd love to play out. They're closet kinksters.

It's fun to share your interests with likeminded people who can support and learn with you. So how do you go about meeting other kinky people?

Keep Yourself Safe

Once you've learned that the secret to incredible sex is freely deviating from the vanilla script without shame or guilt or embarrassment, you may ask yourself, "If shame and guilt and embarrassment no longer stop someone from behaving like a violent psycho and killing me, what does?"

First a bit of bad news. Nothing stops anyone from behaving like a violent psycho and killing you, not even shame, guilt, or embarrassment. If someone has a sociopathic break and decides to shoot up a post office, there's precious little that can be done to preemptively prevent that incident. But this has nothing to do with kink. The desire to harm someone is unrelated to a person's skill with rope. *Fatal Attraction* was about an unstable lover and an affair gone bad, not about a leather fetishist.

Now the good news. The vast majority people are not violent freaks, and you can get a sense of this with a few careful questions. If you're dominant you're probably going to lead the encounter, so ask probing questions of your partner. You can ask extremely personal questions if you establish rapport and offer an escape hatch. Start by saying, "You don't have to tell me anything you don't want." This shows that you don't mean to pry but rather that you want to get to know the other person (and make sure he or she is psychologically capable of edgy sex). Show empathy with phrases like, "I'm not sure if you've been tied up before. It can be scary or exciting. Imagine being tied up now. How would you feel?" Look for things that you have in common, people you both know, and values you share. Rightly or wrongly, if they came from your hometown or if they practice your religion, people just tend to seem more trustworthy.

If you are submissive you should look for a dominant who knows what he or she is doing and is able to take on the responsibility for the interaction, otherwise you'll hold on to control out of simple self-protection and it will be a struggle to yield and let go. Feel free to test your dominant, remain guarded, and trust your intuition until your trust has been won in whatever form that takes for you. I know plenty of female bottoms who are standoffish when they meet new people, because they meet a lot of men who have been **feminized** and are fundamentally not equipped to take control. Once the man has earned the privilege of a dominant position by being congruent and **non-reactive,** once he has shown himself continually in control of the situation, then they can accept his dominant position and submit to him.

A note of caution: don't confuse dominant for domineering, arrogant, or pushy. A dominant person expresses a subtle self-assurance and controls what they can, which usually means being self-possessed under pressure. They are people of strong will. Domineering people are generally egocentric yet weak-willed, looking for recognition, validation and approval from others. They are easily manipulated and difficult to trust. They are the reason we have the word "creepy."

 Race To Paradise

On the subway I once bumped into a very cute, thin, tall girl with curves in the right places. I complimented the tattoos on her arm and her positive energy. "Come on, this is my stop. Let's get a bite," I said. "I already ate," she objected. "Great you can watch me eat." We quickly got past the formalities and found things we had in common: a strong sense of adventure, a tendency to be physical, and a positive outlook.

"Look, I'm only interested in sex, religion, and politics. In that order. So who are you gonna vote for in the next election?" As I described *shibari* things escalated quickly and we went back to my place so I could put her in rope. Forty minutes from meeting to consummation—with time to grab dinner!

Everyday Settings

You can meet kinky partners just about anywhere—if you know what you're looking for. A **shibboleth** (Hebrew שִׁבֹּלֶת: "grainy portion of a plant") is a term, custom, or other signal that distinguishes members of a particular group from outsiders. The word was used in the Bible to distinguish tribes, because its pronunciation revealed a person's origins (like *y'all* indicates an American southerner). Leatherwear, tattoos, piercings, and punk haircuts are typical shibboleths of BDSM scenesters because of their association with counterculture and S&M. Likewise the phrase "Safe Sane Consensual" telegraphs an understanding of kinky sex practices governed by safety and informed consent. I have a shirt that reads *Safe. Sane. Consensual.* that I wear in vanilla settings. Vanilla people ask what it means. Kinky people ask me out.

I had a professional friend who would wear fishnet thigh-high stockings with garters and a vintage hairstyle to her job. Her sex appeal gets noticed to be sure, but the details of her sultry style slip under the radar of coworkers and clients. If you knew what to look for you would catch the Bettie Page homage that telegraphed her kinky interests. Looking for signals like this can help locate like-minded kinky people in vanilla settings.

If you happen to be looking for an over-thirty male dom, look for a goatee and a shaved head, something like Anton LaVey. Or a goatee and long hair, something like—well, like me. I embrace my own stereotype.

Chains Of Loose Change. Here's a tip for tops to test a prospective mate's compliance and receptivity to bondage. Bar games often involve tricks with coins and beer bottles so a female rope top taught me a trick to simulate bondage like a bar game. Ask someone to hold out their right hand, palm up. Place a quarter on the tip of each finger, making sure your partner balances each quarter on their fingertips. Then ask them to bring their left hand over the right, placing each figure on top of each quarter, mirroring their right hand and trapping the coins between each fingertip.

This simulates a cuff restraint. Ask them to close their eyes and describe the sensation. Tell them not to drop any of the coins as you move their hands behind their head or as you lead them around. If a prospective submissive enjoys this bondage simulation and is willing to accept direction and control from you, then you've got a candidate for a possible relationship.

Social norms are changing and people are learning to be more tolerant of sexual orientation and expression, but that does not mean everyone is ready to express their kinky interests or act on their curiosity. Their upbringing may layer on shame and repression. The idea of kinky encounter may so violates a person's social programming that they cannot bring themselves to experience sex while being handcuffed or spanked.

That's fine. It is no one's job to open up another person and insert a taste for kink. Your responsibility as a kinky person is to provide your possible partner with an opportunity for exploration rather than to compel them to try something because it might be good for them.

We summarize the pros and cons of each approach starting with this one:

Pros	*Cons*
• Kinky people have to work, shop, and socialize just like everyone else. If you're meeting people, you can meet a kinky person (or that receptive somebody) in just about any setting.	• Shibboleths are indicators but not guarantees. They can be confused because punk rock hipsters may sport leather accessories and nose rings purely as fashion.
• Meeting in person is more conducive to sparking attraction.	• Young people are more comfortable with body modification because it's cool but are often still sexually reserved. Such indicators can be useful conversation starters such as, "Nice tattoo. What does it mean?"
• Logistics are more practical (people don't usually buy groceries across town) and you connect in a relaxed context.	

Online

On the Internet, nobody knows you're a dog. It's easy to deceive and be deceived so take extra precautions. I've met people online and for the most part it's a great tool to meet people who know what they want and are too busy or too uncomfortable actively meeting people in everyday settings.

You can advertise your interest a kinky partner on one of the following websites, for example.

Alt.com	BDSMSingles.com	BeCollared.com	Bondage.com
Craigslist.org	FetLife.com	SandM.com	TabooPersonals.com

A few tips. Be honest with others and yourself. You don't have to be a swimsuit model or a football player to be effective meeting and dating people online, but if you lie and trick someone into meeting it won't do you any good. It's bait and switch and people feel duped. I've had countless friends and clients complain about someone claiming to have "a few extra pounds" when they're simply fat. As a rule of thumb fifteen is a few extra pounds but fifty is overweight. It's much better to accept yourself as you are and work on improving yourself all the time so you can share your awesomehood with a deservingly awesome person. (Or persons. Or goats. Being inclusive gets exhausting.) Show yourself in the best light, but don't rely on the darkness to mask the obvious.

I once met a woman who created a very appealing profile and detailed the kind of sex she liked. For privacy reasons she was scant on personal details. She shared only pictures of her face and described herself as having an "hourglass figure." She was shaped like an hourglass, but she intentionally omitted the fact that she was 5'6" and 240lbs. No one expects perfection, but "hourglass" has a classic buxom Sophia Loren connotation. To abuse it discredits the abuser.

The psychology behind selective omission is straightforward. **Sexual preferences** determine much of interpersonal attraction and sexual decision making. It's tempting to compensate for shortcomings with other traits, like emphasizing intelligence or personality in place of looks. But regardless of how things work in *Second Life*, attraction is not a conscious decision. Liking the *package* is part of the sexual experience. To miss this is a shame because for everybody, every body type, every quirk and quality out there, there is someone who *loves* it. You don't have to find me attractive (plenty of women don't), and I don't have to find you attractive. But a lot of people find each of us hot, and for some the feeling is mutual. Let's go meet them together and have a threesome.

Mild kink is becoming more mainstream so you can mention your kinky interests on vanilla dating sites without much fear of being creepy. In this setting Be a little poetic: "I love the feel of a silk blindfold between the sheets…9½ weeks is not enough time" is much better than "I want 2 tie u up n make u suck my cock."

If you're looking for a 24/7 master-slave relationship, vanilla sites are simply going to be a waste of time.

It's important to re-emphasize *safety, safety, safety*. I arrange to meet in a public setting to make sure she is not threatened and to allow either of us the chance to walk away if we're not feeling it. As the pursuer my job is to seduce and lead, not to trick someone into a hurried fuck.

For all you dom(me)s, remember to be congruent. I had a friend whose profile read "Dominant male seeks submissive female." But he was getting his dominant act together, having recently recovered from a lifetime of big-pussy-nice-guy syndrome. He contacted a very interested submissive and they arranged to meet. At their first face-to-face he was friendly and considerate but came off as indecisive. He went out of his way to accommodate her and attend to her needs. His confused *ahimsa* squelched his *thelema*. She wasn't feeling him and decided not to meet up again.

After a month or so of working on congruence and extroverting a more attractive, dominant character they caught up by instant message. She reluctantly agreed to meet. This time he was a man on fire, taking initiative, making demands (with which she happily complied), and establishing the frame of reference for their interaction. He remained attuned to her responses but was unafraid to provoke a reaction. From that encounter their relationship took off, and they've both been very happy exploring domination and submission together since.

Accommodating others takes a lot of work. Doing as you will while avoiding harm is much easier.

Pros	Cons
• You're always "on," since your profile is available for viewing and the site matches partners for you.	• You can't convey your personality in full online so you have to be unique or you won't get much attention.
• A good search engine allows you to find people who you wouldn't stumble across in everyday life.	• You don't spark much attraction online. Photos can be deceiving.
• You can telegraph your interests quickly and weed out bad fits. (See the **Sexual Preference Profile** in the next chapter.)	• At worst, you may set up a meeting with someone you don't find attractive and waste an evening.
	• You may come across someone you know and be outed.

Clubs And Dungeons

Fetish clubs and **dungeons** are great places to meet people. Most of them are private membership clubs that collect monthly dues. Some dungeons are completely private and require an appointment to enter. Most dungeons are open to members who are screened to verify age and (hopefully) criminal background. Open play nights permit club members with voyeuristic tendencies become an audience for performances by attention-loving exhibitionistic members. Clubs that have an active social scene are great for meeting people because regulars often mingle and seek out new play partners.

Dungeons usually consist of at least one communal room, a **play space** where people can make use of fetish equipment. A typical dungeon is equipped with a St. Andrew's Cross, medical tables with stirrups, queening chairs, a variety of suspension hardware, and cleaning supplies. Depending on the club, nudity and penetration may or may not be permitted. Each venue abides by its own rules, generally written to comply with local ordinances while catering to members' tastes. Group **play parties** are often held on weekend nights with other times available by appointment.

Most major cities have dungeons that you can join. Rural areas and more conservative enclaves are less likely to have fetish clubs of any kind, and if they do they probably won't make their presence widely known. Dungeons are particularly attentive to member privacy and discretion. Most offer private entrances and forbid any form of photography. You can usually find them online or through word-of-mouth from other community members.

A large number of clubs have a social hour, newbie night, and educational events that people interested in joining can attend to get a feel for the venue. You don't always need to be a member to show up but an RSVP and identification are usually required. These events are fantastic for meeting new people because there are no expectations and no pressure. If you're inexperienced you can ask others what they think of the place and its clientele. If you're a veteran you can invite someone to try out a scene you witness together.

Visiting a dungeon as a couple allows you to share in the experience and look into activities you'd like to try together. This takes the pressure off each partner to initiate something new and potentially awkward. Instead of being the responsibility of the person who brings it up, the encounter becomes something that "just came up," which means if one of you doesn't like it there is less ill will. Float it out there. See if your partner is game.

The first time you visit a dungeon focus on the education rather than the stimulation. Meet the staff, talk to the members, and find out if you like the vibe, the rules, and the regulars. A friend of mine was worried on her first visit about how to dress, how to act, and what to talk about. My advice was that she simply dress comfortably and take the experience in. If anyone asks, she's new and just checking out the place. If anyone invites her to participate in a scene say, "I'm not here to play tonight but I'd love to watch whatever other people are doing."

Street attire and basic black are safe (unless certain attire is required for a theme night). People don't pay that much attention to "new meat" during a play night—unless you're going out of your way to get attention with assless chaps or a leather teddy. Think about how heads turn when you walk into a restaurant. It's human nature. Fifteen minutes later you're the regular and the people who come after are the newbies. Each setting is a little different and you will pick up on the tone of the event quite quickly.

Pros

- Playing in a dungeon gives you a good idea what to expect from your partner.
- You can get very physical in a safe, monitored environment.
- You can watch others play and see things you and your prospective partner might try in private.

Cons

- In a small community you gain a reputation very fast (that can be good or bad depending on your skill level).
- The pool of prospective partners is limited to attendees and the "kinds of people" who hang out in dungeons.
- You have to deal with other people's kinks and perversions.

SIGs And Munches

Special interest groups (SIGs) are groups that get together because members have an interest in common. SIGs are common for alternative sexual practices and queer-friendly groups. With the increase in kink-friendly interests, BDSM student clubs are springing up on college campuses. Look for "kink-friendly," "queer-friendly," and "sex-positive" student groups. The trend on major campuses is toward an awareness of alternative sexual practices, and this tends to encompass kink along with gender and orientation considerations.

Munches are a well-established BDSM social activity. They arose in the 1990s as an informal forum for people to meet in person and share their interests with the recognition that people with kinky tendencies don't spontaneously self organize. By having a regularly scheduled event along the lines of a *Stammtisch* or Meetup group people can come and go as time and interest allows with new members regularly joining the group.

Meeting at a munch or similar kink-friendly event allows you to talk about your sexuality more openly and directly than if you meet in vanilla settings. Once you've gotten comfortable talking about kink in general, SIGs and munches provide yet another arena for you to meet people and learn a thing or two about what others are up to in their sex lives.

Pros	*Cons*
• Munches attract a crowd similar to what you find in a dungeon but without the play space.	• Attractive new members get swarmed while non-participating members can get overlooked.
• Munches are open to all (or to an age demographic) and membership is not required.	• Politics and reputation are based more on gossip than your actual kinky tastes or skill level (in a dungeon others can witness your technique for themselves).
• There is less pressure to perform.	

Conventions

By far one of the fastest ways to come up to speed on all things kinky (or on any topic for that matter) is to attend one of the many conferences that are held across the country each year. The different conventions are too numerous to list, so look for a convention you can attend (preferably in your area if you're looking to find a partner who may live in the vicinity) and one that caters to your interest, be it leather or rope or medical play.

Conventions are great for meeting new people to play with and for starting relationships based on your shared interest. Notice who attends classes with you and get to know them. I say things like, "I noticed you in the advanced suspension class. What brings you to the convention? Where are you from?" Asking simple logistical questions is much easier in this setting that meeting someone attractive on the street. (A note about *tact:* If you've just met the girl or guy of your dreams and you trip over your tongue to meet them, that's on the needy side. Be outgoing and friendly, but play it just a little bit cool.)

At the conventions I've attended, color-coded bracelets help signal that people are looking to play. For example, blue may be worn by tops, green by switches, and orange by bottoms. I don't believe these colors are standardized and given the permutations of sexual orientation and type of play it's best to check the particular color codes at your convention so you don't get arrested after you assume the person wearing a purple wristband wants you to abduct them in the middle of the afternoon and electroshock their genitals.

Pros	*Cons*
• Conventions expose you to a variety of new people and ideas quickly.	• It's hard to date someone who lives halfway around the world. Maybe you can start a *Same Time, Next Year* arrangement.
• Conventions let you focus on some aspect of the fetish scene: rope, leather, spanking, etc.	• Convention-initiated relationships can be difficult to maintain after **con-drop,** the post-convention letdown of being back in the "real world."
• Conventioneers are open to meeting fellow conventioneers and when there's a spark a relationship can grow.	

Now you have a whole range of options and no more excuses so get out and meet someone kinky today.

Devil's Advocate

⟜ Kinky people are so hard to find!

Yes they can be hard to find especially if you don't bring up kink, sex, or other edgy topics in conversation. People tend not to advertise their bedroom behavior on the street so looking for those shibboleths comes in handy.

Most of the clients I work with have trouble meeting kinky people because they have trouble meeting people in general. If you do not meet a variety of people but instead look exclusively for a kinky playmate, the search will feel awkward and forced. In general, the more that you socialize the more you find that people are available to play rough. Even if you suffer from social anxiety or are just introverted, the attitudes and behaviors that lead to effective social interactions can be learned.

↪ There's this one vanilla person that I want to persuade to try my kink...

I strongly suggest talking about sex and communicating your desires with your partner. Just realize that if your kink is incongruent or abhorrent to someone, or if it's a violation of how they express themselves sexually, you're pissing up a rope. Not in a sexy way.

Even the most open-minded people are not willing to give everything a try once. Open-mindedness and tolerance is more about accepting the fact that different people have different beliefs, tastes, and values. It does not mean adopting everyone else's beliefs, tastes, or values as your own. It does not mean that if you find something abhorrent and refuse to do it your mind suddenly snapped shut. It does not mean disabling your bullshit filter and making yourself over as a gullible fool.

Being open-minded means that you evaluate things in terms of whether they work the way they're intended and you're open to considering various alternatives. When it comes to kink, the basic question is *do you like it*? That I have the mental discipline to accept your sexual tastes without feeling threatened does not mean I'm down to have you shove a hamster up my ass. It's usually best to let vanilla folks remain a bland, boring vanilla but the chapter *Melt The Vanilla* discusses things you can do to bring up kink with a vanilla partner.

↪ What if I get it wrong? What if I misidentify a shibboleth and the person is not into kink?

If you get it wrong, so what? There's no harm in getting to know someone new. As long as you're willing to invest a little time and energy in the search you'll find a wonderful and compatible partner. People are generally more accepting and tolerant that we give them credit for provided we don't inflict our values and beliefs on them. Most people seem to believe in "live and let live," particularly in settings where people come together and socialize (i.e., in public spaces, restaurants, nightclubs, and so on).

I'm not suggesting you closet you kink but rather that you offer it to people you're interested in meeting and be congruent with it. When you proposition someone who isn't into kink you may face a little backlash, but who cares? If they don't like it, fuck 'em. (I mean, *don't* fuck 'em.) Move on.

⤷ what if my boss/neighbor/mother finds out I'm into this stuff?

If you're concerned about the scrutiny and judgment of people that are close to you that's understandable. Fostering your own nonjudgmental attitude will help you deal with the self-consciousness but it's up to you to learn what you can live with. If the fear of being outed is too great you best clean up your sex toys when the parents come over for dinner.

If however the issue is that you're repressive tendencies are getting the better of you so you can't comfortably express yourself, try getting *comfortable being uncomfortable*. Try teetering on the edge for a while. Imagine what would happen if you told a stranger in a supermarket that you love putting a saddle on your girlfriend and riding her around your apartment. If you can't handle that because it's rude or you're worried what a stranger might think, then your fear and insecurity control you. I hate to be the messenger here but it's no one's responsibility but your own to figure out what you can live with and what you'll do to handle your issues.

If you're so self-conscious that the mere mention, the mere idea of having crazy rough sex leaves you feeling worried and uptight then you're probably suffering from a general sense of anxiety and could use treatment. Handle this through talk therapy. The reality is that your interest in unconventional sex alone does not make you all that perverted. If mom knew she'd still bake you cookies.

⤷ Does being part of kinky scene give someone carte blanch to do whatever they want to someone else?

Whether you're part of the BDSM community, a veteran of the kink scene, or coming at it from a vanilla perspective, consent is required and abuse is a crime. It can be challenging for vanilla people to relate to kinky folks because the whole idea of informed consent is still new, but it's extremely rare to find a fetishist who breaks the law yet remains on the streets for very long.

People who hang out with other people in a community usually unconsciously adopt the norms and expectations of that community. The kink community emphasizes sexual education (the focus is usually on technical details and includes how-to classes) and does an excellent job distinguishing consensual kink from abuse. As for you, if you internalize the principle of *ahimsa* and check with your partner to make sure he or she or it has done the same you'll be fine.

Think For Yourself

1. Where do you socialize and meet people today?

2. How can you screen for a kinky partner when you're out meeting people?

3. List three clubs, dungeons, munches, or social groups you can visit to meet kinky people in your area.

   1)

   2)

   3)

Choose A Playmate

Once you've found someone attractive who you might be able to start playing with, it's essential that you determine if you're compatible with one another. Otherwise you're coasting along on sheer enthusiasm but it won't take long for your relationship to stall.

Determining if someone is compatible and then building on that compatibility involves a continual negotiation and mutual investigation of one another. It's tempting to launch your relationship as a one-time event and sort out all the details upfront, or to avoid the messy issues completely and simply *react* to relationship drama as it rears its head. Yet if you do this it will lead to frustration, miscommunication, and much messier relationship issues as things progress along a rudderless course for the two of you.

You can take the responsibility for establishing the tone from the onset without too much work if you know how. Building from attraction and liking, you and your partner (or all three of you, all six of you, however many of you are going to dog pile into bed) can start learning how suitable and how compatible your partner is for you.

Ideals, Tastes, And Preferences

Recall some of your earliest sensual memories. Maybe at age twelve you fell in love with your neighbor during your first wet dream. Maybe you had a hopeless crush on your high school chemistry teacher. In the early stages of sexual awakening we often form ideals that influence our sexual expression later in life.

All too often we are unaware of what our ideals are. We spend years seeking something then "suddenly realize" we've been on a quest to reconnect with our first love or find a replacement for a neglectful parent. We instinctively screen people for some quality that conforms to our *ideal*. There is immense value in having a conscious conception of what your ideal partner is like so you can look for him or her (or it or them you sick poly bastard).

Of course, an ideal is an ideal and real people are flawed, imperfect, skin-encapsulated egos. Having ideals doesn't mean you refuse to tolerate imperfection, that you're unrealistically demanding, or that you ignore options as you encounter them. The benefit of knowing your own preferences is that it helps you narrow your search while avoiding painful and frustrating relationship mistakes. If nothing else, your awareness will help you avoid repeating certain predictable mistakes over and over.

As you clarify your own ideals you will begin to appreciate the standards by which you judge your prospective mates. That's right: *judge*. This may seem in conflict with the nonjudgmental mindset described earlier, but nonjudgmental means accepting the *right* of other people to find their own way, to live by their own creed, to have their own values. It does not mean *agreeing* with their way, their creed, or their values. It certainly does not mean *liking* everyone the same. You have tastes and preferences that are all your own. And so you should.

Tolerant people too often get confused and deny their own preferences in an effort to treat everyone equally and see beyond a person's appearance. But having preferences and maintaining personal standards is not a flaw, it's a basic component of interpersonal attraction. Some things turn you on and some things turn you off. If you require physical beauty or a powerful intellect or a strong will from your partner, there is no shame in acknowledging this fact to yourself.

Remember the less defensive you are about your kink or your own sexual preferences the less you'll feel the need to justify your tastes to others. You accept them for what they are: Tastes. Preferences. Turn ons.

Or you can sacrifice your own happiness and satisfaction by settling for someone you *should* like because they have some noble and admirable quality that your misinterpretation of hippie-dippie egalitarianism says you should find attractive. Someone who completely fails to excite you, but someone you *should* like. But doing so would be foolish and leave you both dissatisfied in the end.

Ideal Partner Profile

The best way to improve your own awareness of the qualities your ideal partner should possess is to think about previous successful, exciting, challenging, and rewarding relationships. Chances are you found something of your ideal in the person you were with. If on the other hand your previous relationships taught you about your ideals because the person you were with *lacked* something, use that insight to complete **Appendix 1: Ideal Partner Profile**.

1. **Physical Features and Age Range.** Describe what really attracts you physically to a person. What excites you, makes your nipples or dick hard, and gets your blood boiling? There is no need to justify yourself, just describe it. The better you know what attracts you, the better you will be able to distinguish a good match from fleeting infatuation, particularly if you're looking for more than physical attraction.

2. **Personality.** Describe what kind of personality is compatible with yours—friendly and outgoing, or a sarcastic cynic? Artistic tendencies or more analytical? Outgoing or shy and reserved? Having ideals does not deny your own versatility, but they help you recognize your "type." If you're a top who is drawn to sexually adventurous women who are just a little introverted or reserved in public, note it here.

3. **Sexuality.** Describe the specific sexual characteristics you're looking for in a partner. What kinks and fetishes are ideal? Should the person be into anal, oral, fisting, or multiple partners? Should they keep their sexuality discreet or wear a collar in public? Make sure to consider physical sensitivity and responsiveness if it's part of the deal. If you absolutely need to be with a squirter to get your rocks off, then acknowledge this fact so you can ask about it when the time is right.

4. **Intellect.** Describe your intellectual ideal. Do you want an intellectual peer? Is a superior intellect essential, or can you get it on with someone who is not at your education level. Submissive women often need an *intellectual* dominant, while men are frequently threatened by women smart as them (or heaven forbid smarter). Preferences are just fine as long as you don't deny them, string someone along, and create false hope. Intellectual ideals helps focus your search because a nightclub scene girl and a Rhodes Scholar will travel in different social circles. Looking in the right place helps you both, since it's not your prospective partner's fault if they are not what you hoped.

5. **Social Status.** Describe the social status of your ideal partner. Status is frequently overlooked especially in America, but it can absolutely make or break a relationship. Do you need a person at the same level as you? Do you want a provider or a financially independent partner? Do you want a partner who is at home at the opera? A rock concert? Is the corner dive bar beneath both of

you? **Hypergamy** is the widespread cultural phenomenon in which women "marry up" in socioeconomic status in an effort to locate the best available provider. While differences in social status matter less today, many working-class men can't handle a doctor or lawyer or businessperson, and some women won't settle for less. If a certain social station threatens you or leaves a bad taste in your mouth, acknowledge it.

6. **Religious Beliefs and Spirituality.** Describe the religious or spiritual background you would like your ideal partner to have. Look for compatibilities, similarities, and shared values. If you're a Jew and you'll only date Jews, or if you're an atheist who thinks people of faith are foolish (or vice versa), don't deceive yourself. But do consider whether you can compromise and how willing you are to convert in order to make your relationship work.

7. **Deal Breakers.** Describe any non-starters. For some people this may be smoking, having kids, or being divorced. What must you have to be satisfied and what must you avoid to be in a productive relationship? Deal breakers should be things you will absolutely not tolerate. They cross the line and violate your core being.

To that point, don't confuse deal breakers and **pet peeves.** Pet peeves are the little things that bother or irritate or annoy us about the people. But they're things we can live with. If your partner has a few personality quirks it's no big deal. But if some idiosyncratic belief or habit drives you bonkers list it here. Of course, the more deal breakers you have the fewer matches you will find.

In fact, the more deal breakers you can convert to pet peeves and the more pet peeves you can convert to minor annoyances, the more people you will get along with. This is at the heart of learning to be **tolerant** of your partner. When you examine your ideals, base your entries off of past experiences so you can recognize and look for patterns in your romantic partners when you encounter new people.

Evolving Sexual Preferences

We often say "I want that!" "I need this!" "I can't stand that!" We don't give it all that much thought. We describe our likes and dislikes as they come up. Sometimes, though, we have a strong sense of the relative importance of our likes and dislikes. With experience we learn to distinguish *essential requirements* from *negotiables* or "nice to have" points. Being choosy demonstrates that you have selective tastes while being rigid simply limits your options. The fewer non-negotiable "must have" requirements you have for your playmate, the more tolerant and flexible you become.

A few concepts help clarify how **sexual preferences** factor into our judgment of a prospective partner. The **valence** of your preference indicates whether it's something you like (a *positive* valence means it's something you want to *attain*) or something you hate (a *negative* valence means it's something you want to *avoid*). The **intensity** of a preference indicates its priority compared to other preferences.

Preferences can be latent or explicit, conscious or unconscious, stable or situational. Preference lists are not *static* or *exhaustive*. My preference for a cheeseburger depends on whether I'm starving (*YES! I'll eat anything*), a little hungry (*Oh, cheeseburger doesn't sound bad*), looking for a snack (*No, that's a little heavy*), or if I just ate (*God NO! I'm stuffed*). It also depends on other things on my mind, like if I'm nostalgic (*I'd love a cheeseburger from the soda shop by mom's house*) or whether I'm feeling healthy (*I gotta cut out the red meat*). My preference may be incomplete, limited by low self-awareness and few prior experiences (*I don't know if I want a Teriyaki McBurger with Cheese, is it any good?*).

Similarly I may like rough play or whipping sessions, but if I'm not in the mood or if I have pressing work to do I'm not likely to spontaneously search for a spanking partner. Some preferences are more stable than others. Dirty talk may get me in the mood for bondage, but *nothing* will get me to shove my dick in a puppydog. Preferences can be loosely categorized based on the combination of intensity and valence.

- **Need.** A need is a strongly positive preference, or a *must have*. This is something you absolutely must include in your sexual repertoire either all the time or on special occasions. Some people need penetration and orgasm to make sex worthwhile while others must have emotional closeness or aftercare. This is not the same as being *needy* of course; it just means there are a few things that really get you off and you're actively looking for them.

- **Want.** A want is a distinctly positive preference, or a *turn on*. This is something you would really like when you're with your partner. Some people want a long-term commitment; others want variety or adventure or multiple partners. Distinguish your wants from your needs. Your wants are nice to have but you can live without them, whereas your needs are essential elements of your sexual experience.

- **Fact (No Preference).** If you're ambivalent to "being tied up" and you could take or leave it, it's merely a fact that you're open to it. You may be **indifferent** to the issue and be just as happy being a top as a bottom. You may be **uncertain** of your preference, as with someone who has never experienced erotic spanking and is not sure how they might respond. You might have a **latent** preference that you're not ready to explore. For example, someone who is deep down bi-curious may find it too threatening to their sexual identity to seriously consider a homosexual encounter and may decide it is a deal breaker in a relationship.

- **Dislike.** A dislike is any negative preference, or a *turn off*. This is something you really prefer to avoid as part of your sexual experience. Your dislikes can include pet peeves, unpleasant experiences, or self-sacrificing activities that are done for someone else's benefit. You may dislike you partner's anal sex games but tolerate it in return for some other benefits (i.e., emotional closeness). Be willing to discuss your dislikes with your partner.

- **Deal Breaker.** A deal breaker is a strongly negative preference or a *violation*. This is something you simply must avoid in a sexual relationship. Deal breakers can include **hard limits** such as bestiality, pedophilia, raptophilia, or necrophilia—since consent cannot be given for any of these acts. (At least not in America where underage sex is illegal and puppy howls do not mean "I agree.") Deal breakers are non-starters in any new relationship and can abruptly terminate existing relationships should they arise.

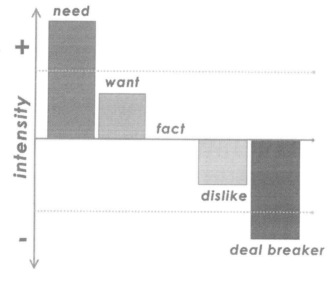

Sexual Preference Types

This categorization is immensely useful tool for communicating your preferences with your prospective partner as long as you remember that the categories are not perfectly rigid or absolute. What feels like a need one day can turn into a deal breaker another depending on your (or your partner's) mood, physiology, outlook, experience, or personal circumstances. Talking about what you want, what you need, and what turns you off as your sexual preferences change over time is fundamental to maintaining your relationship.

A person's **Sexual Preference Profile** can be thought of as a snapshot of this ever-changing constellation of preferences. This is useful because it helps partners discuss the *variety* of sexual preferences, attitudes, and experiences you both may have and what you might want to explore together, rather than narrowing the focus and risking serious miscommunication. True as is the adage "you can negotiate anything," it's just as true that unfulfilled needs have the tendency to dissolve relationships and deal breakers have a way of stopping them dead in their tracks.

Interpreting a Sexual Preference Profile

The individual needs, wants, dislikes, and deal breakers that are indicated in your Sexual Preference Profile may be broad categories such as being into pain, humiliation, and bondage; or they may be fine grained desires such as enjoying public rope suspensions and genitorture as part of **knife play**. Keep in mind that sexually adventurous people may think that more sexually reserved individuals have unnecessary hang-ups. People respond to sexual stimuli in their own way and we're each entitled to get our needs met and seek what we want while avoiding serious turn offs. Your partner need not be a psychopath to be a freak.

Some preferences are so fundamental to a person's identity there is no room for negotiation. In the psychology of decision making, multiple attributes like wants and needs, dislikes and deal breakers all carry a certain weight so some dislikes are more important than others. *Dominating factors* are those items that outweigh other items—thus the intensity of your preference may determine how imperative it is to incorporate or exclude some dominating factor even if everything else "looks good on paper."

So if you wine and dine your date in the hopes of off showing your best side so you can make the reveal of your "kinky little secret" less disturbing—e.g., you're a closeted transvestite who wears bras to your job as a corporate attorney—the simple fact is that if your secret so violates your partner's worldview that they cannot imagine living with themselves if they continue their relationship with you, then your secret is a *deal breaker*. That factor dominates her perception of you. There's really no softening the blow.

For instance, I've tried to be conventional and start off vanilla with women I thought were good girls, only to bring up rope and handcuffs after a few fairly tame romantic encounters. But with their picture of me firmly established the proposal seemed wildly out of character. You won't talk someone into experimentation if they're not ready to go there. If you've learned to be congruent you will avoid this problem. People will have a sense of what you're like from the onset. Congruence leads to less miscommunication, less frustration, and much less disappointment.

You are best served if you learn about your partner's preferences in an effort to better understand them rather than to hold what they claim to be curious about over their heads. Experiments show that we routinely *mispredict* our own mental and emotional response to different situations, and we suffer from *miswanting*— we desire things that provide little or no satisfaction once we actually experience them. Even better information about what makes people happy won't eliminate miswanting; psychologists who *study* this phenomenon day in and day out experience miswanting themselves! We're a puzzling little species in this regard. So saying, "C'mon baby you said you'd be cool with me putting clothespins on your scrotum!" is just trapping a person in their words. You'll only get reluctant compliance, and that kind coerciveness violates the spirit of informed consent.

Sexual Preference Compatibility

Your Sexual Preference Profile gives you a picture of yours and your partner's sexual tastes. A few concepts help clarify how people find sexual matches.

Compatibility. A partner is *compatible* with you if that partner satisfies your needs while presenting you with no deal-breakers (and vice-versa). Now just because someone appears to be compatible with you does not mean that you are in fact compatible with them. For example, Jack and Jill may appear to be compatible except that Jill refuses to become exclusive and Jack requires that level of commitment for a relationship to proceed. If they don't talk about this, from Jill's perspective everything is fine. From Jack's point of view it's doomed to failure.

Fitness. A partner P is a better *fit* for you than partner Q if partner P is compatible with you and partner P satisfies more wants while presenting fewer dislikes than partner Q. For example, Jack could be compatible with both Jill and June but Jack really likes public sex and Jill loves fucking in the back seat of cars in parking garages while June refuses to do anything remotely sexual outside of the bedroom. In this case, Jack and Jill are a better *fit* than Jack and June.

 Entitled To A Stupid Response

I once spent weeks trying to get together with a sexy and confident girl I met briefly on the street. We got together, had chemistry, flirted, and built sexual tension. Back at my place the intensity was through the roof, yet things weren't gelling. She hustled to the couch and I said, "Oh, I love when you play hard to get!" "Who's hard to get?! Come here!" she demanded. I bit her neck and she pulled my hair to yank me off balance. Somehow we were blocking each other's moves. "Seriously, loosen up," I said to her confused stare. After a while she said in frustration, "This isn't working!" and left. I was pissed too, but I respected her response. Her stupid, irrational, irritating response.

It wasn't until the next day I realized the issue: we were both *natural dominants* and we were trying to *top* one another! Ultimately there was no harm or foul, just misaligned expectations. Ah, the complexities of liberated masculine-feminine energies.

Compatibility and fitness are major factors that you need to consider in the process of selecting a partner, although we'd prefer not to couch things in such clinical terms. Initial attraction (which becomes the retrospective experience of "love at first sight") drives that first spark. After all, why spend time screening someone as a partner if you're just not into them in the first place? Don't forget that we're highly emotional, and our sexual decisions are rarely calculated. While sexual preferences help determine compatibility, compatibility alone does not ensure great sex and a connection. Even the most compatible partners may not be into each other. The reason you consider compatibility and fitness is because you want to find a great partner and you don't want to suffer **buyer's remorse**—the sense that you made a bad choice and there's someone better just waiting for you. If only you had kept looking…

It's tempting to think people are logical and consistent, but we're really a bundle of mixed emotions, desires, fears, uncertainties, and doubts. That itself is normal and healthy. If you accept this fact about your partner you'll be able to navigate their needs, wants, dislikes, and deal breakers more openly to see if your kinks will lead you to satisfying sex.

A final thought about partner selection and decision making. Ultimately we are each responsible for the consequences of our decisions. It's tempting in power exchange to think that you might insert your will in the mind of another person, to persuade, cajole, or pressure them doing as you wish. Sometimes it works but usually gives them buyer's remorse—or worse. When people behave in an erratic, inconsistent, or conflicted manner I call them out on it. I can make them aware of their own behavior and its consequences. I can suggest ways they can change their behavior and get better results if they choose to. But I can rarely get someone act against their own will for long. And remember if you don't like what you're doing, *stop doing it.*

Once I figure out how to get people to do my bidding, of course, you'll be the first to *bring me a beer.*

Devil's Advocate

⟶ Why is talking about needs and wants so difficult?

Intuitively a person can feel he or she *is* their collection of needs and wants. Just like sex forms identity, so we tend to identify with these interior aspects of our personal self—our feelings, our fantasies, our personal history, and our preferences. Sexual preferences make up a person's sense of self just like fantasies and core values do. Intimacy is often the experience of *crossing boundaries* by getting to know what goes on inside a person, what gets them hot (literally, what elevates their blood pressure during sexual arousal), and how they feel about various erotic situations. It's a wonderfully intimate experience to learn how a woman feels toward me as her partner.

Much like sex crosses the personal boundary of the body into intimate physical areas, so conversation crosses the psychological boundary of the mind into intimate emotional arenas. For some people that level of intimacy is just too revealing. What if they get judged or scrutinized or attacked for their internal makeup? That fear can make it difficult for many people to open up.

I've found that the more I'm genuinely curious about my partner and the more I express my nonjudgmental, non-defensive attitude the more we can explore these intimate spaces safely. She knows that I'll accept whatever we find there. There's a whole lot less tension and fear when you know your partner has your best interest at heart.

⟶ There's so much qualification and relativism in all this discussion of kink. Where are the universal truths? The standards?

People can be very smart, but we're quick to over-generalize and jump to conclusions. (Did I just generalize there?) We think to ourselves things like: *I bet this girl's into rough play. Will it be shocking that I'm into paddles and pain?* And we assume other people know our intention: *I'm not going to harm anyone. I know where the fantasy ends and real life begins. Can't she tell I'm really a good person?* Like there's some correct procedure to follow and nothing more to discuss.

The problem is that we don't all think alike, feel alike, or act alike. Suppose someone comes up and asks you: *Hey, should I eat this candy bar?* You see immediately that the answer depends on a lot of other questions. Do they like candy bars? Are they diabetic? Are they starving and don't have fruits and vegetables? Are they on a diet? Notice that they didn't ask: *Hey, do you yourself like candy bars?* or *Do I have your approval to eat this candy bar?* You opinion about candy bar deliciousness is hardly a useful predictor of blood insulin reaction.

If I were to play doctor for a minute (you can be the nurse), I might say that I need to *diagnose* a patient and understand what will improve their health before I *prescribe* medicine or a course of treatment. But of course most of us are not doctors. Most of us are unsolicited advice dispensers. The best unqualified advice there is about kink is: 1) know yourself, 2) know your partner, and 3) sort out the rest. Hardly a simple prescription but there you have it.

How do I predict someone's preferences from their culture (or heritage, education level, job title, etc.)?

You can't. You just have to ask. Look, even if you have a whole lot of information about a person's personal history, at best that will tell you the *likelihood* of a certain response, an attitude, or a belief. Probabilities will not tell you what this *individual specimen* thinks or feels.

I know, it seems like *all* European men are wild sex machines and *all* women crave a take-charge manly macho dude. Except it's simply *not true*. It may be a good rule of thumb because that's fairly common, even likely—it's certainly mostly true in my experience. But there are so many exceptions that if you treat an individual like some averaged stereotype you disrespect that individual and demonstrate your own ignorance.

Heuristics are rules of thumb that work most of the time, but when they're wrong they're really wrong. With all these exceptions, instead of struggling to predict how the different combinations play out, the cooler mental trick is to be resilient and *let it go* when things don't turn out as you expect. Then your rules of thumb don't cause any trouble because you don't *assume* they're true. Instead you realize your rules of thumb are probably true so they guide you while you get to know your partner, yet you're ready to change your mind when you get better information. I bet you've always thought like this intuitively, and from now on you can do it on purpose. Talk about a powerful mind!

What if Jesus reads my mind and finds out that I have perverted sexual needs from my partner. Will I go to hell?

You're not going anywhere. You're already there.

Think For Yourself

1. Complete **Appendix 1: Ideal Partner Profile.**

2. Identify your top three needs and your top three deal breakers.

   Needs   Deal Breakers
   1)   1)

   2)   2)

   3)   3)

3. Think about your top three needs and top three deal breakers, along with other wants and dislikes. How can you go about discussing these with your prospective partner?

Start Your Relationship

Maybe you're the kind of person who only opens up to kinky sex when you're already in a relationship. Or maybe you feel it's best to take a test drive with your potential playmate before you feel serious enough to bother defining your relationship. If you're going to get into a kinky relationship the critical question you have to answer for yourself is "What kind of relationship do I want to be in?"

A relationship involves time spent with one another, and it means continuing contact. Recurring encounters over time. Maybe not forever, but not a one-time rendezvous. Repeat business is good business.

Leather. Rinse. Repeat.

What To Expect

A kinky relationship is like any other sexual relationship except that the sex is kinky.

> *Well why didn't you just say that on the first page and save me the trouble of reading all this crap?!*

Because traditional relationships presuppose the traditional masculine-feminine polarity as their template and kink blows it to bits. By challenging this basic relationship template, all the things people get to take for granted about relationship structure comes into question. Your world crumbles, black becomes white, and God vanishes in a puff of logic. Welcome to the freedom of kinky sex and the burden of taking responsibility for your own romantic satisfaction.

Relationships can be thorny, messy and difficult. Relationship maintenance is relationship maintenance whether it's kinky or otherwise. Relationships change over time so if you learn and grow together then you can find a partner in crime who can grow with you. If on the other hand you've done this for twenty years and you know exactly what you like and the other person does not provide it, the best plan is probably to let them go, free them so they can find someone who will be a better fit for them, and go find yourself your own ideal partner.

This means it's up to you to **define the relationship** in terms of what you want. Do you want something stable and recurring? Do you want a series of short-term flings? Do you want a lifestyle master-slave arrangement? A harem of women or a bevy of men to have coming and going each week? You also want to consider how you will talk about all this with new playmates.

New relationships are exciting and uncertain. New relationship energy can stir a feeding frenzy of anticipation and excitement in both of you. You don't want to appear too needy and yet you want to stay engaged and show you care. You don't want to seem too available and yet being aloof will just frustrate the other person. Each relationship blossoms at its own speed, so move yours along by talking, meeting, flirting, and making sure you're a good fit for one another. Define things as you go, but resist the temptation to *contractualize* the terms of your relationship. Instead, clarify your own expectations.

The same advice from kinky play applies to your kinky relationship: do it (define it, pursue it) because *you like it.* And if you don't like where it's going, *stop it.*

Relationship Types

Once you've dispensed with the traditional heteronormative template it's not a trivial matter to redefine the parameters of your relationship. Questions come up like, "So what are we doing?" "Are we dating?" "Are we boyfriend and girlfriend?" "Is this getting serious?" These questions demand some kind of clarification and elaboration. Your challenge is to define a new arrangement that works for you.

To this end it's useful to consider the range of relationship types to facilitate communication between two (or more) partners. The relationship can and should develop at its own speed and this is most likely to happen by setting reasonable, fair, mutual expectations. That way certain *essential* or assumed requirements are made explicit, giving each partner something they actually want to invest time and energy into. While the relationship will grow through the natural expression of the interests of the people involved, poorly defined relationships are like poorly built houses: if you stand in a field and start cobbling a bunch of boards together, you get the mess you deserve. Kinky relationships that suffer from misset expectations and miscommunication are all the more sucktacular.

In fact every relationship you have with someone important uses some kind of relationship template yet grows organically. Your "coworker polite" relationship is different from your "college roommate party animal" relationship, which is yet different from your "adult child of permissive parents" relationship. So too your with kinky partner. Each relationship carries its own expectations, its own protocols, its own history and so forth. Why not give a new relationship the best chance of success by defining the basics from the start?

Kink does not absolve anyone of relationship responsibilities. On the contrary it makes relationship expectation setting and communication all the more essential. Assumptions must be clarified, roles defined, and terms negotiated in order to avoid harm. With the mold broken the wet clay affords you the chance to sculpt and form things to your mutual liking. Communicate your desires. Ask rather than assume so you set *realistic* expectations.

It helps to have vocabulary to convey what you want. Saying that you'd like to be "open" or "serious" is not all that specific. Suppose you've ditched the *boyfriend-girlfriend* template. If you're in an open relationship can you fuck the bartender after a night on the town? Or do you have to agree to sex outside the relationship before it happens? Do you expect exclusive access to your partner but refuse to reciprocate? Will you wear rubbers when you're together? When you're with other people? Will you get tested every six months?

Power Exchange	Level of Involvement	Exclusivity
Master (Mistress)/slave	Spouse	Monogamous
Parent/child	Live-in partner	*Nonmonogamous:*
Dominant/submissive	Lover	Polyfidelity
Sadist/masochist	Going steady	Polyamorous
Owner/pet	Dating	Swinging
Switches	Friend with benefits	Open
	Fuck buddy	Celibate (!)

Duration	Public Visibility	Sexual Contact
Life	Public	Intercourse
Long-term	Collared	Penetration
Regular	Vanilla glossed	Masturbation
Short-term	Community only	Orgasm control
One-night	Private/discreet	No genital contact

Some Dimensions Of A Kink Relationships

It may seem overwhelming when you realize that all of these dimensions of your relationship (and many more) are negotiable. But you tacitly negotiate them all the time in vanilla relationships anyway. You just choose from the "traditional" defaults. There's no self-evident definition of "being together" so we make one up using the vocabulary of pop culture: friend with benefits, lover, significant other. Not long ago people would "go steady," which led girlfriends to ask each other, "So are you guys seeing other people?" Even the simple terms "boyfriend" and "girlfriend" have that adolescent ambiguousness we exploit from time to time.

Q: What's the story with Stacey?
A: Well, she's my friend and she's a girl but she's not a *girlfriend* girlfriend. We've slept together, but it's not *serious* serious.

A relationship is built up from the time you spend and the history you create together. It's foolish to think that just because you're in a kinky relationship that somehow you're not in a relationship. The mere introduction of kink does not license anyone to cheat or engage in irresponsible behavior. Not without putting the relationship itself at serious risk at any rate.

That the degree of sexual contact in a relationship is entirely negotiable is bound to catch some people off guard, but an erotic relationship may not involve sex outright. Play partners who avoid genital contact can go through every aspect of sexual escalation in a domination scene by tying up a submissive, but without any penetration or sex. Pro-dommes do this all the time. As noted before, a lot of people are into kink for the meta-sensation and the sheer exhilaration of playing together. Some people jump out of airplanes to experience a rush of adrenaline; others climb mountains. Some of us have sex hanging upside down from the ceiling. It's titillating and tempting to be sure. But much like going to a strip club teases and excites without offering actual intercourse so a play encounter can focus on arousal. It's up to you.

Trust And Intimacy

A sexual relationship must address each person's basic desires for trust and intimacy or it will not last. **Trust** means providing comfort and reassurance so your partner rightly believes you care and are concerned about their well-being. People entrust things of value to trustworthy sources, just like money goes into the bank and secrets get shared with close friends. When someone breaks their word consistently you have no way of believing in their future promises or commitments. That's why lying damages credibility. Anything other than glib humor—anything of substance—has no reliability. Society is constructed out of a series of promises (like money which is just an IOU for goods and services delivered). People who don't follow through with what they say they'll do are untrustworthy. It's always good to give people the benefit of the doubt but a pattern of broken promises shows absent minded incompetence or outright deception. Either way trustworthiness is lost. Trust is *mandatory* if we are going to share our most intimate selves and expect any level of personal safety.

You know it when you experience it but do you have a clear idea of what intimacy means? **Intimacy** (Latin *intimus*: "innermost, within; interior") can be thought of as crossing personal boundaries to get *inside* a person's physical or emotional space. Physically we do this through sex, petting, and physical touch (girls brush each other's hair to bond while guys slap each other's asses after well-executed sports maneuvers). Closeness doesn't need to involve penetration.

Psychological intimacy is achieved though conversation and sharing in joys and hardships. Why do you think we gossip about friends and gawk at the unfortunate fashion decisions of passersby? In sharing our opinions we reveal something of ourselves. That deepens our mutual sense of intimacy.

Demonstrating trustworthiness is straightforward. Be honest with people, be congruent, own your intentions, and say what it is you want. Don't

Trust Me

When I take a girl who I don't know very well home I consistently get asked things like, "How do I know you're not a serial killer?" While taking my word alone is hardly prudent verification, the intuition behind the question is solid: How can I trust that I will be safe with you, and that you will not harm me? How do I know will keep your word? *How can I trust you?*

I have a standard answer. "You don't, and if I said I was safe that'd be like letting the inmates run the asylum. But I've already told you I'm a dickhead, a sex fiend, I think you're cute, and I'd like to tie you up. What exactly do you think I'm hiding? Secretly I wanna get you home so we can play naked Yahtzee? You're sick." That disarms the underlying assumption and breaks the tension. When you're congruent with your intentions it is easiest to simply describe the truth. Making it plain that you have no ulterior motive increases trust.

mislead someone, don't deny your desires, and don't shirk responsibility. In a relationship governed by trust and open to intimacy, two consenting adults can do just about anything their filthy hearts can dream of, provided they don't kill each other. Personally, I reserve the right to incorporate *poetic ambiguity* when hitting on women so as not telegraph too much interest. The truth is I find many women physically attractive and curiosity motivates me to meet them. But I'm not all that taken with someone until I get to know her. For me, the first stage of seduction—the initial meeting—means doing my job and screening her for compatibility.

Trust shades so many aspects of a relationship. When you start dating it's a safe assumption that the other person is seeing (or is free to see) other people. But once you've defined your relationship will that same freedom still be there? You may be comfortable with the idea of having multiple partners as long as neither of you is working from a template that requires exclusivity. You're just dating or you're fuck buddies or something along those lines. If you imply that you're exclusive and one of you is seeing other people, the misled partner is certain to feel violated. You can agree to keep your relationship *open* and see other people, maybe because your schedules don't permit seeing each other as regular as your sex drives would demand or you're not in a position to get that involved emotionally.

Similarly there is a basic safety concern as to whether you are drug and disease free. It's not hysterics for someone to become enraged over any deception regarding your sexual health. Your life may depend on knowing the truth about your partner's STI status. If you do have an infection you had better let your partner know upfront so they can decide whether to engage in sex knowingly, or you face serious emotional (and possibly legal) consequences.

As your relationship starts it's up to both of you to set **expectations** so the other partner knows what you want and what you don't. Don't remain silent with regard to your needs and your deal breakers. Communicate early and often with your partner. Disappointment always follows the *failure* to meet hopes or expectations. You thought she would be available for sex three times a week but her schedule only allows it once. You though he'd be cool with anal but he's grossed out by any form of ass play. If you're using the traditional template, you expect your partner to follow the script—couples have lunch and watch movies but they don't fornicate in the park. All of this has nothing specifically to do with kink. If you're operating from some relationship template but the other person isn't, you're expectations are misaligned. You're guaranteed to be disappointed.

Effective communication is all about setting expectations. Lawyering the relationship may work in the short term, but using people's words against them will be less successful than letting people "opt-in." Blaming and judging stifles the natural tendency to be trusting and open and inhibits relationship development. I'm not saying you hold no one accountable—quite the opposite. I'm saying hold people accountable to their intentions, not to the intentions you *want* them to have. Hold people accountable to what they mean and what they say, not to what they *should* have said. And remember, relationships get redefined as they grow. When the time comes to talk about where your relationship is heading, embrace it as a chance to set new and better expectations.

Cheating

Remember the business about *reputation management* and how it was largely obsolete? Well now reputations count again. Your reputation is what other people say about you. It establishes a line of "social credit" where people are willing to give you things of value (their time, their friendship, sex) because they trust you will exercise care with them. But violating that trust discredits you. It gets your account closed. Just like your credit score is based on your payment history, so your social credit is based on your personal history and it may just precede you.

In any relationship, cheating undermines trust and creates a hostile setting for both partners. In a kinky relationship, cheating no longer simply means having sex with other people. (Is a wife who has a rope top tie and spank her for education cheating on her husband?) **Cheating** literally means lying, deceiving, swindling, or otherwise breaking the rules *you agreed to*. In the context of an open sexual relationship, the rules are negotiated by both partners, probably on an ongoing basis. Cheating involves betraying the trust you've established and taking advantage of the intimacy that served as the basis of the partnership. Cheating calls into question all of the expectations that have been established during your time together. In other words, cheating means *breaking your word.*

If you really want to cheat, cheat "legally" and *renegotiate* the terms of your relationship with your partner so you don't recklessly break the rules you've agreed to. Talk about the possibility of seeing other people, taking a break, or breaking up altogether. This way you preserve the trust and intimacy you've earned while avoiding unintentionally harming your partner. And if you get caught breaking your word, own up to your mistake. The essence of congruence is taking responsibility for your own desires and the consequences they produce. Admit what you did and don't turn it around on the other person. Politicians know all too well that it's not the crime but the cover up that does the most damage.

The best, most mutually beneficial relationships are the ones where each partner discovers out how to satisfy themself *through* the relationship rather than sacrifices themselves for *the sake* of the relationship. At some point we quit looking for a magic mate who *makes* us feel happy and instead find a partner who *permits* us to feel happy and healthy and satisfied. A partner who helps you grow as a person and realize your full sexual potential will make sex an opportunity for personal growth. Instead of thinking of a **soulmate** as that elusive one-in-six-billion person who alone completes you, think of a soulmate as a compatible partner who is good for your soul. That is, someone who lets you express your own intrinsic happiness. Shackled to the bedpost, of course.

Taking Your Relationship Public

The decision to take your relationship public is a big step. Sharing your relationship with others reinforces your bond. Public proclamations of sexual commitment—going steady or getting married—create social pressure on your union that can keep the relationship intact during the inevitable trials and tribulations of emotional co-existence. It's much harder for Jill to break things off when she knows her friends will ask, "So how are you and Jack?"

Expressing your relationship can be done kinky-style or with a **vanilla glossing**. If you're vanilla glossed you're passing as vanilla in public. You keep your kink a secret. It's not something that comes up when you and your partner attend birthday parties and work functions as usual so from the outside your life together may look like a Normal Rockwell painting. Power exchange is a sweet little secret between the two of you.

When you express your kinky relationship publicly, there are a number of ways to go. Some slaves wear a collar in public to demonstrate their commitment to their master just as married people wear wedding rings to symbolize commitment to their spouse. In fact, for some people the **collaring ceremony** takes on significance akin to marriage. Collared slaves tend to see themselves as the property of their masters. Rightly understood, this level of involvement (a **total power exchange** or a **24/7 lifestyle**) can turn the play of kink into a full-blown spiritual or self-discovery path. For those who participate, the declaration of servitude carries at least the same implications as a marriage vow.

Whether casual or collared, you can share your relationship in many of the same settings you meet people: online, at dungeons, at munches, at conferences, and so forth. A number of dungeons have **roundtables** for tops and separately for bottoms so they can share their experiences and concerns regarding the lifestyle among supportive and likeminded people.

Before you share your relationship with friends and family or the general public make sure you and your partner are on the same page. Are they committed in the way you expect them to be? Are they willing to attend those work or family functions where you're expected to bring a date? Think about how you'd feel if someone you've been seeing very casually invites you to their parent's for the holidays. You've got to wonder, "Are we serious now? I'm going to meet the parents—what will they think of me?" Kinky people are not immune from relationship anxiety, so talk through your social expectations.

With all that said, it bears repeating: *A kinky relationship is like any other sexual relationship except that the sex is kinky.*

Devil's Advocate

⤷ I'm in a relationship that I want to spice up with kinky sex.

The focus of this book is on starting kinky relationships because it's much easier to introduce kink in the relationship early or to get away from it entirely while things are still very fluid. That said, the chapter *Melt The Vanilla* discusses ways to bring kink into an existing relationship.

⤷ The person I'm with would never go for an open relationship. How do I open my relationship up?

Again, changing a relationship once you've established the template you're working with is difficult because the emphasis is on the *loss of commitment* or stability in the relationship, not on the *gain of freedom* and the opportunity for new sexual experiences. People are instinctively loss averse and that inherent fear of loss usually cancels any benefit your partner might perceive. The best approach if you are really interested in an open relationship is to be open from the start. From there, learn to talk about what gets you off sexually. That level of communication will make your sex life so much better.

⮩ I'm not looking for a relationship. How do get a kinky girl in bed as quickly as possible?

I'll write that book next year but for now keep reading this one, it's pretty good.

⮩ I want a normal relationship not anything kinky! Except I want my girlfriend to peg me every other Thursday...

Incorporating one kink or fetish you enjoy into your relationship doesn't make you any more or less perverted than anyone else. It's not a matter of what you enjoy sexually or the "degree of kink" you exhibit, but simply what will make your relationship sexually satisfying. If you know yourself and can express what you want, and you're not worried about what others think, then the label "kinky" is irrelevant. I have no agenda to recruit card-carrying kinksters into my secret sex cult. (If you really want to join my secret sex cult email me.) As long as you're clear and can constructively discuss what gets you off with your partner do so using whatever terms you like.

The central benefit of considering the variety of relationship types available is that you make a more informed decision that you can coherently articulate to your partner when you start seeing them. Remember, once you break the template it's your job to reconstruct an expectation of how the relationship will be structured so you can both enjoy yourselves.

⮩ I want a kinky relationship but I have baggage—an ex-spouse, kids, work issues, etc.

Look, a relationship is a relationship is a relationship. Kinky relationships are like any other kind of relationship, they just happen to involve kinky sex. Personal issues can and will come in any relationship so it's up to you to handle them or avoid them as you would in any other partnership.

Now if you establish that your relationship is strictly sexual then whether it's kinky or not, I suggest you *encapsulate* your personal life if you want to keep the arrangement working. That means just presenting a certain side of yourself (call it your *lover persona*) to your partner. It will be a less comprehensive experience than if you gabbed about all your issues, but it doesn't need to be any less intimate or fulfilling. If you want to avoid all the messy feelings find a fuck buddy. The bargain you make when you take on a fuck buddy is that you keep the emotions, the personal issues, and the unnecessary drama to a minimum.

Good luck with that baggage, by the way.

Think For Yourself

1. What kind of kinky relationship are you looking for or open to?

2. Do you want to keep your relationship private or make it public?

3. How will you communicate your expectations for your relationship with your partner(s)?

Negotiate A "Scene"

So you've found a kinky playmate, defined the basic terms of your relationship, discovered some things that you really want to try together, and agreed to meet at your place at 8pm on Friday. This is your chance to perform. Now what?

When it comes to sex, if you know exactly what you want to do AND you can read the minds of other human beings, skip this chapter. But if you want to know how to share what you like and learn what your partner likes so you can get together and have everyone like it all, read on.

You want your first encounter to be the starting point for a satisfying sexual relationship. You need to navigate the thicket of trust and intimacy, informed consent and limits, expectations and disappointments.

You, dear friend, need to negotiate a scene.

The Theatrics Of A Sexual Performance

Quiet on the set. Roll film. And, *action!* Movies capture slices of human experience. Most movies are scripted, rehearsed, and acted out over many takes to get just the result the director desires. We tend to think of scenes as "things that happen in movies," but why is that? Movies merely record those moments when roles and settings come together to create dramatic action.

We may not script life to its exact words like some Hollywood screenplay, but we often take on roles with clearly associated expectations (office worker, wife, college student) and interact in staged settings (office, kitchen, classroom). We call drawing unwanted public attention "making a scene" for a reason. Is it therefore all that strange to think of segments of our everyday life in terms of scenes?

Ah, right. There's that stuff about what you *do* and who you *are*. Following a social script would seem inauthentic, except you know intuitively when to act according to what script. Think about how these conversations might play out.

- *What seems to be the problem, officer?*
- *Hey boss, got a minute?*
- *Honeeey, where'd you put the car keys?!*

The words and setting trigger an automatic response based on previous experience. You know what to do. Familiarity with the situation and personal history give you a pretty good idea what's to come and you know your role. There's nothing unnatural about it. Why not immerse yourself in your role rather than struggle to distinguish your real, authentic self from your play acting self?

Sociologist Erving Goffman called this spillover of theatrical interaction in everyday life *dramaturgy.* We are always performing. Always. We perform ritual acts and execute social scripts because we've seen them done by others, we've tried them ourselves, we've become comfortable incorporating them into our repertoire, and they are justifiable (any properly educated audience would understand our actions and realize we are competent in our role). We're the best species of cultural imitators this planet has ever produced. Not to bruise your ego, but you didn't *invent* the fashion you wear or the sex positions you love so much. It's in our DNA to imitate others. It's no wonder we replay in private behaviors we learned by watching others in public.

We are bound to "act out" our social reality in this dramaturgical sense. We are participating in scenes whether or not we choose to consciously acknowledge it. In fact this accounts for much of a person's apprehension about new experiences. When there is no set script to follow our behavior is determined on the fly. We're suddenly incompetent, feeling hyper-aware of everything we do. We become unsure of ourselves. It's much harder to get into a comfortable, relaxed state of *flow* because so much attention is dedicate to **impression management,** self-consciously and with great effort to trying construct a certain appearance of ourselves for the sake of others. When you can wear a role or adopt a persona and follow a script, you free yourself from hyper-vigilant attention to your own self-presentation and can turn your attention to your partner in a scene.

Negotiation may be less *spontaneous* than unreflective action, but it's no less authentic than any interaction you have with another person. Maybe every Thanksgiving like clockwork you and your mother argue about uncle Al's drinking problem. It's not spontaneous—you know it's coming—but the emotions and the words are perfectly real. The argument is perfectly authentic. So authenticity is not the same as spontaneity, though they tend to be associated—being too calculated and detached, too rehearsed, seems disingenuous.

Similarly be careful not to confuse authenticity for *originality*. Authentic expression is rarely original, but rather it incorporates the "greatest hits" of our experiences from various sources. You speak English (or are reading it at any rate) at a sophisticated level, yet you didn't *originate* English. You express yourself using language and maybe you have a few original pet phrases that are all your own. But you can be perfectly *authentic* using commonly-spoken, unoriginal English. No, originality isn't all that useful. Self-mastery and congruence trump originality in the authentic expression of your will.

Well-negotiated sexual activity is much like any other social encounter in that it plays out under a shared set of expectations. Your sex only gets better when you clarify your intentions and sort through those thorny issues that produce confusion and cross-purpose miscommunication.

Setting The Scene

For the purposes of kink, the scene is the backdrop and setting for those fantasies or activities that we engage in together. Not every scene needs to be negotiated but when you want informed consent, negotiating the scene is much more effective than leading a new partner into an unpredictable and potentially unsafe sexual situation. Sometimes a scene has nothing but a thematic element: bondage, a St. Andrew's Cross, a spanking session. Often that's enough to get started if you're not planning to push hard limits.

The expectations for erotic fulfillment are being established between you and your partner as part of the negotiation. Setting expectations includes a discussion of both of your limits.

- *Spanking is okay but you can't leave any marks.*
- *My ass is okay but my nipples are off limits.*
- *Clothes pins hurt too much.*
- *You can do anything you want but anal penetration is a real comedown.*

 Short And Sweet

"Come over at six. Wear a white blouse, short skirt, stockings, heels. No bra. If you care whether it gets ripped, leave it at home. By the way, you're a second-shift secretary and work starts at five so when you come at six you're late. You'll be reprimanded."

Negotiating a scene need not be complex.

There are as many types of scenes as there are ways to have sex. The primary consideration in scene negotiation is *degree of specificity*. Will your scene be a loosely scripted improvisation along a theme (incorporating anal sex or playing cops and robbers) or staged in detail, blocked out based on the configuration of equipment in your play space. Is this your first time through, or are you replaying a kidnapping scenario you've done in the past? If you're a veteran of abduction and ravishment scenes and you're with a new partner, that partner is going to interpret the script in their own way. They bring themselves to the scene. Often women I advise say things like, "He's not doing it right! He's supposed to do this!" It's a matter of personal style how your partner fleshes out the scene. If it were scripted down to the color of his underwear, that's one thing. A well-negotiated scene allows both of you room for interpretation.

As a performer, respect your audience. Don't forget that you're performing for each other's gratification and excitement. First and foremost play in a scene because you want to play with your partner. Enjoy yourself and get off. Second, perform for your partner, and give him or her what *they* need. The more you can step into the performance and own your role even for a little while, the more exhilarating the experience. You'll both love it.

Benefits Of Negotiating

By negotiating your scenes upfront you are able to share expectations, to *preconsume* the experience (that is, to savor the anticipation and relish the excitement), and to discuss boundaries. Don't let the analytical tone rob your encounter of its drama. In the moment during the act itself, your *feelings* and *experiences* are totally spontaneous and authentic. The fact that the scene does not spontaneously *coordinate* itself shouldn't detract from its fundamental sexual impact. Sexual scenes are meant to be arousing and not overly calculated. You're not programming a computer or assembling a bookshelf.

It's a bit like driving a car. With a little driver's education and a few months practice handling the car becomes second nature. You maneuver around sharp corners and learn to navigate highways while the actual mechanics of driving no longer distract you. That you masterfully shift gears doesn't make a leisure drive "inauthentic" any more than knowing you want to play with handcuffs and ball gags makes your sex mechanical. If the central aspects of your sexual experience are not discussed—what turns you on, what turns you off, what you hope to experience—then miscommunication or missed expectations can leave you or your partner feeling frustrated, let down, and unsatisfied. Avoiding this disappointment is worth the extra effort.

There's a kind of beauty in the romantic fiction that we can read each other's thoughts and feelings and find the perfect complement who responds telepathically to our unstated desires. However psychologists call this belief the **illusion of transparency,** in which we massively overestimate the degree to which other people can actually know our mental state (in this case, how well our sexual partner knows how we feel without us giving any feedback). It's nice to feel *simpatico* with another person. Then you don't have to create roadmaps with words. But it's rare and most of us don't share enough common history with our new partner to skirt the job of negotiating. Think of it as a give and take. The iterative process of asserting, explaining, and clarify your *thelema* will go a long way toward bringing you and your partner closer together.

Incredibly good sex is not unspoken magic. Sexual communication is a skill. As author Janet Hardy said, hoping another person will somehow guess what you like is "good formula for very shitty sex." So to avoid shitty sex, improve this skill.

Think of negotiating as expanding your **sexual repertoire.** Your experience, your preference, and your skills come together to determine what you're proficient at sexually and what you have to work on. If you decide that sex is the kind of skill you want to develop there are various steps you can take to get yourself out of your comfort zone. It's not mandatory, of course. As an actor you can take your part seriously and perform with great dedication or you can just let your hair down and get silly. Over time you'll find what works for you and what doesn't. You'll learn what kind of people make the best play partners in the relationships you hope to foster.

Miscommunicating And Not Communicating

Communication is an ongoing process of expression, interpretation, and clarification. I cannot read your mind, so without some insight into your personal history and your worldview I simply don't know what to expect from you. The fact that we both have a rope fetish does not mean it's reasonable to assume that we have perfectly identical perspectives on every aspect of our sexuality. Your notion of kink may be based on vampire novels whereas mine is based on Japanese cartoon porn. We may have come from the same culture but different sides of the tracks. We may not have all that much in common, much less share some sort of "common sense" to unite us. Common sense is just not that common.

People from other cultures experience this acutely when they hang out with friends who subject them to American pop culture references. For a long time the Fonz *defined* the cool rebel. Britney Spears *embodied* the nasty school girl. As non-natives, foreigners are left confused and not sure why everyone laughs when we say, "Not that there's anything wrong with that!" They have no frame of reference to appreciate a culturally-bound joke. This follows from the differing cultural history, norms, and idiomatic phrases we use to communicate. So too people with less experience in the kinky lifestyle will find their ability to understand your intentions to be limited by their own experiences.

For example, a woman may want a rapid take-down and hogtie because the thrill for her comes from being overpowered by a top as she struggles to resist. Suppose her partner wants to practice a new chest harness that requires patience to weave, and she'll need to move her arms to accommodate his knot work. If they don't share their personal expectations but instead just go at it, he'll think she's trying to sabotage his rope play and she'll think he's an inexperienced dom who doesn't have the balls to treat her rough.

The root of so much frustration and disappointment, and so many missed expectations, is poor communication. Miscommunication all too often comes from assuming certain facts or details based on common sense rather than *personalizing* a script to a partner's wants and needs. If all the communication seems like unnecessary hassle, think about how valued you feel when your partner goes out of their way to learn what your needs and deal breakers are so they can incorporate that into the your sex play in a way that satisfies both of you. It's dealing with miscommunication that's not worth the hassle.

Communicate Using Worksheets

One way to talk about what you want with your partner, while taking the pressure off either of you to "guarantee" the other a good time, is to use **best practices** to script your scenes. Best practices are not "right ways" but ways that have worked effectively for other people in the past. Your mileage may vary.

- **Appendix 2: BDSM Worksheet** is comprehensive checklist of things you might want to try that involve bondage and discipline.

- **Appendix 3: Role Play Worksheet** is similar but focuses on the setting and the psychology of role playing.
- **Appendix 4: Spanking Partner Worksheet** is for you truly sick bastards to decide between an open hand or a tennis racket.
- **Appendix 5: Humiliation Activities Worksheet** will help you to turn your sub into a groveling mess.

If you're with a new partner you can use these worksheets to talk about what you enjoy, what you're curious about, and what is off limits.

I use these worksheets with a new partner to establish the *tone* for our freaky escapades. I let her read over the worksheet so I learn what turns her on and what's just not sexy. I point out some of the more extreme things on the page (what's "extreme" depends on the girl) and say, "Can you believe some people are into that?!" This helps forge a shared sense of "us" based on our mutual sexual interests and disinterests. It also shifts some of the burden off me for bringing up kinky kinds of play. The worksheet itself "floated the idea," and I'm just talking about it. This relieves the potential pressure associated with initiating kinky play.

The act of letting go of responsibility and following the direction of another's intentions is referred to as going into an **agentic state**. This involves becoming an *agent* of some outside will, not unlike a submissive serving a dominant. Taking the responsibility off either of yourself and going into an agentic state is a little like using alcohol as social lubricant. The alcohol is what takes the blame when things "just happen." It can resemble subspace, although the agentic state has the negative connotation that a person blindly follows orders (even harmful commands) compared to the same person's behavior in their hyper-attentive ego state.

You can use the worksheets in this book and role playing to induce a partial agentic state in our partner, not to manipulate them (keep in mind the principle of *ahimsa* and the *New York Times* test) but to reduce those inhibitions and discomfort that can arise at the mere thought of getting wild while they entertain the idea. Look, if want to pursue my kinky desires but I feel a little guilty about having them, it's going to be a challenge for me to take full responsibility for the outcome. What if I don't like it? What if my partner doesn't like it? What if something goes wrong?

Whether it's with the guidance of a worksheet via sheer intuition, you need to communicate to steer the course in your relationship so your desires and concerns are clear. The more you talk about your fantasies and turn ons, the more room you create for the kind of experimentation that will keep your relationship sexually fulfilling. Communication is much healthier, much more satisfying, and much safer than not talking about sex.

By the way, releasing either partner form complete responsibility for raising sensitive and taboo subjects is the primary task of a couple's therapist. Use this insight and the worksheets in the appendix to function a little like a surrogate therapist to guide and improve your kinky relationship.

Fantasy Chain: A Subtle Negotiation

A person who has more experience can guide a newbie and negotiate a scene without ruining the moment's spontaneity. You don't have to say "Hey let's negotiate a scene" to *actually* negotiate a scene. You can be subtle without being sneaky. If someone says, "It sounds like you're planning this out," I find the best response is not to reject the suggestion but to acknowledge what I'm doing. "Maybe I am, it depends on whether we like where things take us. A kinky boy scout is always prepared." It's truthful and playful without denying my intentions.

Fantasy chains are conversations that involve shared storytelling where two or more people add to the fantasy's theme until a chain reaction occurs and the fantasy takes on a life of its own. This becomes the basis for inside jokes and a shared sense of history. I like to build a fantasy chain that's fairly silly then give the fantasy a kinky twist. I'll suggest fantasy topics and throw random things out there to essentially create a scene on the spot.

Me: This bar feels like the lower decks of a pirate ship. Here, I'm a pirate and you're my slave cargo!
Her: Ooh, no I'm a princess and you're taking me away from my kingdom!
Me: Even better. I bet you're stuck up and naughty. You're in need of a serious spanking.

The story we come up with together allows us to take our imagined situation into the bedroom and open up through fantasy to one another sexually.

One caveat: Develop a shared history to get a sense of what's arousing, exciting, and possible, but don't think because you've chatted about it like this that you've secured implied consent. If she says she has a ravishment fantasy, you don't suddenly have license to blindfold her and fuck her ass. Fantasies are often just that, and there's no precise way to explain how to progress from having a fantasy to acting on it physically. Guys often make the mistake of thinking that if a girl finds some taboo hot and she talks about it, he has permission to execute. It's better to find out what gets her juices flowing and what she's willing to try, but make sure you respect the fact that *no means no.*

Usually your new partner wants to know the sex will be satisfying (or at least a cheap thrill) and that you're safe. Safety can mean no bodily injury, no emotional damage, no STIs, or no subsequent stalking. People are typically pretty adventurous and fairly open to playing sex games, so take the time to negotiate a scene where she comes home from work wearing stockings and lacey Agent Provocateur underwear instead of just pouncing on her unannounced because last week rough play came up during pillow talk.

Furthermore, don't be too clinical *while* you negotiate. You're negotiating sex, not the price of a car. Be passionate, enthusiastic, and just a shade poetic in your erotic exchange. If you're so desensitized to sex that you can't get excited about anything other than masturbating a donkey while seven naked wood nymphs sing the praises of Bacchus taking turns licking your asshole, then try faking it you sociopath. When it comes to acting out your sexual fantasies, clarify rather than assume. It may seem a bit stiff, but err on the side of caution until you've gotten to know your partner's needs, wants, deal breakers, and personal limits.

Early on make a habit of selecting a safe word and don't be resentful when your submissive *actually uses* the safe word. (As a sub, don't be afraid to use the safe word when you feel you have to.) That's what it's there for. If the sub calls out the safe word it's because something is wrong. Realize the sub is continually calibrating his or her own experience and learning about their likes and limits as they go. If the sub calls red, they're getting really uncomfortable with what you're doing. If you punish the sub too far, you risk terminating the relationship. Why do that? It's better to ease up and play nice now so you can play with each other again and again.

Devil's Advocate

↳ This negotiating business seems so calculated. Doesn't that detract from the pure spontaneity of the moment?

If you set expectations you can look forward to what's coming and savor the moment, but the fact you're planning may reduce the surprise and can come at the expense of that thrill of the unknown. Of course you don't have to detail the scene like a legal contract. Negotiation and fantasy chaining allow you to set a general tone and play with a theme, and if you know your partner fairly well you can just talk about what's working and what's not *while* you're fucking.

However, giving feedback on-the-fly can be very difficult. The challenge is to communicate your likes and dislikes without turning someone off, shutting them down, or blaming them. If you're a world-class communicator this will not be an issue for you. For the rest of us it's better to establish the requisite levels of trust, demonstrate consideration and respect for the other person ("you can stop the sex, I won't hold it against you"), and define the tools for sexual communication. Granting the sub veto rights with a safe word usually gives them enough power and you can negotiate less up front.

Sometimes my entire negotiation is simply, "I'm gonna do freaky shit and you're gonna like it. The safe word is Apple Jacks." Since I'm good at reading people and talking about what I want this works fairly well for me.

↳ What about trying something I saw in a movie? Or read online?

A really hot scene can involve imitating something you saw somewhere else. Use a movie to script your scene or ask your partner to read an erotic novel so you can act out the bedroom bondage scenario on page 69. Just remain flexible and understanding. Things don't always play out in real life exactly as they do in the movies. There's no point in letting the fantasy *detract* from the encounter itself.

↳ What if things don't work out as planned?

Don't let your inner control freak tell you that to adapt to the circumstance is to fail. This isn't about perfect execution for the cameras, but about enjoying yourself and getting off with your partner. Things need not go without a hitch in order for the two (or three or four) of you to have a blast.

I've done abduction scenes with a chest ties and suspensions where my partner started to go numb from the ropes. On a couple of occasions I released her arms, readjusted the position, and retied her wrists but it was still not coming together. When that happens we abandon the script and improvise. I make sure she's comfortable continuing with me and we do oral or spankings and nix the abduction element. It's great. Scripts are best used as *guidelines* not as exacting specifications. Overly specific sexual blueprints are kind of a comedown.

What if something goes wrong?

Safety is at the heart of kink education and central to the fetish community. Safety, risk management, and the mental and physical health of your partner have become such an essential element of fetish play that I don't think a book, conference, or dungeon omits them—or if they do, they assume safety to be well understood and practiced by everyone in attendance.

Not surprisingly, new dom(me)s who come onto the scene are evaluated in terms of their technique but reprimanded and ostracized when they fail to take safety into account. The stigma of being a wannabe stems from the fact that inexperience as a top can be *dangerous* for the bottom. Sexual domination is built around careful control of your erotic plaything. No one wants to break their toys. So learn to play safe, take a class, and make sure your playmate takes off their blindfold before they run around with scissors.

What a great idea. Why doesn't everyone negotiate their scene when they have sex?

I have no idea. But you're cute. So, um, are you here for the education or the stimulation...?

Think For Yourself

1. What kinds of scenes turn you on?

2. How can you make yourself comfortable discussing and planning a scene with a new partner (i.e., handling any awkwardness or feeling it's forced and unnatural)?

3. Imagine a really arousing fantasy of yours. How can you plan it and put it into action while keeping it authentic and exciting?

Melt The Vanilla

Suppose you're in a vanilla relationship and you want to add some sexual cinnamon to spice things up. What can you do to broach the topic so neither of you feels threatened, yet allows you to test your partner's receptivity to the kind of hot stuff you have in mind? It would certainly seem much better to talk it out before springing it on them unexpectedly. How do you do this without coming across as a perverted sex maniac?

Remember not to identify your *whole being* with your *interest*. Curiosity about taboo is natural and normal. You are entitled to entertain your curiosity in kink simply because you're sexual—it is neither "abnormal" nor "deviant" as discussed earlier. Instead of *being* your interest, disidentification and depersonalization help raise the question without unwarranted shame.

Ultimately we can't get our partner to participate in something they refuse to even consider. They have to be willing, enthusiastically or with some reservations, to give your proposal a try. Melting the vanilla is about testing your partner's receptivity and not pressuring an unwilling partner.

The basic approach is to convey the thought, "There's something I'd like to try. I want to get your feelings about it." Your partner's response is accepted nonjudgmentally, clarified, and negotiated. But you can be subtle and seductive in your approach.

Start With Fantasy

Bringing someone from vanilla to kink requires crossing the boundary into their fantasy life. Everyone has different personal histories and attitudes about kinky behavior. Engage the fantasy aspect and tell your partner something like this.

> *I love having sex with you. I'm always looking for ways to make it more fun, and I've been thinking of ways to spice things up...without going overboard. But there's no harm in naughty fantasies. Have you ever had any fantasies that are a little kinky?*

Ask this in a safe setting—not while you're in the middle of screwing or during a family reunion—and remind your partner that you are not going to judge them based on their fantasies. You just want to get to know them better. Whatever they say is okay with you.

Once you've heard your partner's thoughts, work with what they offer you. Restate what you heard in your own words.

> *If I heard you right, you'd like playing with scarves or blindfolds and it would be fun to be a little more spontaneous, like if we have sex in the living room after work.*

By repeating what you heard you'll demonstrate that you're paying attention and listening. If there are things you want to bring up, ask your partner how receptive they are.

> *Would it be sexy if we did some light bondage? How would it make you feel if you pulled my hair?*

Your goal here is to explore the emotional and erotic content of the fantasy, not to get premature commitment. Remember this is still fantasy talk at this point. Acting on your fantasies requires further clarification and negotiation. When you zero in on something you want to try see how receptive your partner is.

> *What would happen if we did that? Could we even make that happen? Maybe we should visit the sex shop together and see if we can find a strap-on dildo.*

Remember that most people are comfortable talking about taboo subjects as long as the conversational tone is safe, and you're just *talking* and not *committing*. As always, safety and consent are of utmost importance. It's very threatening to imagine your serious partner losing respect and love for you. If your vanilla partner feels like a slutty whore for being tied up or if tapping into masculine energy makes him an evil domineering cocksucker it's a major turn off. The sex will be lousy and could do more damage than it's worth. The fear of spoiling the relationship overrides the practical questions of when and where you're going to play cops and hookers.

If you're not advocating something outright then you're just investigating. Being curious about the unknown is an admirable characteristic of open-minded people. It's not that difficult to entertain the thought of something you may find threatening or disagreeable as long as you're just talking. Discuss your fantasy life with your partner and if it's not arousing for both of you it's probably not something you should pursue. One person's turn ons are another's hang-ups, and sexual preferences don't need to be "fixed." Instead, keep talking about it. See if you can uncover the source of any resistance or anxiety. Then you may be able to work it through, so both of you take an interest in your kinky agenda. But if you try to get them to act against their interest or against their will, in a coercive and threatening way, you risk messing up the whole relationship. Or going directly to jail.

Experiment Together

When you decide to probe your own kinky interests, bring your vanilla partner along for the ride. It makes sense for you to visit sex shops, read books, and go to conferences as a couple. As the kinky instigator it's easy to get ahead of yourself. Think of how frustrating it is for a novice to play a game of strategy against a master who anticipates and matches their every move. The more you grow your interest with parity the more "buy-in" and excitement you'll get from your partner.

As you delve into erotic opportunities together, look to get information from different sources. Go online. Buy dirty movies. Use the **Appendix 3: Role Play Worksheet** to talk about what you'd like to try and what you want to avoid. Take the fantasy of movies and romantic fiction with a grain of salt. In a novel a 24/7 S&M relationship progresses with romanticized elegance. In real life, people get

 But What If They Catch Us?

One fairly tame girlfriend invited me to a coworker's wedding. I said no. She persisted and I made her a deal. "Make it fun for me. Wear your gold silk dress, your matching gold shoes...and that's it!" The night was titillating as I saw her pert nipples show through her dress and held her close on the dance floor. But the fun came late in the evening, after all the toasts and the feasting as people were mulling in a post-celebratory haze.

"Come on," I ordered and dragged her to the banquet hall entrance. Looking for a secluded location we popped into an empty dining room, lights off and doors unlocked. I led her to the bar at the far side of the room and with a little limber gymnastics we enjoyed a treat that put the pricey dessert tray to shame.

sick and fart. A lot. Erotic arousal is a *state* couples enter into together, rather than a permanent *trait* of the relationship that is at its peak all day, every day.

As you gather new sex toys, costumes, and props consider incorporating everyday items into your sexual play. Household objects can help sexualize everyday activities and can remind you and your partner of your adventure after your scene is over. In doing so you make a **pervertible** out of just about any convenient object. Use neckties, telephone cords, and computer cables as restraints. Silk scarves make comfortable blindfolds. Dessert staples like whip cream and strawberries can turn a bland evening at home into a treat if you're willing to make a mess of each other. Offer it up. Your partner may just be into it.

As you try new things make an extra effort to pay attention to your own feelings and responses both during and after your romps. It's very easy to improve your whole sensual experience with a few simple techniques like conscious breathing, more comfortable positions, the angle of penetration, and so forth. Since you've opened the door to kinky experimentation you might as well improve your overall lovemaking skills. Be sure to talk with your partner about what you're experiencing and ask about their feelings and responses too—outside the bedroom, of course, when the pressure to perform is off. Encourage your partner to practice similar self-awareness techniques. You'll be making better lovers of each other in the process.

Keep in mind there's no accounting for taste. Some people are strictly vanilla and they're determined to stay that way. Offer them an option and allow them to explore along with you, but resist the temptation to coerce or judge. Nonjudgmental starts with you and if you find you're in an unsatisfying relationship, most marriage counselors and relationship experts will tell you to change the situation. If your differences are not yet irreconcilable you should find a qualified counselor, coach, or therapist who can help you work through your troubles. Sexual differences are often surprisingly straightforward to work through with honest and open communication along with the help of a good therapist.

Ease Into It

Pacing and intensifying your trysts can be tricky. Make an effort to escalate at the rate that makes you the most comfortable; that usually means testing the waters with your partner and easing into things. At the same time if you get a wildly enthusiastic response from your partner, seize the opportunity to dive into the deep end and introduce more kink into your sex.

Easing in allows a gradual and natural escalation of kinky activity rather than thrusting everything on your unsuspecting partner all at once. This is a safe way to determine the level of intensity that will work for both of you and get your partner to play along. Maybe you arrange every Wednesday as "dress-up night" and start with costumes and a little role playing and take things from there.

Make sure you've taken psychological and sexual safety issues into account before you launch into a carnal freak show. If you're not sure how to tie hemp rope take a course or visit a reputable bondage instructor. If you want to experiment with edge play, make sure appropriate safety precautions have been taken (e.g., keep a fire extinguisher around if flame is involved). If you engage in edge play like blood play or breath play and you don't know what you're doing, you can inflict serious damage on your partner.

"Easing in" does not mean you demonstrate annoying persistence in the face of your partner's unwillingness to play along. If you partner is dead set against what you have in mind it can be a struggle to accept the fact that your curiosity is a deal breaker for them. Discovering your differences sooner will help avoid the frustration of having unmet needs sabotage your relationship. If you find this to be the case and couples therapy doesn't let you reach a suitable arrangement, consider playing separately. It can be tough to reconcile such a sexual and romantic disconnection, but if you and your partner find a way to agree that you'll have another playmate for the kinky stuff with terms spelled out (maybe you stipulate that there will be no penetration, for example), that may minimize the frustration and damage to your relationship. But both of you have to agree. Getting your rocks off behind your partner's back is cheating, pure and simple.

If worse comes to worse, consider terminating the relationship so both of you can seek partners that will fit you better. I hate to break it to you, but romantic relationships that involve fundamental sexual incompatibility are recipes for cheating, lying, resentment, and mistrust. You may love your partner and want to be with them, but if you're being denied sexual gratification in an exclusive relationship you're not likely to be happy for very long.

Easing into the sensual world you're creating with your partner helps you because you can continually communicate and reset expectations on an ongoing basis. By playing, talking, playing harder, and talking more you each develop a greater sense of each other's likes and dislikes and hopefully bring yourselves closer to one another sexually and emotionally.

Shift The Burden

Kinky sex is taboo so bringing it up for consideration can be awkward. It would be nice to test the waters and gauge your partner's receptivity without adding unnecessary pressure. Do this by letting the subject come up on its own rather than by suddenly demanding your partner insert a butt plug into your lubed rectum.

One of the primary responsibilities of a relationship therapist is to guide the conversation about sensitive subjects and take the weight of "being the instigator" off each partner's shoulders. While both people still need to contribute for counseling to be effective, raising difficult subjects is usually just too painful for the people actually living with relationship troubles. Once a couple has agreed to work with a therapist it becomes much easier for the therapist to facilitate a fairly frank and intimate discussion of those things that make the relationship both satisfying and challenging. The therapist *accepts the burden* of responsibility for raising the issues that need to be considered. The therapist frees the couple to respond and share their feelings without the fear that the other partner will hold it against them for simply bringing it up some difficult topic.

As the person initiating kink play you can shift the burden in a number of ways. Use the worksheets in the appendix of this book. Explain to your partner, "I stumbled across these in a book I'm reading. Some of these look really fun. What do you think?" Similarly, you can recount something you've seen and heard without demanding that the two of you hurry up and try it. "I saw the craziest thing on television last night! I was watching Cinemax late and an episode of Emmanuelle came on..." Or, "A friend told me about a newbie social night they had at this dungeon a few weeks ago. It sounds really fascinating! One couple was play acting a corporal punishment high-school scenario, spanking each other with a wooden ruler! Sounds hot, huh?" Sometimes your suggestion plants the seed in your partner's imagination. From that germ of an idea, give the thought time to sprout.

Of course as grown adults we take *full responsibility* for the consequences of our actions. Shifting the burden of responsibility for *initiating* the conversation simply makes it far less threatening and safer for you and your partner to consider sprinkling a little kink into your sex life.

No Means No, Yes Means Yes

Until you're in the midst of a scene with safe words in place, "no" means no. Coercion, pressure, and prodding (or the passive equivalent of such aggressive behavior) on the part of either partner will damage your relationship. Even though some of what you'd like to try may feel awkward to talk about it's better to talk it through than take a wrecking ball to your sex life and hope somehow you end up with a lovely chalet.

Sex-positive activists have taken the phrase *no means no,* which implies the lack of consent, and extended it to integrate the notion of **enthusiastic consent.** *Yes means yes* suggests that both partners are totally informed and *eager* to undertake the sexual adventure that awaits them. Suppose you're discussing a spanking scene. In the "yes means yes" paradigm both of you feel an urge to play out this spanking fantasy. One may want an open hand, while the other may like a hairbrush. This leaves room for negotiation. Contrast this to begrudging consent, where the spanker whacks the spankee despite the whole situation being a huge turn off for the person being spanked, all in some misguided effort to make the spanker happy. The spankee agrees because saying "no" would amount to rejecting the other person. Here "yes" basically means "I love you," it does not mean "I like this" or "I agree because I want to do this."

As the person who feels the urge to commence playing kinky games in your otherwise vanilla relationship, it's up to you to do it in a way that doesn't twist your partner's arm (unless you learn that they're really into the rough stuff, in which case use a go word along with a safe word). The non-defensive, nonjudgmental mindset will make this far easier for you. Enthusiastic consent may be something you arrive at after easing in and building your sexual history together. In the mean time don't rush, force, or pressure things unless you're ready to send your relationship to an early grave.

Devil's Advocate

↝ What if I'm really not comfortable talking about my kink? I just want to get to the action.

You can try rough unnegotiated sex but that'll probably end with a huge freak out or jail time. We build relationships by sharing time together (experiencing our *physical* selves) and sharing our thoughts and feelings (expressing our *inner* selves). If talking about this is just not worth your time or it makes you feel too weird, your partner will be prone to misconstrue your intention. People cannot read minds.

Even when people think they're on the same page they're really coming at things from very different personal histories. Part of the fun of aggressive sex is sorting all that out. I think talking about sex is sexy. If you don't and you want to cut to the chase you can try using a safe word and your best judgment. When you're in an existing relationship that's vanilla, springing kink on your partner is risky. It might be great, but it's just as likely to cause problems that would have easily been avoided with a simple conversation.

↝ My partner is so vanilla but I think they'd really like kink if they give it a try.

Even if someone *might* like something once they really got into it, they can so overwhelmed with shame, guilt, or social programming that they cannot open themselves up to the possibility. If they do, they often experience *severe* buyer's remorse after the fact. If you induce that kind of regret in your playmate you threaten to damage your relationship.

Now I'm all for pushing people to their limits and encouraging them to step outside their comfort zones. I think that helps people grow intellectually, physically, and sexually. I'm also willing to end the sexual aspect of a relationship and stay friends if the person I'm with isn't a good fit for me (or me for her). So if you're willing to accept the consequences, whatever they may be, of trying to convert your vanilla partner then go for it. But remember, coerce someone into something will often get them to try it once. *Exactly* once.

⟵ What if my vanilla partner refuses to even entertain the possibility?

This is hard. There's insight in the art of negotiation: if you can't walk away, you can't bargain. If you're committed to a relationship and refuse to end it under any circumstances, particularly over sexual compatibility (which just may be the most critical element in the success of a romantic relationship), well my friend, you're screwed. In the missionary position if you're lucky. Or maybe not at all.

Ask yourself what price are you're willing to pay to get your partner to play as you'd like, in order for you to see if it's any fun for them. If you're not willing to put something on the line—like denying them vanilla sex—then there's not much incentive for him or her (or it or them, damn with all these gendered pronouns) to give it a try. I don't mean for this to be a moral problem, just a practical fact. You can whine and cajole and prod someone hoping for an adventurous side to come out, but without the ability to walk away, bitching about it is pretty much your only option.

⟵ What if I cross someone's boundaries or seriously push their limits?

Kill 'em. Wrap the body in plastic. Dump it in the ravine by old man Brown's farm. The authorities shouldn't find it till spring. Lie low till the heat dies down.

Seriously, people are more resilient that we often give them credit for provided we act under the principle of *ahimsa*. Be open to aftercare and a debriefing following your encounter. Discuss what you each liked and what you didn't. Do more of what you both like and eliminate what you don't.

Think For Yourself

1. How can and will you bring up the subject of kink with a new (possibly vanilla) or long-term partner?

2. Identify three books, movies, stories, or web sites you can use to help you communicate your kinky inclinations.

    1)

    2)

    3)

3. *Reverse The Roles:* If someone brought up kink with you, what would you want to know? What reassurances would you like to hear?

Maintain Your Relationship

The purpose of this book is to get you into a kinky relationship. Now comes the hard part: what do you do to *stay* in that relationship?

Your kinky relationship raises the same variety of issues as a vanilla relationship, and navigating romances is the stuff of Cosmopolitan, Maxim, Oprah, and countless self-help books. While much of that advice applies to your relationship too, several guidelines that are specific to kink will help you make sense of your own experience and better understand your partner so your relationship can grow in a way that satisfies both of you.

I-Statements

Nonjudgmental, non-defensive language can be hard to master. You want to *offer* your partner an option but not sound like you're *telling* them what to do. You want to express your *feelings* but don't want your partner to argue with you as if you're relating an absolute *fact*. You can articulate much of this with an **I-statement**. I-statements allow you to take responsibility for your own feelings while reporting subjective truths (how you feel) and asking your partner to change their behavior.

Format Of An I-Statement

1. *I* feel this **emotion**   (take responsibility for how you feel)
2. When *you* do that **action** (describe the behavior involved)
3. *Because* of this **reason**   (explain why the behavior troubles you)
4. *I'd like* you to **substitute** (provide an alternative behavior)

For example, "I feel uncomfortable when you strip me in public because I'm still self conscious and I keep imagining the neighbors will see us. Can we do the next flogging scene at the dungeon instead?" You can also express *approval* after a scene. "I liked it when you went down on me and did that thing with your fingertips. It tickles in a good way. Do that again next time!"

You can see how describing your feelings using I-statements can help you avoid the blame and accusation (and potential defensiveness) that gets associated with expressing something as personal and subjective as your feelings about sex. Importantly, I-statements offer an *alternative* to the current situation. Instead of cursing the darkness you light a candle. Then drip the wax all over your partner's bare stomach. That's hot.

Avoid Lawyering

It's helpful to regard the communication style of your relationship as a chance to describe your ever-evolving experiences instead of turning your partner's words into one-time contracts to be executed by each party. **Lawyering** means holding your partner(s) strictly to their words as if they are obligations. You treat them like defendants—and by putting them on the defensive you can't help but to provoke hostility and resistance. The adversarial system is not very effective at settling disputes amicably. It's designed to put parties in opposition. That's why courtrooms are tense and mediators are often used before resorting to lawyers.

You can tell when the lawyering talk has started when you hear words like *technically* and *actually* and *proof* being used to scout for loopholes or skirt responsibility. It's as if there's a contract being enforced with phrases like, "*Technically* we're not married," and "Well how can you *actually* prove I was out with Jack?" People in relationships will always disagree, but you'll be better off if you use I-statements and make sure you both understand each other than if you "win" an argument with your partner. Even if you're in a 24/7 lifestyle situation both partners' needs have to be met or one of you is going to leave.

If someone tells you, "I'm not looking for anything serious," but in the course of play they start to develop feelings, that's natural. After a month or two, guess what? Things got serious. To try to lock them into that earlier not-so-serious arrangement because they said they weren't out looking for a relationship is nonsense. People experience relationships at different speeds. Be willing to renegotiate expectations, because relationships will inevitably grow and change.

Most of the women I've been with have at some point or another tested the "exclusive" waters. Sometimes it's direct as in, "I don't want you seeing other people." Sometimes it's indirect as in, "Sooo, um, what did you do last night?" Evolutionary psychology tells us that women on average tend to seek an *emotional investment* from their partner while men look for *sexual fidelity* from theirs.

Sure, we have prophylactics and the pill today but forty years of readily available contraception have not deleted hundreds of thousands of years of evolution.

Thus if a man has sex on the side it isn't such a big deal, the reasoning goes, as long as he doesn't divert resources (like his love and money and time for little league practice) from his existing progeny. *Opportunistic mating* gives his genes a better chance of being passed into the next generation. If the bastard offspring is the other woman's problem his primary partner may harbor resentment, but as long as he remains emotionally invested her offspring will be secure. Straying sexually is usually pretty easily forgiven if it "doesn't mean anything." (Whence the cliché question about the mistress, *So do you love her?!*)

From the male's perspective, paternity takes nine months to test and even then family resemblance is not a guarantee of fatherhood. The male doesn't mind if the woman's *heart* wanders, provided she stays sexually faithful. She can crush as hard as she wants on the new sexy neighbor as long as she just lusts from afar. This helps him avoid becoming a cuckold.

If you're in a polyamorous relationship, it's not all that useful to discuss, or for Christ's sake compare, your other lovers. That's just begging for drama. Resist the temptation to bring up other lovers, even past lovers, unless you're secure enough in your relationship that you're sure everyone is okay with your nonexclusive arrangement.

The Couch Test

A friend of mine describes an exercise he uses to keep the peace among multiple partners: If you were to put your partners, and their partners, all together on a couch and watch a movie, would everyone get along? If not, it's best not to rub your partner's nose in the fact that they are not your one and only.

There's no reason for animosity, anger, unnecessary drama to interfere with the healthy progress of each relationship on its own terms.

If you've transcended the blame game God bless you because you're probably having shockingly potent thirty-minute orgasms together. Congratulations. The rest of us can manage the risk of lawyering by easing into it and shifting the burden when experimenting with new ways to play as discussed in the chapter *Melt*

The Vanilla. The initiator usually gets blamed if things don't go well so initiate things together and the blame goes away.

The advantage of shifting the burden in an existing relationship is that you can try new things and get rid of boring routines that have you stuck in a rut without having to lawyer each other and defend your interest in trying something new. Which of these would you rather hear?

a) We always do role playing before bed, and I'm exhausted. It's starting to get old so knock it off!
b) I read in this magazine that if you're always having sex right before bed you can mix it up by making an afternoon of role playing.

While you're at it throw in an I-statement and say, "Sometimes I feel unsexy when you initiate sex right before bed because I'm exhausted when it gets that late. I'd love to try a bank robber scene in the afternoon, though. How does that sound?"

Praise Each Other

Praise is one of the most effective ways to show your gratitude and appreciation to your partner. For some reason we don't do it very much. We'll say, "I love you," or "You're so thoughtful," but that hardly conveys the depth of your feelings if you're in a satisfying sexual relationship. Part of the reason praise is given infrequently is that we have assumptions about how people should act or we don't know how to take compliments ourselves.

* *If I'm not complaining, then everything is great.*
* *Can't my partner tell I love the way we play dress-up every Thursday?*
* *I can't praise my sub, that'll make me look like a weak dom.*

Recall the *illusion of transparency* where we assume others have access to our mental state. That cognitive bias factors into much of this thinking and it's not very useful. Silence does not imply consent in the fetish community, so it shouldn't imply satisfaction in a sexual relationship. Everyone is somewhat insecure about their sexual prowess, physique, or bedroom performance. Praise and compliments reassure your partner that you're happy with them and your sex life together. Praise can also positively reaffirm for your partner those attitudes and behaviors that you truly enjoy.

Even if you're a sadist whose sole purpose in life is to humiliate your sub, if you reward what pleases you with praise and punish what displeases you with discipline the relationship you foster with your sub is going to be a whole lot more likely to make both of you a couple of happy perverts. All sticks and no carrots makes Jack a dull dom.

These are some things to keep in mind when delivering praise.

1. **Be specific.** It's hard to act on overly general praise. If you say, "That was awesome!" after sex add, "The thing you did with your hands when you were sucking on me was incredible." This will reward the behavior you want and your partner is more likely to repeat it next time.

2. **Be authentic.** Empty praise can be more damaging that silence, since people are adept at detecting disingenuous words and discounting them as lies. That can hurt your credibility and reduce trust. If something makes you happy or impresses you just speak from the heart.

3. **Praise publicly.** This can be hard if your partner is shy and you don't want to put them on the spot, but it's very effective at demonstrating that you value them. Praising some aspect of your relationship among friends or kink-aware compatriots puts your words on the record and gets others to value your partner along with you. That doesn't mean you brag and say, "Jill can do more tricks with rope than your dog can do with a ball." It means you are specific and authentic in your appreciation of your partner.

4. **Don't be manipulative.** Buttering someone up is not necessarily inauthentic but it's certainly manipulative. If you hit your partner up with a demand after every compliment it will trigger the reverse effect and make them guarded every time they see praise coming. It's also incongruent. If you want something learn to ask for it.

If you aren't used to giving or receiving praise, or if your family was unexpressive, it can feel awkward and forced to praise your partner at first. Start by noticing what you like and what you genuinely appreciate about your partner. Maybe it's their body, their attitude, or the graceful way they move. Then take a minute to acknowledge your gratitude to yourself. Maybe you find yourself saying, "Wow, I'm lucky to have someone this smart around spanking me when I get horny." Finally, get your partner's attention with, "Honey, I've got something I want to tell you..." and just say what's on your mind. If you've never done this before you're in for a real treat.

Bond Outside The Bedroom

Relationships are built of *common interests*. Your mutual attraction and interest in each other drew you together. But whether it's a knitting circle, a book club, or a political cause, shared interests keep people together. The key to maintaining *any* relationship is to have some interest, cause, or concern you can share. That way your time is not spent entertaining each other but you both get to enjoy fun things while you're together.

Most people connect more deeply when they connect on multiple levels: physically, emotionally, intellectually, and spiritually to name a few. That's why it's so important to get a drink with the gang after work and attend the office Christmas party. For sexual partners, the challenge is simply to find things you can talk about other than just kinky sex if you want to have more in common than just kinky sex. I get bored spending time in the company of people I don't fundamentally care about—people that I can't find something in common with. I

Friends First—And Last

I mostly have sex with girls who are friends and who I find fascinating and fun outside the bedroom. Before we get into a relationship I like them as friends, and if things don't work out I make every effort to avoid acrimonious breakups. Together we do things that build on our fantasies and bond us in a spirit of exploration.

It's much easier to stay friends (or at least friendly) with an ex-lover if you were friends to begin with.

prefer to connect on some level so I feel my time with them is an investment rather than just time wasted.

If you're only out for bedroom action that's fine, but you're depth of connection will be limited. You restrict the amount of outside experience you and your partner can build upon. Sexual cues come from the environment all the time so if you socialize together you have a chance to share those "Wouldn't it be hot?" moments. Your sexual creativity and intensity rise dramatically.

Furthermore, strictly sexual relationships are not easy to sustain. People instinctively look to invest themselves emotionally in their relationships so keep this in mind as you navigate yours. Remember that nothing grows without maintenance, particularly relationships. Even if you set the expectation that things will be purely physical from the onset, be prepared for feelings to develop. Try to lay it all out at the beginning. But don't be oblivious to the fact that peoples' hearts follow their genitals.

I often tease girls when I meet them and say, "Oh you'll be like all the rest. You'll be stalking me after a week because you'll crave the ridiculously mind-blowing sex and confuse it for love!" These comments break the ice but the humor lies in the recognition that this really does happen all the time. As tempting as it is to keep it just physical, the heart wants what the heart wants. Anticipating this means establishing appropriate boundaries for yourself and maintaining them.

Of course, if you happen to have the perfect just-physical relationship there's no need to ruin it. Remember the Abilene paradox? Be clear about what you want and talk about it. If you want to spend time with your partner in vanilla settings and grow your bond of trust and intimacy, do it. But don't do it because you think they want it. Don't do it out of a misguided sense of obligation. Do it because it's something you want to do. Self-sacrificing will leave both of you more dissatisfied and unhappy than if you each act under your own *thelema*.

If you're sufficiently comfortable and a shade analytical you can conduct a periodic relationship assessment. Each month or so check in with your partner specifically about your relationship status. Don't simply ask, "Is everything alright?" and hope for the best. See where things are now and where they're going. Talk about what's working for you and what needs help. It's rare that relationship difficulties automatically correct themselves, and couples therapy routinely involves checking in to confront such smoldering matters. Laying bare our needs and wants leads to less anxiety, less resentment harboring, and less disappointment when we're together.

Counseling And Therapy

If you're relationship is serious enough, don't rule out couples counseling or relationship coaching. Counseling is not just for relationships in trouble. It can be an exceptionally helpful forum for airing those questions and concerns that make healthy relationships even better. A new trend in therapeutic circles called **positive psychology** focuses on helping healthy people lead happier and more satisfying lives. Whether it's from a life coach, a community support group, or a professional therapist, it may enhance your relationship to look into counseling.

Look for a therapist who is kink-friendly. Be forthright and direct about your kinky practices. Therapists are bound by an ethical code and a professional standard that keeps your conversation confidential. But some counselors are not well trained in the safe and healthy expression of alternative sexual practices. If they classify your spanking sessions as abuse but you and your partner are playing nicely, your counselor won't help much. They'll advise you to quit or split up.

Counseling makes sense if things start to become uncomfortable or abusive for either of you. For example, couples acting out D/s roles can sometimes find the lines between fantasy and reality blurred in a way that is fundamentally unhealthy. Maybe you've set the expectation that he licks your boots before bed. If you've agreed that your relationship will be vanilla glossed and discreet, but you start testing him in public by demanding foot worship at a restaurant, guess what? You'll piss away a lot of the trust you've built. Trust is the foundation for safe physical arousal, and when it's missing the relationship suffers. Hopefully neither of you feel that the endorphin rush is worth betraying and humiliating your partner. At least, not without their *enthusiastic yes* in advance.

These relationship issues may seem like a big to-do about nothing, but we've had thousands of years of cultural reinforcement of traditional institutions like marriage. Maybe in a few thousand years society will create elegant institutions in support of kink's alternative sexual unions, but for now it's up to you to do your best and have fun now. When you throw away the mold it is your job to create a new relationship template together. Coaching, community support, and counseling from a competent professional will help you do that.

Trustworthiness: Keep Your Word

When you're writing your own relationship template rather than relying on the standard ones such as *just dating* or *marriage minded,* what you promise and what you agree to becomes more important than ever. Saying "I'd like it if you pulled my hair" serves as a request and as a standing preference. You are free to revise it, but if you make this remark I'm not likely to keep on asking, "So do you want me to pull your hair today?"

Remember that trust forms the foundation we need to feel confident in the belief that things of value will be kept safe. In other words, your word is your bond. Once you break your word the trust you've worked to establish has been violated. If we agree to a light bondage scene and nothing more, but I relentlessly slap you around or drip wax on your ass, consent is neither informed nor implied. I broke my word. I am not trustworthy. Similarly if as the dominant I say I will punish the misbehavior of the submissive but fail to enforce my own rules, I am not trustworthy. It would have been better had I not set up such toothless rules in the first place.

In a healthy and supportive relationship, both people actively seek to trust one another. Communication reinforces the feeling of trust that partners have toward each other. It's when the relationship is strained that having a track record of doing what you say can make or break things. If you've managed to avoid resorting to lawyering then you'll forgive the sincere misstatements of your partner. But when things get ugly or hostile, human instinct is to attack and to defend against whoever is causing you grief.

Unfortunately there's no way to be genuinely open and intimate while being guarded and bulletproofing yourself against having your words twisted. The reality of intimate relationships is that they're vulnerable to violation. But if you always act in a way that is congruent with your *thelema* and respects the principle of *ahimsa*, while doing your best to say what you mean and to keep your word you'll be fine. That way, while your particular words may not perfectly capture your meaning, your intentions are indeed beyond reproach.

Talking about sex requires a level of openness and trust, and that trust has to be earned and maintained. Power exchange is all a trust game. People have to wonder, "Am I safe in the hands of this person? Will he or she hurt me? I'm not calling the shots...I hope this person knows what they're doing." The tools of kink (e.g., restraints, pain, and control) are trust manipulation devices used to play in the most intimate of physical and mental spaces. Sex continually crosses interpersonal boundaries. When you're entrusted with someone's most intimate being, treat it with respect.

Check In, Communicate, And Grow

It amazes me in the vanilla world how ready people are to have sex yet how reluctant they are to talk about what they're doing and even after the first physical encounter the sex talk can be surprisingly awkward. Becoming physically intimate does not mean you're going to instantly and effortlessly grow closer mentally or emotionally. Communication is how your relationship grows.

If you don't communicate, if you don't express your thoughts and feelings as your relationship moves forward, then you're holding something back from your partner. Your changing emotional landscape is not likely to keep pace with your partner's. It's common to **project** your feelings on others and attribute the kind of emotional investment that you want to see, rather than to accurately perceive the emotional investment that is actually there. If you're hoping for commitment or exclusivity or true love, your **wishful thinking** can give you the impression this person is coming along for the ride with you. Interpreting into the words "I'd love to get with you," as "I love…you!" is selective editing. You hear the words you want to hear.

As you change and as your needs mature, make sure your partner is on board with you. You can take the lead in pursuing new kinks or changing the way you do things today. The key is communication. Talk about what's on your mind. If it feels a little uncomfortable for you, that's okay. Discomfort is just the price we pay to stretch ourselves and experience new things. That feeling of discomfort tells you that what you're doing is unfamiliar, that you're in uncharted territory. You're exploring something new. That's just how change works. If you let fear of discomfort limit you then you are no longer in control of your own actions. Your moods control you.

Furthermore, scene negotiation and consent involve an ongoing dialog and not a one-time formality. When your partner agrees to try something, it does not provide blanket permission for you to do whatever you want whenever you want. If you fuck someone without consent it's rape. People change. Preferences

Mindgames

Mismatched expectations lead to frustrations that can kill a relationship. I had a great booty call and explained I was in no position to offer emotional support. She said she was cool with that and things were nice and intense for about a month.

One day she started sending reminder texts. "I had such a long day!" "Don't you love the weather?" "Hey how's it going?" Since checking in was not part of our bargain, I decided to text her back once 24 hours had passed from her last message. I went seven full days playing my waiting game before enough time elapsed. We met once more to break things off.

If we had talked about her emotional needs in more detail we might have worked something out. Lack of communication led to misaligned expectations that broke the deal.

change. Permission changes. Discuss it so you're not blindsided by change when it happens.

At the same time, don't be afraid to introduce new thrills into your relationship now that you have an understanding partner who provides you an outlet for your kinky desires. Pluralistic ignorance makes everyone unhappy. If you believe, "He'll never go for this—he'll think I'm a freak," or, "She's a good girl—good girls don't like naughty sex," then you are condemned to uncertainty and you're certain to miss out.

Be direct. Acknowledge your interests. Accept your own sexual curiosity and encourage that of your partner's. Own your love life. Then tie your partner up. It's insanely fun.

Devil's Advocate

⊸ *It sounds like a lot of work to keep the communication lines open.*

It is, but it's not a great deal more work communicating with someone who likes it kinky than it is communicating with someone who is vanilla. Communication is messy, imprecise, and in continual flux. It's just part of being a person.

Kink can actually make it easier to talk about sex because many of the things that are otherwise taboo become candidates for explicit negotiation. Instead of assuming sexual scripts based on romantic comedies or plotless porn we share our sexual turn ons and turn offs far more frankly. Rather than adopting relationship templates designed to create legal structures to protect assets and offspring (marriage is not just for religion anymore) we base our relationships on what we want and what we want to avoid. Talking about kinky sex can help a person become a better communicator overall.

⊸ *It's just a given that I can count on my partner for emotional support.*

That's certainly true of the *soulmate* template and in certain types of close relationships like friendship, and maybe family. But just because you're having sex that does not mean there's a significant emotional investment on the part of either partner. Whether kinky or otherwise, people invest sexually and emotionally because it satisfies *their* needs, not because it's some rule. Kink blows up the template anyway. As a responsible adult you have the obligation to set clear expectations and maintain clear boundaries so that your need to be loved and your urge to have sex are not inadvertently commingled. Commingle them because you agree to it, not because you mistakenly assume it will happen.

⟶ *Look, I just want a physical relationship. No strings. All this other stuff doesn't interest me.*

"No strings" has the advantages of a relationship with no serious commitment, and the disadvantages of a relationship with no serious commitment. That means if your partner finds someone who is a better fit, they're going to spend their precious time with someone else. Basically you're saying the relationship is not worth the effort to maintain anyway, so as long as you're cool with that you don't need to do a lot of extra work to maintain your relationship.

As far as I'm concerned, the people who I have sex with are first and foremost *people*; second they are *friends*; third they are *sexual* partners. This forces me to consider their personal well-being regardless of my sexual interest in them. When I do things with no strings it's usually infrequent (once a month or less) and intense, a heat of the moment thing.

Keep in mind that comfort, trust, and great sex have a funny way of sprouting unexpected strings on you.

1. Do you tend to use "I-statements" now or do you need to work on taking responsibility in your communication style?

2. Have you actively worked through relationship issues in your past relationships, or have you let issues "sort themselves out"?

3. What specific relationship difficulties have you encountered in the past that could arise in a kinky relationship?

Conclusion

Congratulations, you've covered quite a lot of ground in the last ten chapters! At this point you have all the tools you need to find a suitable partner and start a kinky relationship. To recap, the exercises have allowed you to do the following:

- In **Why Do It Kinky?** you identified what about kink turns you on.
- In **What *Exactly* Is Kinky?** you figured out your own limits and what you can handle in your sex life.
- In **Essential Kink: BDSM** you learned where you fall in the bondage & discipline, domination/submission, sadism & masochism continuum.
- In **The Kinky Mindset** you discovered what elements of the kinky mindset you possess and seek in a partner.
- In **Meet Kinky People** you decided where you can meet kinky people.
- In **Choose A Playmate** you determined what you are looking for in a kinky partner.
- In **Start Your Relationship** you established just what kind of relationship you want to have.
- In **Negotiate A "Scene"** you made plans to discuss how you would go about doing what you like with your partner.
- In **Melt The Vanilla** you considered various ways to express your kinky interests to a new partner in a constructive way.
- In **Maintain Your Relationship** you equipped yourself with tools to work through communication and interpersonal issues that can impair new relationships.

You now have a fantastic basis on which to build your relationship. There's nothing stopping you from going out and meeting an exciting, attractive, complementary partner today and having the best sex of your life.

As you learn more about yourself and your own sexuality, review this workbook in a few months. Share what you've learned with your partner. Review the chapter material and your *Think For Yourself* answers. You're bound to uncover things you didn't know about yourself and your partner, which makes the experience of getting to know someone all the more exhilarating.

Top Ten Do's And Don'ts

Fortunately for you, gentle reader, everything that's been said in this book can be completely captured in the form of a Top Ten list. Captured. That's hot.

Well, maybe not "completely captured." Maybe neatly summed up. Or maybe just gratuitously force-fit into list form for laughs. Enjoy.

Do

1. Do as you will. (See *thelema*; own your intentions.)
2. Do get out and meet people.
3. Do negotiate your scenes.
4. Do continually communicate to increase trust, intimacy, and arousal.
5. Do it kinky because you like it.

Don't

6. Don't harm yourself or others. (See *ahimsa*; safety and respect.)
7. Don't assume but ask instead.
8. Don't be ashamed, embarrassed, or afraid of your kink.
9. Don't avoid responsibility for your actions.
10. Don't keep doing it out of habit. If you don't like what you're doing, stop it.

Glossary Of BDSM Terms

[From *http://www.xeromag.com/fvbdglossary.html* courtesy **Franklin Veaux**.]

This glossary is intended as a guide to many of the terms you might hear in the BDSM community. Don't assume everyone who is involved with BDSM is into everything listed here; many of the specific practices described in the Glossary are quite rare.

Nobody is into everything, and even in the BDSM community, not everyone has the same tastes, the same limits, or the same ideas.

If you see something described in here which you personally find disturbing or offputting, that's fine; it doesn't mean that you aren't or can't be interested in BDSM.

The definitions given here reflect the usage I am most familiar with. Some terms contain commentary; anything following the word *Commentary* indicates my own views on a particular subject, and should not be assumed to be part of the formal definition.

Comments or additions? Email Franklin at: **mailto:mtacitr@aol.com**.

Terms

24/7: *Colloquial* Of or related to a **total power exchange** relationship.

A-FRAME: A type of **bondage** furniture consisting of an upright triangle, usually made of wood and typically about seven to eight feet tall, sometimes with cross slats. A person can be **bound** to the frame with wrists together, arms above the head and affixed to the pinnacle of the triangle, and ankles bound to the base of the triangle with legs apart.

ABASIOPHILIA: *Psychology* Sexual attraction to people in or who use wheelchairs, casts, braces, or other orthopedic fixtures.

ABRASION: Any form of **sensation play** involving stroking or brushing the skin with rough, textured objects such as sandpaper, emery boards, and the like.

ABSOLUTE POWER EXCHANGE (APE): *See* <u>total power exchange</u>. *Usage:* Less common than **TPE**.

ADULT BABY: *Colloquial* A person who engages in <u>infantilism</u> in the role of a very young child or infant.

AFTERCARE: A period of time after intense <u>BDSM</u> activity in which the **dominant** partner cares for the <u>submissive</u> partner. *Commentary:* Some BDSM activities are physically challenging, psychologically intense, or both. After engaging in such activities, the submissive partner may need a safe psychological space to unwind and recover. Aftercare is the process of providing this safe space.

AGE PLAY: A form of <u>role play</u> in which a participant assumes the role of someone of a different age. Typically, the <u>submissive</u> partner will assume the role of a very young (and hence powerless) child. *See related* <u>adult baby</u>, <u>infantalism</u>. *Commentary:* One common misperception about **age play** is that it appeals to pedophiles or is intended to simulate pedophilia. For those who engage in this activity, it is the powerlessness aspect of childhood and the inherent power imbalance between an adult and a child, rather than the childhood itself, that is appealing.

ALGOPHILIA; *also,* **ALGOLAGNIA:** *Psychology* Sexual arousal from receiving pain. *See also* <u>masochist</u>; *See related* <u>pain play</u>, <u>sadomasochism</u>, <u>sadist</u>.

ALPHA SUB: *Colloquial* In a relationship in which one <u>dominant</u> has more than one <u>submissive</u>, the **submissive** accorded the greatest power or respect among all the **submissives.** *See related* **polyamory:** <u>primary/secondary</u>. *Commentary* Not all relationships which have more than one submissive include a hierarchy among the submissives; that is, not all such relationships have an **alpha sub.**

ANAL HOOK; *also,* **BUTT HOOK:** A smooth, blunt metal hook, typically about an inch thick and six inches long, with a small loop on one end. The shorter side of the hook is inserted into the anus, and a rope tied to the loop on the other end can be tied to an overhead fixture to force the wearer to kneel with his or her butt in the air, or can be secured to the wrists to bind the wearer's hands. Some **anal hooks** include a ball on the end that is inserted.

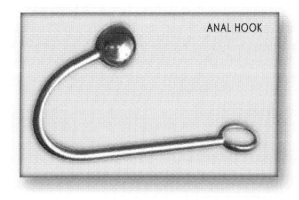

ANILINGUS: Any sexual activity involving licking, kissing, or tonguing another person's anus.

ANIMALISM: Any form of role play in which a participant assumes the role of an animal to be trained, such as a horse or dog. *See related* pony play, puppy play.

ANKLE CUFFS: Any cuffs (def. 1) specifically designed to be affixed to a person's ankles. Ankle cuffs are often made of leather, but may also be made of cloth, rope, metal, or even wood.

ARMBINDER: A restraint device consisting of a long sleeve into which both arms are placed, often fitted with laces or straps to hold the arms securely together. An armbinder may also include an integrated collar to prevent the wearer from withdrawing the arms. Also referred to as a **single-glove** or **monoglove**.

ASPHYXIA: *see* breath control; *see related* auto-erotic asphyxia.

ASS PLAY; *also,* **ARSE PLAY (British):** Any form of sexual stimulation of the ass, including anal sex, anilingus, and the like.

ASYMMETRIC BONDAGE: Any bondage technique in which a person is bound in an asymmetric pose; for example, with one leg extended and one leg bent. Many forms of shibari include **asymmetric bondage.**

AUCTION: *See* slave auction.

AUTO-EROTIC ASPHYXIA, *also* **AUTO-EROTIC ASPHYXIATION:** A specific form of breath control in which a person who is by himself or herself constricts his or her own breathing, often with a rope or similar implement, while masturbating. *Commentary:* Often considered among the most dangerous forms of edge play(def. 1). According to some estimates, between five hundred and a thousand people a year die in the United States doing this. It is almost impossible to do safely.

BALL BUSTING: *Colloquial* Any form of genitorture applied to the testicles, as by squeezing, impact, or tight binding.

BALL GAG: A gag consisting of a ball, usually made of rubber, which is attached to a strap. The ball is placed in the mouth and the strap is placed around the head to hold it securely in place.

BALL HOOD: A specific type of hood, often without openings for the eyes or ears and sometimes containing integrated bladders designed to be inflated with air to press the hood tightly against the head, used as a means of rendering a person unable to hear, see, or speak.

BALL TIE: A specific form of bondage in which the person is bound in a seated position with the knees up, the head bent down over the knees, and the hands behind the back. *Commentary:* This posture quickly becomes fatiguing and should not be used for extended periods of time on people who are not accustomed to it.

BANDAGE SCISSORS: Specialized scissors, often used by emergency medical personnel, consisting of a pair of scissors with one sharp blade and one blunt blade with a rounded end. The blunt blade can be slid beneath bandages or anything else wrapped tightly around a limb without risk of cutting or injuring the person. *Commentary:* Often used in BDSM to remove a person from tight **bondage** or <u>mummification</u> very quickly in the event of an emergency. A sturdy pair of bandage scissors will make quick work of even thick rope; a person totally wrapped in rope can be freed within seconds with bandage scissors without injury.

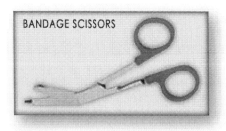

BASTINADO: Any form of <u>pain play</u> involving inflicting pain on the soles of the feet, often by striking, <u>cropping</u>, or <u>whipping</u> them.

BAT: A thin, flexible instrument used for striking, consisting of a rigid but flexible shaft wrapped or braided with leather or cloth, very similar to a <u>crop</u> but usually slightly shorter and with a wider leather striking tip.

BDSM: A composite acronym for "B&D" (<u>bondage</u> & <u>discipline</u>); "D&S" (<u>dominance</u> & <u>submission</u>); and "S&M" (<u>sadomasochism</u>). Used to refer to any consensual activities or lifestyles between adults which include some or all of these things. The term "**BDSM**" is used in a general sense to describe any situation or practice which includes erotic <u>power exchange</u>, **dominance** and **submission**, <u>pain play</u>, **bondage**, <u>sensation play,</u> or anything related to these.

BELTING: The practice of striking a person with a belt or with any long, narrow, belt-like strap.

BERKLEY HORSE: A type of <u>bondage</u> furniture consisting of a padded bench with integrated restraints and a pair of arms to which a person's legs can be affixed. A person is bent over the **berkley horse** and restrained in place; the **berkley horse** is designed so that it can be elevated, rotated, or moved into any position, and the arms to which the ankles are bound can be opened or closed. *Etymology:* The **berkley horse** was allegedly invented in 1828 by Theresa Berkley, a <u>prodomme</u> in London who specialized in <u>flogging</u> her clients.

BIMMY: *See* <u>sennet whip</u>.

BIRCH: An implement used for striking, consisting of a bundle of light, thin wooden rods, typically made of birch. *Also, verb* To strike with a birch.

BIT: *See* <u>mouth bit</u>.

BLADING: *Colloquial; see* <u>knife play</u>.

BLINDFOLD: Any implement designed to prevent a person from seeing by covering the eyes. *Also, verb* the act of using a blindfold on a person.

BLOOD PLAY; *also,* **BLOOD SPORTS:** Any activity involving drawing blood. Specific types of blood play include <u>needle play</u> and <u>knife play</u>, among others. Often considered <u>edge play</u>

(def. 1). *Commentary:* This is a high-risk activity which may transmit HIV and other infectious diseases. Persons who engage in blood play should be aware of these risks and take appropriate precautions.

BODY BAG: A long, heavy bag, often shaped like a narrow sleeping bag and typically made of canvas, rubber, or latex, used to restrain a person very tightly. Sometimes includes integrated straps which wrap around the person within the bag. *See related* **mummification.**

BODY HARNESS: A harness consisting of a series of straps designed to be worn around the torso, which may optionally include a mechanism for locking the harness into place and may also include rings or other attachments for ropes, **cuffs**, or **chastity belts**.

BODY MODIFICATION: Any practice, including piercing, tattooing, **branding**, and the like, intended to modify, often permanently, the appearance of one's body.

BOI: *Colloquial* 1. A person, usually biologically female and often boyish or "butch" in manner, appearance, or dress, who is **submissive**; commonly but not exclusively used in lesbian **D/s** relationships. 2. An effeminate man.

BONDAGE: Any practice involving tying or securing a person, as with ropes, cuffs, chains, or other restraints. **Restraint bondage,** the most common form of bondage, involves immobilizing a person, by tying or otherwise restraining him or her to an object or by binding his or her limbs together. **Stimulation bondage** is any form of tying in such a way that the subject is not immobilized and has freedom of motion, but the ropes or ties shift and move against the body, often in sensitive or erogenous areas; certain forms of **shibari** are stimulation bondage. A person in bondage is said to be **bound**. *See also* **bondage, predicament**, **ball tie**, **breast bondage**, **bondage tape**, **box tie,cock bondage**, **device bondage**, **frog tie**, **hogtie**, **lacing** (def. 4), **self-bondage**, **strappado bondage**, **steel bondage**, **suspension**, **mummification**, **punishment tie**. *See related* **bondage belt**, **bondage bunny**, **mitt, one**, **psychological bondage**, **rigger**, **spreader bar**, **spreadeagle**, **straitjacket**, **two-column tie.**

BONDAGE BELT: A belt used to restrain a person, which consists of a heavy band of leather or a similar material which can be strapped or locked about the waist and which has several attachment points to which the subject's wrists may be **bound**.

BONDAGE BUNNY: *Colloquial* A person who enjoys being tied or **bound**. *Usage:* Often implies that the person described is not necessarily **submissive** or **masochistic**, but enjoys **bondage** because he or she takes pleasure from being restrained.

BONDAGE MITT; *also,* **BONDAGE MITTEN:** A fingerless mitten, often made of leather, canvas, heavy vinyl, PVC, or similar materials, which is placed over the hand and then fastened in place with an integrated buckling or locking **cuff**. The **bondage mitt** holds the hand flat or balled up, and prevents the wearer from being able to pick things up or otherwise make use of his or her hands.

BONDAGE TAPE: A vinyl tape material, available in many colors, which sticks only to itself but not to other materials such as skin or clothing, making it ideal for **bondage**.

BOOTBLACKING: Polishing and spit-shining a pair of boots, sometimes as a gesture of sub-mission, sometimes as a part of military-style uniform play, sometimes as part of boot worship, and sometimes to mark the beginning of a scene (def. 1). *Commentary:* In some corners of the old leather community, **bootblacking** was used as part of a ritual between a dominant and submissive; the **submissive** partner would shine the **dominant's** boots while the **dominant** sat above the **submissive**.

BOOT BOY: *Colloquial* A male submissive, usually but not always a gay male, who engages in activities such as boot worship or bootblacking.

BOOT WORSHIP: A specific type of shoe fetishism centered around boots, in which the submissive partner may kiss, lick, polish, or otherwise adulate the **dominant's** boots. Often, but not always, includes some elements of uniform play. *See related* bootblacking.

BOTTOM: A person who receives spankings, floggings, or other forms of stimulation in situations which specifically exclude power exchange. For example, a masochist may be interested in receiving some kind of stimulation but may not be interested in giving up psychological control; whereas **submissive** has given up authority and may receive some kind of stimulation on the instruction of a dominant, a **bottom** does not give up authority and may control exactly how, under what circumstances, and to what degree he or she receives some form of stimulation. *Contrast* top; *see related* submissive.

BOTTOM DROP: *Colloquial* A sudden, abrupt feeling of depression, unhappiness, or similar negative emotion in a submissive which may occasionally occur immediately after a period of BDSM activity. May include feelings of shame or guilt, especially if the **submissive** has traditional ideas about relationship or socially appropriate behavior; after a period of intense pain play, **bottom drop** may be related to the reduction of levels of endorphins in the brain as well.

BOX TIE: A specific form of bondage in which a person brings his or her arms together and grips each forearm with the opposite hand, and then ropes are brought around the forearms to tie them together. Often combined with ropes between the upper arms to prevent the **bound** person from slipping his or her arms sideways out of the tie.

BRANDING: Body modification by the use of a heated metal implement to brand a person's skin, leaving a permanent mark in the form of a scar. Occasionally done as a way for a dominant to "mark" his or her submissive.

BRANK; *also,* **BRANKS:** *Archaic; see* scold's bridle.

BRAT: *Colloquial* A submissive who may refuse to obey a dominant's commands, tease or taunt the **dominant**, or engage in other activity intended to provoke a response, often a punishment response.

BREAST BONDAGE: A specific form of bondage involving binding around or over the breasts. *See related* breast press, karada, shinju.

BREAST PRESS; *also,* **BREAST CLAMP:** A type of device, often consisting of two horizontal wooden planks with an adjustable screw or clamp mechanism between them, which can be clamped over the breasts.

BREAST TORTURE: <u>Pain play</u> involving the breasts and/or nipples.

BREATH CONTROL: Any practice in which a person's breathing is constricted or interrupted, as with a hand or ligature around the throat or with a covering over the face, for the purpose of increasing sexual arousal or sexual climax. Often considered an extremely dangerous form of <u>edge play</u> (def. 1), as it can and often does lead to permanent injury or death. Also referred to as **asphyxia, erotic asphyxiation, gasping**. *See related* <u>auto-erotic asphyxia</u>.

BUCK HAMMER: A medical instrument used to test reflexes and neurological function, consisting of a metal handle with two cylindrical, rubber-tipped metal hammerheads. Typically, one or both hammerheads can be detached and replaced with a short metal spike or needle-like attachment, or with a short, soft brush, both of which can be used to test sensation and neurological function in the skin. Sometimes used for <u>percussion</u> or <u>sensation play.</u>

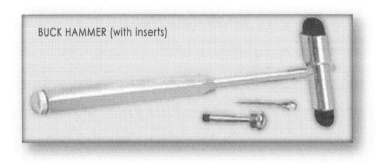

BUCK HAMMER (with inserts)

BULLWHIP: A type of <u>singletail</u> consisting of a woven or braided leather whip, usually longer than 4' and sometimes 6' long or more, with a short rigid handle. *Commentary:* Requires extensive practice and great skill to use safely.

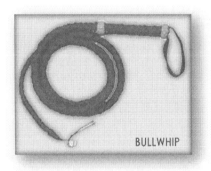

BULLWHIP

BUKKAKE: (from the Japanese 打っ掛け, "to splash water.") A sexual practice, originating in Japan, in which a very large number of men masturbate and ejaculate onto a person.

BUTT PLUG: A sex toy intended for anal stimulation, consisting of a flared dildo, usually quite short, with a wide base, designed to remain securely in the anus until removed.

BUTTERFLY CHAIR: A chair which contains two horizontal planks to which the legs can be secured, affixed to a pivot such that the legs of the secured person can be spread apart.

CABLE LOOP; *also,* **CABLE SLAPPER:** An implement used for striking, consisting of a loop or occasionally two loops of thick wire, coated with plastic, rubber, or leather, and affixed to a handle. A cable loop can be used much like a <u>crop</u> or similar implement, and produces intense sensations.

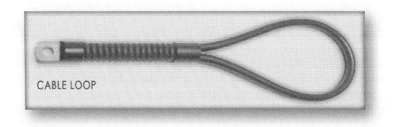

CABLE LOOP

CABLE TIE; *also,* **CABLE CUFF, PLASTICUFF, ZIP TIE:** A type of <u>cuff</u> consisting of a thin plastic strip with a row of teeth in its surface, and a small ratchet on one end. The end of the cable tie can be placed through the ratchet to form a loop which can be pulled tight but not loosened again. Sometimes used by police in favor of <u>handcuffs</u>.

CANE: A thin, flexible instrument used to strike a person. Canes are often made of rattan or a similar material, but may be made of other types of wood or even of flexible plastic such as polycarbonate. They are quite painful, often leaving marked welts. *Also, verb* to strike with a cane.

CAPTAIN'S DAUGHTER: *Archaic, colloquial; see* <u>cat o' nine tails</u>. *Etymology:* The **cat o' nine tails** was used as an implement of discipline aboard British Navy sailing ships beginning in the late 1600s. The term "captain's daughter" was a slang term for the cat o' nine tails popular among sailors, likely because it could not be used without the captain's express authorization.

CARABINER: Any device used to connect two chains or ropes together, often in the form of a D-shaped metal ring with a spring-loaded lever which can open the ring. *See related* <u>panic snap</u>. *Commentary:* Carabiners are not usually appropriate for <u>suspension</u>, as they cannot easily be removed if the suspended person's full weight is bearing down on them.

CAT: *Colloquial; from* <u>cat o' nine tails</u>: A generic term for any <u>flogger</u> whose lashes are braided or knotted, regardless of the number of lashes. *Commentary:* Knotting or braiding the lashes makes the **flogger** considerably more painful.

CAT O' NINE TAILS: A specific type of <u>flogger</u> consisting of a handle, often made of wood and wrapped with cloth, with nine lashes affixed to it. The lashes are usually made of rope or of leather cords, and are braided or knotted. Generally more painful than many other types of floggers. The cat o' nine tails was commonly used aboard British Navy sailing ships beginning in the 17th century. *Commentary:* The original **cat o' nine tails** was made by unbraiding a section of the rope used aboard British sailing ships. Each rope was made of three sections twisted together, each section of which consisted of three cords twisted together, so the rope when untwisted had nine tails.

CATHERINE'S WHEEL: A large, upright wheel, usually made of wood, to which a person may be <u>bound</u> and then rotated to any position.

CATHETER: Any thin, flexible tube designed to be inserted in the urethra. *See related* sound.

CATHETERIZATION: The act or process of inserting a catheter, often as a part of a medical role play.

CBT: *see* cock and ball torture.

CHASTITY: The practice of disallowing any form of sexual release or sexual activity, sometimes imposed on a submissive by a dominant. Some forms of imposed chastity include the use of locking devices such as chastity belts to prevent direct sexual stimulation of the genitals. Also sometimes called **chastity play**, **enforced chastity**.

CHASTITY BELT: Any device intended to prohibit contact with or stimulation of the genitals. Female chastity belts often take the form of a lockable harness which passes between the legs and around the waist; male chastity belts may include a locking enclosure into which the penis is placed.

CHASTITY PIERCING: Any body piercing intended to prevent sexual intercourse; as, piercings along the labia which can be locked together to prevent penetration, or a piercing of the foreskin which can be used to pull the foreskin over the head of the penis and lock it in place.

CHEMICAL PLAY: Any form of sensation play involving the use of mild irritants such as wintergreen oil, menthol, Tabasco sauce, and the like to create sensation.

CHDW: (Acronym) *Colloquial* Clueless Horny Dom Wannabe. A derisive term for a person who proclaims himself or herself a dominant, but who has little or no real-world experience, and/or behaves with reckless disregard for the needs or safety of the submissive. Pronounced "chudwa." *Usage:* Invariably indicates disdain for the person so named. *Etymology:* Originated on the now-defunct Usenet newsgroup alt.sex.bondage.

CICATRIZATION: 1. *Formally, medicine* The process of wound closure by means of scar tissue formation. 2. *See* scarification.

CINCHER; *also,* **RIBBON CORSET, WAIST CORSET:** A specific type of corset which is shorter than a full corset and wraps around the wearer's waist.

CINCH KNOT: A specific type of knot made by passing a rope or line through an opening, then around and around itself several times, and finally through a loop near the opening.

CINCH: 1. To wear a cincher, often very tightly and sometimes as a form of **body.** 2. To tie with rope by making several windings of rope around two limbs, or around a limb and a fixed object, then passing a loop of rope around the windings. The loop of rope is used to regulate the tightness of the binding. 3. To tie a cinch knot.

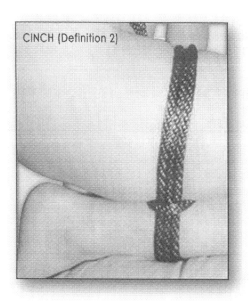

CINCH (Definition 2)

CLEAVE GAG: A type of <u>gag</u>, usually mode of cloth, that is pulled tightly between the wearer's teeth and tied behind the head. The **cleave gag** forces the mouth partway open and is quite effective in preventing speech.

CLOVER CLAMP: A specific type of <u>nipple clamp</u> consisting of a clamp with a lever mechanism to which a chain or cord is affixed in such a way that pulling on the chain or cord increases pressure on the clamp.

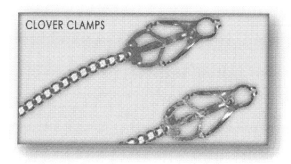

CLOVER CLAMPS

COCK AND BALL TORTURE (CBT): Any of a number of different practices involving pain play of the penis and testicles, including such practices as binding, compressing, striking, or stretching the penis or testicles. *See related* **parachute.**

COCK BONDAGE: Tying or restraining the penis.

COCK RING: A ring (often made of metal or rubber) or strap designed to be affixed around the base of an erect penis. The ring allows blood to flow into the penis but constricts the penis sufficiently to prevent blood from flowing out, preventing the penis from becoming flaccid once it is erect.

CO-DOM: 1. A person who acts in conjunction with or as an assistant to **dominant** during a specific <u>scene</u>. 2. A person who shares a <u>submissive</u> with another **dominant**, often in the context of a <u>polyamorous</u> relationship. *Also, verb* to act in concert with another **dominant.**

COFFIN: An item of furniture consisting of a long, narrow box, sometimes shaped like a conventional coffin, padded on the inside and usually featuring built-in restraints, a lockable lid, or both. The lid of a **coffin** typically features small openings or flaps at the level of the face, breasts, and genitals, allowing people outside the **coffin** to reach in and stimulate the person inside, or to allow the person inside to perform oral sex on those outside.

COLLAR: An item worn around the neck, sometimes equipped with a locking device to prevent its removal, and often worn as a symbol of <u>submission</u>. *Also, verb* To put a collar on, often as part of a ceremony indicating a committed relationship between a <u>dominant</u> and a <u>submissive</u>. *See also* **collar, drop,** <u>posture collar</u>, <u>training collar</u>; *see related* **ceremony. Commentary**: Some people outside the BDSM community associate collars with animals or pets, and erroneously believe that a collar is a sign of humiliation or is used to dehumanize a submissive; however, the symbolic value of a collar within the BDSM community is completely different.

COLLARED: The condition of having engaged in a committed, long-term relationship to a <u>dominant</u>, often by means of a <u>collaring ceremony</u> of some kind.

COLLARING CEREMONY: A formal ceremony celebrating or symbolizing a commitment between a <u>dominant</u> and a <u>submissive</u>, typically during which a <u>collar</u> is placed around the submissive's neck. *Commentary:* There is no single type of collaring ceremony, and not all people in committed relationships in the BDSM community practice collaring ceremonies. A collaring ceremony in the BDSM community has many of the same kinds of social significance as something like a marriage or a wedding; often, the process of collaring is used to indicate a committed long-term relationship, particularly in **TPE** relationships. A submissive who has participated in such a ceremony is often said to be "collared to" his or her dominant. A collar in this context has symbolic value not unlike that of, say, a wedding ring. Collaring ceremonies may be public or private, and may include whatever elements the people involved find appropriate. Collaring ceremonies may or may not imply a monogamous relationship; one dominant may have more than one collared submissive, but it is extremely uncommon for one submissive to be collared to more than one dominant. A collaring ceremony is sometimes used to mark the formal beginning of a **TPE** relationship.

CONSENT: Affirmative permission, assent, or approval. In a <u>BDSM</u> context, "consent" is an affirmative assent to engage in a particular activity, freely given without coercion or distress. **Informed consent:** Consent freely given with full and prior knowledge of the conditions and potential consequences of the assent. *Also, verb* To give affirmative permission to engage in an activity. *Commentary:* Consent is one of the hallmarks of BDSM, distinguishing it from abusive activities which may appear superficially similar. Consent is based on the active, willing participation of everyone involved in a particular activity; for example, if two people are engaged in something like <u>pain play</u>, a key defining characteristic which differentiates this play from physical abuse is that all the people involved know exactly what they're doing, want to be there, and give specific assent to the activities in question, whereas the victim of abuse does not specifically and affirmatively assent to the abuse. Consent is valid and meaningful only if it is **informed**, meaning that all the participants have full knowledge of the activities to which they are consenting (including but not limited to the circumstances under which the activity will take place and the possible risks, if any, inherent in the activity); if it is **uncoerced**, meaning that the participants give the consent freely without threat, force, or intimidation; and if the people involved give that consent from a condition of sound mind, meaning their judgment in not impaired by drugs, disease, or any other condition which might cloud or distort their ability to make reasonable, rational decisions.

CONSENSUAL NON-CONSENT: Any situation in which one person knowingly and voluntarily gives up the ability to prevent another person from doing whatever he or she wants; as, for example, deliberately engaging in activities which the <u>submissive</u> may be physically prevented from resisting and does not have a <u>safe word</u>. Some forms of <u>rape play</u> are consensual non-<u>consent</u>. *Commentary:* Consensual non-consent is still consent. A person who gives consent in this way is giving affirmative assent to engage in an activity that he or she will not be able to stop in the middle; it can be thought of as consenting to an activity in such a way that the consent may not be revoked.

CONTRACT: A mutually negotiated, written agreement between a <u>dominant</u> and a <u>submissive</u>, outlining the **submissive's** <u>limits,</u> the activities the participants wish to explore, and the like. *Commentary:* <u>BDSM</u> **contracts** are not legally valid or enforceable, but are useful tools for defining what activities are and are not acceptable and in what contexts.

CONTRAPOLAR STIMULATION: *Physiology* Of or relating to any form of stimulation which produces both pleasure and pain sensations simultaneously.

CORPORAL PUNISHMENT: Any activity involving disciplining a person through physical means, as by spanking.

CORSET: An article of clothing, often made of leather, PVC, or vinyl and sometimes including strips of rigid "boning," which is tightly laced and designed to narrow the waist and lift the breasts, creating an "hourglass" figure. *See related* <u>corsetry</u>.

CORSET COLLAR: A specific type of <u>posture collar</u>, typically made of leather, vinyl, PVC, or similar material and sometimes containing rigid inserts or rigid metal sides, which is designed to lace up the front, back, or sides rather than buckling or locking closed.

CORSET PIERCING: A form of <u>body modification</u> in which multiple rows of rings are placed through a person's skin, then laced together with a silk cord or similar tie. **Corset piercings** can be done on the back, down the sides, or even on the labia, tying it closed. The piercings themselves may be temporary or permanent.

CORSETRY: The practice of wearing a <u>corset</u>, often laced extremely tightly, and sometimes constraining motion, as a form of <u>body modification</u> or for the purpose of control. *See related* <u>lacing</u> (def. 1).

CO-TOP: A person who acts together with or as an assistant to a <u>top</u> during a specific <u>scene</u>. *Also, verb* to act in concert with another **top.**

CRACKER: 1. A short piece of cord on the end of a <u>whip</u>, which makes a loud cracking sound as the whip is snapped. 2. *Archaic, colloquial* One who wields a whip. *Commentary:* The colloquial term "cracker" when used to describe a person from the rural southern United States originates with def. 2.

CRASH: *Colloquial* An abrupt feeling of depression or unhappiness immediately following the end of a **BDSM** activity. This feeling may be triggered by a number of different factors, including feelings of guilt (especially among people raised with traditional ideas about sex and relationships), confusion, unexpected psychological response to the activities, or even physiological processes such as a drop in the levels of **endorphins**. *See related* **top drop**, **bottom drop**.

CROP, *also* **RIDING CROP:** A thin, flexible instrument used for striking, consisting of a rigid but flexible shaft wrapped with leather or a similar material, with a handle at one end and often with a small leather loop at the other. *Also, verb* to strike with a crop.

CROP

CROSS-DRESSING: Sexual arousal or gratification from wearing clothing appropriate for the opposite sex.

CROSS-ORIENTATION PLAY: *See* **orientation play**.

CROTCH ROPE: *See* **sukaranbo**.

CUCKOLD: One whose partner practices **cuckoldry**.

CUCKOLDRY: The practice by which a **dominant** takes one or more sexual partners other than his or her **submissive**, for the purpose of humiliating the submissive. *Commentary:* Cuckoldry is distinct from the practice of **polyamory** in the sense that it is done in a context where the **submissive** has no direct control over the **dominant's** other partners, and the primary purpose is to humiliate the **submissive**. Those who are aroused by cuckoldry are most often attracted to the humiliation and powerlessness aspects of it. The majority of the people who practice **cuckoldry** as a sexual fetish are women, who humiliate their male partners by having sex with other men.

CUFF: 1. Any restraint which has a band or band-like structure, which may be made of metal or of a flexible material such as canvas or leather, intended to be strapped or locked around an extremity such as a wrist or ankle for the purpose of securing or immobilizing it. 2. *Archaic* the fist. *Also, verb* 1. To restrain or immobilize by means of a cuff or cuffs. 2. To strike a rapid blow, as with the hand. 3. *Archaic: Cuff with,* to engage in a fistfight with.

CUPPING: A type of **sensation play** involving the use of small glass or plastic cups which are placed over the skin and then evacuated to create a vacuum, and hence suction. Some cups have an integrated valve to which a hand-operated vacuum pump can be attached; in other cases, the vacuum is created by dropping a flaming cotton ball, usually soaked in alcohol, into the cup and then placing the cup over the skin in such a way as to extinguish the flame. The vacuum is created by the contraction of the cooling air.

D/s: **Dominance** and **submission**.

DACRYPHILIA; *also,* DACRYLAGNIA: *Psychology* Sexual arousal from seeing a partner cry.

DEVICE BONDAGE: *Colloquial* <u>Bondage</u> involving highly specialized equipment, furniture, or devices, often very elaborate, to immobilize a person.

DEVIL'S FIRE: *Colloquial* An unusual branding technique involving taking a pointed needle that has been heated red-hot and touching it lightly to the surface of the skin for a brief instant The point of the needle creates a tiny round burn on the skin. Hundreds or thousands of these tiny marks are combined to create a pointillistic design which may persist for several weeks to several months.

DIAGONAL CROSS: *See* <u>St. Andrew's cross</u>. *Usage:* Primarily British; uncommon in the United States.

DISCIPLINE: 1. Any activity in which one person trains another person to act or behave in a specified way, often by enforcing rigid codes of conduct or by inflicting punishment for failure to behave in the prescribed way. 2. *Archaic* Any instrument used to enforce discipline or to punish physically, such as a <u>whip</u> or <u>crop</u>.

DOMINA: A female <u>dominant</u>.

DOMINANT: A person who assumes a role of power or authority in a <u>power exchange</u> relationship. A dominant takes psychological control over or has power over another person, and may, for example, give that person orders which are to be obeyed. *Contrast* <u>submissive</u>; *see related* <u>top</u>, <u>switch</u>.

DOMINATE: To assume or exert control over; to take psychological power over. A person who controls another person or takes control of a scene is said to dominate that person. <u>Dominant</u> is a noun or an adjective; **dominate** is a verb. **Domination, dominance:** the act of wielding authority over another.

DOM: A <u>dominant</u>. *Usage:* Often indicates a male dominant; however, may be applied to a dominant of any sex.

DOMINATRIX: A <u>dominant</u>, usually female and often a <u>prodomme</u>.

DOMME: A female <u>dominant</u>.

DOOR HANGAR: An implement for <u>bondage</u> consisting of a short piece of flat webbing, usually an inch or two wide, connected to a thick metal or wooden dowel on one end and a metal ring on the other. The webbing can be hung over the top of a door; when the door is closed, the dowel prevents the webbing from being pulled through the door, and a person may be **bound** to the ring.

DOUBLE WEAVE: *See* <u>florentine</u>.

DRAGON'S TAIL: An unusual type of <u>whip</u> consisting of a handle, often made of wood and wrapped with leather, to which a wide triangular piece of thin leather or suede is attached. This leather or suede forms a lash which is a hollow tube tapering to a point at the striking end.

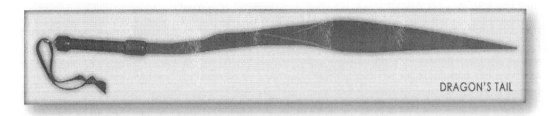

DRAGON'S TAIL

DRAGON'S TONGUE: An unusual type of <u>whip</u> consisting of a handle, often made of wood and wrapped with leather, and a lash made of a single wide piece of leather or suede wrapped around another, thinner suede lash. The outer lash is rolled into a tube around the inner lash, and tapers to a point at the striking end.

DREAD KOOSH FLOGGER: *Colloquial* A <u>flogger</u> made from a rope handle tied to several Koosh balls, which are children's toys consisting of a small, hard rubber ball with a very large number of long rubber "whiskers" attached. The **dread koosh flogger** was invented by a participant of the Usenet newsgroup alt.sex.bondage, and is generally considered the definitive standard for <u>thud</u> in a **flogger.**

DROP COLLAR: A specific type of <u>collar</u> which is shaped in such a way as to descend in the front, so that the frontmost part of the collar rests in the hollow of the throat rather than around the front of the neck. A **drop collar** may be constructed of a rigid material like stainless steel, or made of more conventional materials such as leather. Some **drop collars** feature a medallion, charm, or other ornamentation on the frontmost part of the **collar.** *Commentary:* Some people find that **drop collars** are more comfortable than collars that go around the neck, particularly for extended wear.

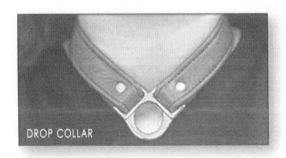

DROP COLLAR

DUNGEON: Any place specifically set up for <u>BDSM</u> activities, often equipped specifically for BDSM play, as with furniture such as <u>racks</u>, <u>crosses</u>, and the like.

DUNGEON MONITOR: In a <u>play party</u>, a person charged with ensuring that the participants adhere to safety rules and treat one another with respect.

EDGE PLAY: 1. Any practice which involves significant risk of injury or physical harm; as, **breath control**, **fire play**. 2. Any practice which challenges the **limits** or boundaries of one or more of the participants.

ELECTRICAL PLAY: Any of a variety of different practices involving the use of electrical current or electricity to stimulate a person. Some common forms of electrical play include using high-voltage, low-current devices such as **violet wands** or the use of controlled pulses of electricity to induce muscle contractions as with a **TENS unit**. *Commentary:* Many forms of electrical play are not safe to use above the waist, as even small amounts of electrical current across the chest may induce heart arrhythmia or heart attack.

EMT SCISSORS; *also,* **EMT SHEARS:** *See* **bandage scissors.**

ENCASEMENT: *See* **mummification.**

ENDORPHINS: Naturally-occurring opiate-like chemicals produced in the brain in response to pain, which block pain and can produce a euphoric sensation. The euphoria sometimes described by people who engage in **BDSM** is often attributed to endorphins.

ENEMA: The act of introducing water or other liquid into the bowel or lower intestine, often by means of a nozzle inserted into the anus and connected to a liquid-filled bag or bulb. *Commentary:* In a BDSM context, enemas may be given for pleasure (some people find the sensations enjoyable or arousing), as a form of **humiliation play**, or simply as a precursor to anal sex.

ENGLISH: *Archaic* **caning**.

EVIL STICK: *Colloquial* An implement consisting of a thin rod of carbon fiber, typically about the diameter of a mechanical pencil lead, attached to a small, rigid handle. The carbon fiber rod is flexible and very strong; when laid against the skin and then flicked with a strong upward motion at its tip, it causes a sharp pain and typically leaves a thin, well-defined welt that can persist for days.

EXECUTIONER'S HOOD: A specific form of **hood**, almost always made of leather, which covers the head and the upper part of the wearer's face but not the wearer's mouth.

EXHIBITIONIST: One who is sexually aroused by showing others his or her body or by being watched, particularly in a sexual setting or while engaged in sexual activity.

EXHIBITIONISM: The act of engaging in **exhibitionistic** behavior, such as sexual behavior, for the sexual gratification of the person being watched.

FACESITTING; *also,* **FACE SITTING:** *See* **queening.**

FALL: 1. The striking end of a **singletail**. 2. *See* **lash** (def. 2).

FEMDOM: A **power exchange** relationship in which the **dominant** is female. Often (but not always) used to refer to a relationship between a female **dominant** and a male **submissive**.

FEMINIZATION: The practice of enforcing activities or behaviors on a male <u>submissive</u> which are typically associated with women, as <u>cross-dressing</u>, requiring the **submissive** to sit when urinating, and the like. Often used as a form of <u>humiliation play.</u> Also referred to as **sissification.**

FERULA: *See* <u>tawse</u>. *Usage:* Originated in Catholic schools; uncommon among people who have not attended Catholic school.

FETISH: 1. Formally, *Psychology* a non-sexual object whose presence is required for sexual arousal or climax; informally, anything not generally considered sexual which arouses a person, as a *foot fetish* or a *leather fetish*. 2. Anything of or relating to <u>BDSM</u> in general; as *a fetish convention, a fetish event.* 3. Items, practices, or apparel relating to **BDSM**; as, *fetish photography, fetish clothing.*

FETTERS: *see* <u>leg irons</u>.

FIDDLE: A type of restraint consisting of a short metal rod that has a locking <u>collar</u>, usually made of metal, affixed to one end and a pair of locking <u>cuffs</u> on the other, or a rigid yoke with openings for the neck on one end and the wrists on the other. Used to bind the wrists together and prevent freedom of motion of the hands and arms.

FIGGING: The practice of placing a piece of carved ginger root into the anus or vagina. The result is a burning sensation which many people claim can intensify orgasm, and which other people use as an adjunct to physical discipline such as <u>spanking</u>. *Commentary:* This practice is believed to date back to Victorian times, when it was used in conjunction with <u>caning</u> as a technique for disciplining errant women.

FIRE PLAY: Any of a number of practices involving the use of fire or flame in <u>BDSM</u> or sexual play. One form of **fire play**, for example, involves placing an accelerant such as alcohol on a person's body, then igniting and quickly extinguishing it. *Commentary:* Very dramatic, but also dangerous. Not appropriate for inexperienced people.

FIRE WHIP: 1. A <u>flogger</u> with multiple lashes made of flat woven Kevlar, designed to be soaked with a flammable accelerant such as lighter fluid and then ignited prior to use. The **fire whip** is used by keeping it continuously in motion, so that it strikes the target for very brief periods of time so as to avoid burning the person being whipped. 2. A type of <u>singletail</u> consisting of a rigid handle connected to a long, flexible Kevlar rope, often with a short length of Kevlar string on the end, designed to be soaked in an accelerant and then ignited prior to use.

FIRST GIRL: In the <u>Gor</u> novels, one of a group of female sex slaves owned by the same master, who is considered 'first' or predominent over the other sex slaves. In <u>Gorean D/s</u>, a woman who identifies as a <u>slave</u> and has status or rank over any other women who consider themselves **slaves** to the same person.

FISTICUFF: *Archaic* 1. To strike with the closed hand. **Fisticuffs:** *Archaic* 1. The fists. 2. *Colloquial* A fistfight. *Get into fisticuffs:* Engage in a fight with bare fists.

FISTING: The practice of inserting the entire hand into the vagina or (less commonly) into the anus. *Commentary:* Vaginal fisting is actually quite a bit easier to do than most people realize;

the human body is quite accommodating. Contrary to common misconception, fisting is not done by making a fist and shoving it into the vagina; rather, the fingers are placed together and inserted slowly; as the hand is inserted, the fingers tend to curl into a loose ball. Many women experience intense orgasms from vaginal fisting.

FISTING SLING: A sling designed in such a way that the person within the sling is reclined with the legs spread apart, in a posture convenient for fisting.

FLAGELLATION: A generic term for any sort of activity involving flogging or whipping.

FLAGGING: The act of wearing a specific clothing, insignia, jewelry, or other sign as a means of expressing interest in a specific form of BDSM activities. *See related* hanky code.

FLOG: To strike with a flogger.

FLOGGER: An implement used to strike a person, consisting of a handle with multiple lashes attached to it. The **lashes** are typically made of leather, but may also be made of materials such as rope, suede, horsehair, or even Koosh balls. *See also* cat, cat o' nine tails, dread koosh flogger, fire whip; *See related* thud, sting.

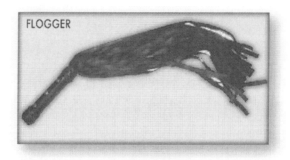

FLOGGER

FLORENTINE: A flashy flogging technique involving the use of a flogger in each hand. The floggers are swung in a figure-8 pattern. Sometimes called a **double weave**. *See related* triple weave.

FORCED ORGASM: An orgasm induced in a person against that person's will or as part of resistance play, often by means of bondage combined with sexual stimulation. *See related* consensual non-consent.

FORNIPHILIA: (literally, Latin *fornire* furniture + Greek *philos* love): a specific type of bondage combined with utility D/s in which a person is **bound** and immobilized, and then used as furniture, such as a table or footrest.

FORNIPHILIA GAG: *See* utility gag.

FOUNTAIN OF VENUS: *Colloquial* Water sports involving urination by a woman.

FREEPLAY: BDSM activities in which there is no domination or submission. *See related* top, bottom, sensation play.

FROG TIE: A specific form of <u>bondage</u> in which the person kneels and the ankles are bound to the thighs, preventing the person from rising; the wrists are then bound to the ankles.

FUCKING MACHINE: Any device or machine which is designed to simulate the act of sex; often consisting of a dildo affixed to a reciprocating motor so as to thrust in and out of a person. Many varieties of fucking machines exist, some designed so that the subject straddles or sits on them, others designed to be used when the subject is prone or <u>spreadeagle</u>.

FUNNEL GAG: A <u>gag</u>, usually consisting of an oblong or penis-shaped rubber or plastic bit, which has a tube running through it connected to a funnel. When the gag is placed in the mouth, any liquids introduced into the tube will pass into the mouth, and the person wearing the **gag** has no choice but to swallow them.

GAG: Any device or object designed to be placed in the mouth, most commonly to prevent a person from speaking or making loud sounds, sometimes to hold the mouth open. *Also, verb* 1. To place an object into the mouth to prevent a person from speaking. 2. To choke, particularly by placing something in the mouth. *See also* <u>cleave gag</u>, <u>ball gag</u>, <u>ring gag</u>, <u>rope gag</u>, <u>mouth gag</u>, <u>mouth bit</u>, <u>pump gag</u>, <u>funnel gag</u>, <u>spider gag</u>, <u>utility gag</u>.

GASPING: *colloquial; see* <u>breath control</u>.

GASPER: *colloquial* One who participates or engages in <u>breath control</u> or <u>auto-erotic asphyxia</u>.

GATES OF HELL: A male <u>chastity</u> device consisting of a series of metal rings connected by a leather band which are placed around the penis.

GENITORTURE: <u>pain play</u> inflicted on the genitals.

GIMP: *Colloquial* A <u>submissive</u>; most often, a gay male **submissive**. *Usage:* Almost always refers to a **submissive** who frequently wears tight-fitting vinyl, leather, PVC, or rubber suits with a <u>hood</u> or mask. Sometimes used insultingly or to indicate derision of the person so named.

GIMP MASK: *Colloquial* A specific form of <u>hood</u>, often made of heavy leather or rubber, which entirely encloses the face and head, and which often lacks openings for the eyes, mouth, or ears.

GIMP SUIT: *Colloquial* Any tight, formfitting suit, typically made of black rubber, PVC, heavy leather, or a similar material, which encloses the wearer's entire body. May have straps, rings, or other accessories which can serve as tie-down points.

GOLDEN SHOWER: A form of <u>water sports</u> involving the act of urinating on a person.

GOR: A mythical planet created by science fiction writer John Norman and used as the setting for an entire series of science fiction novels. The novels describe a civilization in which women occupy an extremely submissive position in society and are often used as sex slaves. The novels describes a formalized, ritualized set of social structures centered around female submission and male superiority, which have been adopted by a subcommunity of people within the <u>BDSM</u> community.

GOREAN D/S: Male domination and female submission according to a formal system adapted from the fictitious society described in the Gor novels, and characterized by strong hierarchy, male superiority, and an elaborate system of protocols. Includes such elements as ritualized postures and positions which women are expected to take in the presence of men under certain circumstances. Also **Gorean master, Gorean slave**: one who adopts a dominant or submissive role in a manner which reflects the society described in the novels. *See related* kajira, first girl.

GREEK: *Colloquial* Of or related to anal sex.

GROPE BOX: A long, narrow, enclosed box, often made of wood, with many openings along its front and sides, into which a person may be placed and then groped or fondled by people outside the box. A person within a grope box is helpless to prevent the fondling and often cannot see the people doing the fondling.

GYNARCHY: 1. Formally, *Sociology* A political or governmental system ruled by women. 2. *Colloquial* Femdom, particularly **femdom** in which all females are assumed to be superior to the male.

HAIR TIE; *also,* **HAIR BONDAGE:** Any bondage technique in which a rope, twine, or cord is woven or braided through a person's hair, then tied in such a way as to limit mobility of the bound person's head.

HANDCUFFS: Narrow metal cuffs with a pivoting hinge and a ratcheted locking mechanism, connected to each other by a short length of chain and often used to restrain people's wrists together. Commonly used by law enforcement and security personnel. *Commentary:* Handcuffs are not always safe to use in BDSM scenarios, particularly if resistance play is involved, as their narrowness and hardness can cause injury to the wrist if the restrained person pulls or struggles against them.

HANDBALLING: *Colloquial; see* fisting. *Usage:* Less common than the term **fisting**.

HANKY CODE: A covert technique developed largely by the old leather community for advertising one's BDSM preferences and to indicate the activities in which one was interested. The code worked by using a system of colored handkerchiefs, usually worn in the back pocket, on the left side for dominants and the right side for submissives. Each class of activity had its own particular color; for example, a person who was interested in pain play might wear a black handkerchief, whereas a gray handkerchief might indicate an interest in bondage, and so on.

HARD LIMIT: A limit which is considered to be absolute, inflexible, and non-negotiable. *Contrast* soft limit.

HARNESS GAG: A ball gag with additional straps which pass around the wearer's face and head to hold it securely in place.

HEDGEHOG: A device used for sensation play consisting of a short metal cylinder with numerous spikes attached to a handle in such a way that it can be rolled over the skin, producing a sensation somewhat similar to that of a wartenberg wheel.

HOBBLE SKIRT: A item of clothing consisting of a very tight skirt that ends below the knee, which prevents freedom of motion of the legs, allowing the wearer to walk slowly in a hobbling motion but not to move quickly.

HOBBLE STOCK: Any device intended to restrain a person by the genitals, such as a fixed bar or blank with an attached <u>cuff</u> designed to be locked around the penis and testicles, or a fixed rod ending in a dildo to which a woman's legs may be bound so that she is penetrated by the dildo and cannot move. *See related* <u>impalement</u>.

HOG SLAPPER: An implement for striking, consisting of a strap of thick, heavy rubber, often wrapped in burlap or some other coarse material.

HOGTIE; *also,* **HOG TIE:** A <u>bondage</u> technique in which the bound person's ankles and wrists are bound together, usually behind the back; then the ankles are bound to the wrists while the person lies on his or her stomach. *Also, verb* to tie in a **hogtie.**

HONOR BONDAGE: *Colloquial; see* <u>psychological bondage</u>.

HOJOJITSU: (Japanese 捕縄術) A martial art, originating in medieval Japan, for tying and restraining prisoners. Seldom used or taught any more, but the art of **hojojitsu** may have been the origin of <u>shibari</u>.

HOOD: Any covering designed to go over the head, often partly or completely covering the face as well.

HORSE: 1. A piece of bondage furniture consisting of a plank supported by two legs on each end, similar to a sawhorse. A person may be bent or tied over the horse and <u>flogged</u> or <u>spanked</u>. 2. *See* <u>wooden horse</u>.

HOUSE BOY: A male <u>house slave</u>.

HOUSE GIRL: A female <u>house slave</u>.

HOUSE SLAVE: A <u>submissive</u>, who may often live with the <u>dominant</u>, who acts as a maid, cleaning up the **dominant's** house and performing other household errands, often while nude. A **house slave** may sometimes be punished for failure to perform satisfactorily; with this form of <u>D/s</u>, sexual submission may or may not be part of the arrangement.

HUMBLER: An implement consisting of a locking metal ring which fits around the testicles, connected to two wings which go between the legs and behind the buttocks. A person wearing a humbler cannot stand straight without placing painful pressure on the testicles; the humbler forces the wearer to walk bent over or on all fours.

HUMILIATION PLAY: Sexual arousal from activities which include an element of humiliation, shame, or embarrassment for one or more of the participants. *Commentary:* Humiliation play is a relatively unusual taste that is often very difficult to explain to someone who doesn't understand it. While humiliation play may carry little or no risk of injury, it can be psychologically very intense, and is sometimes the psychological equivalent of <u>edge play</u>.

HUMILIATRIX: A female **dominant** skilled at **humiliation play**. *Etymology:* The word was coined by Edmund Bohun in 1853, from the Latin for "woman who humiliates."

IMPACT PLAY: Any activity involving striking or hitting, as for example **flogging**, spanking, **whipping,** or **percussion.**

IMPALEMENT: A practice in which a person is **bound**, usually while standing, and penetrated anally or vaginally with a dildo attached to the end of a fixed pole or rod in such a way that the person cannot escape or remove himself or herself from the dildo. *Commentary:* This practice can be dangerous if not done correctly. The person must be bound in such a way that he or she cannot fall if he or she loses balance.

INFANTILISM: A type of **role play** in which one of the adult participants takes on the role of an infant, and may be dressed in diapers, suck on a pacifier, and so forth. *See also* **age play**; *see related* **adult baby.**

INFIBULATION: 1. **Chastity piercing**, particularly of men. 2. In some cultures, the practice of female genital mutilation, typically forced on women at the onset of puberty and often for religious reasons. The practice consists of surgical removal of the clitoris and/or sewing the labial lips together to prevent sexual penetration. 3. In some historical contexts, particularly in ancient Rome, the practice of sewing the foreskin over the head of the penis to prevent a male slave from engaging in sexual intercourse.

INFLATION: A practice involving injecting saline solution into the scrotum to "inflate" the scrotal sac, sometimes to a very large extent. *Commentary:* A sometimes painful practice that is not safe if not done by a skilled and experienced person.

INFORMED CONSENT: *See* **consent**. *Commentary:* Consent is not valid if it is not informed; in order to be valid, a person who gives permission to engage in an activity must know and understand what the activity is, what the circumstances surrounding the activity are, and what the potential consequences are, including any risks involved in that activity.

INVERSION TABLE: A piece of furniture consisting of a flat table to which a person can be **bound**, suspended between upright supports on a pivot in such a way that the table can be rotated upright, inclined, or completely upside-down.

IRONS: *See* **leg irons**. *Archaic, colloquial* **locked in irons, thrown in irons, clapped in irons:** restrained with leg irons.

ISOLATION HOOD: Any type of **hood** designed to be used for **sensory deprivation** by removing the wearer's ability to see, hear, or speak. *See related* **ball hood.**

JAPANESE BONDAGE: *See* **shibari**.

JAPANESE CLOVER CLAMP: *See* **clover clamp**.

KAJIRA: In the **Gor** novels, a female sex slave. In **Gorean D/s**, a woman who identifies as a **slave**.

KAMI: In shibari, any technique or tie that involves the hair, such as by weaving ropes through the hair to hold the head immobile.

KARADA: A rope harness, originating in Japan, that is tied around the torso in a series of diamond-shaped patterns. Often used as a foundation in shibari. The karada does not restrain the subject, and can even be worn under clothing.

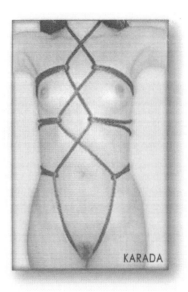

KARADA

KENNEL PLAY: A specific form of puppy play in which the submissive is confined to a kennel or doghouse as part of the play. *See related* animalism.

KINBAKU: *See* shibari. *Usage:* Most technically, **shibari** is the act of tying, and **kinbaku** is artistic bondage. In general use, however, **shibari** and **kinbaku** are often used as synonyms.

KOTORI: A rope harness intended to support a person's weight from the torso and upper legs, used for suspension in shibari.

KNEE PILLORY; *also,* **KNEELING PILLORY, KNEELING STOCK:** A stock on a very short frame, such that a person may be restrained by kneeling in front of the **stock** and then bending over. The top of the **stock** is then closed around the person's neck and wrists, restraining him or her in a kneeling position.

KNIFE PLAY: Any activity involving use of a knife. Sometimes done strictly for psychological effect, as with a dull knife; sometimes done for the purpose of cutting or breaking the skin. *See related* blood play, edge play (def. 1).

KNOUT: A specific type of whip with multiple lashes made of wire or of leather thongs twisted with wire and usually knotted.

LADDER: A structure consisting of either a triangular wooden frame with wooden slats running across it or two vertical wooden planks with several horizontal cross members, to which a person can be bound.

LACING: 1. The practice of extreme **corsetry**; particularly, very tight corsetry done as a form of **body modification.** 2. A specific and unusual type of **bondage** done by **suturing** a part of the body to or around a fixed object. 3. Any functional tie used to close an article of clothing, such as boots or **corsets.**4. Any style of **bondage** involving restraining a person by tying a cord or rope over the person and around many fixed points. *See related* **lacing table.** *Commentary:* In the sense of def. 2, the practice of **lacing** is often considered **edge play** and may not be safe if done by a person who is not skilled and knowledgeable.

LACING TABLE: A table or other flat, horizontal table-like object specifically designed for **lacing** (def. 4), usually consisting of two or more rows of eyehooks affixed to the table in such a way that a person lying between the rows of eyehooks can be restrained to the table by a rope or cord that is laced back and forth between the eyehooks.

LASH: 1. Any long, flexible implement, often made of leather or cord, used to strike a person. 2. The flexible striking part of a **flogger**. *Also, verb* To strike with a lash (def. 1).

LEATHER BAR: A drinking establishment catering to the **BDSM** community, often specifically to the **old leather** community, which may have strict dress codes for entrance.

LEATHER BUTT: *Colloquial* A condition where prolonged, repeated stimulation of a particular part of a person's body, most often pain play involving paddling or striking so as to leave deep bruises, makes that part of the body less sensitive. *Usage:* Used generically, not necessarily only to describe one's butt. *Commentary:* In some cases, repeated, prolonged, and very hard striking, as with a paddle or a crop, can create bruising deep enough that the area that is bruised becomes less sensitive. If this is done repeatedly over a period of time, this decrease in sensation can reportedly become permanent, resulting in **leather butt**. As the people I know tend to enjoy forms of play that do leave very deep bruises, and as I've never seen any cases of permanent reduction in sensation, I am of the opinion that such permanent reduction in sensation is probably rare.

LEG IRONS: A set of locking **cuffs**, often made of iron fastened together with rivets, with a length of chain about a foot long between them. Designed to be locked around the legs or ankles in such a way that the bound person can still walk, in a slow, shuffling gait, but cannot run. May also include additional chains designed to be affixed to a belt and to cuffs fastened about the wrists. Leg irons which attach specifically to the ankles or feet are also called **fetters**.

LEG STRETCHER, *also* **LEG SPREADER:** *See* **spreader bar**.

LIFESTYLE: 1. *Colloquial; often "the lifestyle"* Of or pertaining to involvement in **BDSM**, as in *How long have you been in the lifestyle?* 2. Of or pertaining to a **TPE** relationship, as in *We practice lifestyle D/s.*

LIMIT: A boundary, which may be set by a **dominant** or a **submissive**, which specifies a point past which any activity will not go. *See* **soft limit**, **hard limit**. *See related* **edge play** (def. 2).

LITTLE: *Colloquial* One who takes the role of a submissive younger person in **age play**. *Usage:* Used as a noun; as, *Bob is a **little**.*

LITTLE PLAY: *Colloquial; see* **age play**.

LUNGE WHIP: A specific type of <u>whip</u> consisting of a handle attached to a long, flexible shaft, often made of fiberglass and typically about 65" long or so, with a single long, narrow lash. Lunge whips often telescope or disassemble for easy storage.

LUNGE WHIP

MANACLES: Any metal <u>cuffs</u> with a length of chain attached, which either connects the **cuffs** together (as in a pair of <u>handcuffs</u>) or which may be used to affix the **cuffs** to a wall or other restraint point.

MARTINET: A specific type of <u>whip</u> (def. 1) consisting of a short, rigid handle with many short leather lashes, each of which is square in cross-section.

MARTYMACHLIA: *Psychology* Sexual arousal from being watched during sex; <u>exhibition-ism.</u>

MASOCHIST: One who experiences arousal, excitement, or sexual gratification from receiving pain. *Contrast* <u>sadist</u>. *Commentary:* Contrary to popular misconception, a masochist does not experience arousal at all forms of pain; stubbing a toe, for example, is unlikely to be arousing. The context of the pain is important.

MASTER: A <u>dominant</u>, usually in a <u>TPE</u> relationship. Usually male; the female equivalent is a **mistress.** *Contrast* <u>slave</u>.

MASTIGOTHYMA: *Psychology* Sexual arousal from being <u>flogged.</u>

METACONSENT; *also,* **META-CONSENT:** *See* <u>consensual non-consent</u>. *Usage:* Uncommon.

MESSALINA SYNDROME; *also,* **MESSALINA COMPLEX:** A seldom-used synonym for nymphomania. *Etymology*: Derives from the alleged promiscuous sexual appetite of Valeria Messalina, the wife of the Roman Emperor Claudius.

MILITARY PLAY: A specific form of <u>role play</u> which involves military-style settings, uniforms, hierarchy, or <u>protocol.</u>

MILKING: 1. The practice of stimulating the male prostate, often with a finger or with an implement such as a dildo, or of stimulating the perineum in such a way as to produce ejaculation without orgasm. 2. The practice of inducing orgasm repeatedly in a man, often by sexually stimulating him over and over, until he is no longer able to produce ejaculate. 3. Stimulating the prostate by means of an electrode built into a dildo or similar probe, inserted into the anus and connected to an electrical stimulation device such as a <u>TENS unit</u>. The electrode causes involuntary contraction of the muscles around the prostate, causing ejaculation without arousal or orgasm.

MISTRESS: Female equivalent of a <u>master</u>.

MONOGLOVE: *See* <u>armbinder</u>.

MOUTH BIT: Any of a style of <u>gags</u> with a long, cylinder-shaped bit, usually made of soft rubber or latex, in place of a round ball. **Mouth bits** may include an integrated harness; such bits are often used in <u>pony play</u>.

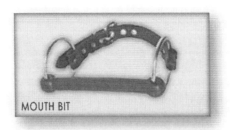

MOUTH GAG: A dental instrument designed to hold the mouth open for long periods of time, sometimes used as a <u>gag</u> in <u>BDSM</u> play.

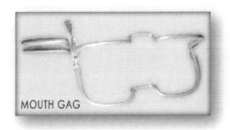

MUMMIFICATION: A form of <u>bondage</u> in which the subject is immobilized by being entirely wrapped quite tightly, as with Saran wrap, rope, fabric, or similar material.

MUNCH: An informal social gathering of people interested in <u>BDSM</u>, usually in a public place such as a restaurant or cafe, for the purpose of meeting other like-minded people and socializing. A munch is generally a low-pressure gathering without overt **BDSM** overtones. *Commentary:* The word "munch" was coined by the same person who gave us the word <u>squick</u>.

MUZZLE GAG: A specific type of <u>gag</u> which has a flat panel, often made of leather or latex, that is held over the wearer's mouth by straps which go around the wearer's cheeks, and sometimes containing additional straps that pass over the top of the wearer's head, straps that pass around or under the wearer's chin, or both.

NAWA JUJUN: *Japanese; see* <u>bondage bunny</u>.

NEEDLE PLAY: Activity involving placing needles through the top layer of skin, or using needles for temporary piercings. *See related* <u>blood play</u>, <u>edge play</u> (def. 1).

NEWBIE: *Colloquial* A newcomer to <u>BDSM</u>; or, more generally, a newcomer to any sport, hobby, or subculture.

NEW LEATHER: Anything of or related to a specific part of the <u>BDSM</u> community which began taking the place of the <u>old leather</u> community in the late 1980s and early 1990s. The new leather community abandoned many of the rigid hierarchies and strict **protocols** of the old leather community, and welcomed lesbians and heterosexuals interested in **BDSM**. *Commentary:* The old leather community began to fade for a number of reasons, including the fact that many of its members were aging, the fact that both homosexuality and BDSM became much more mainstream during the late 1970s and 1980s (a trend which is continuing today), the fact that BDSM began reaching a wider and wider pool of interested people thanks to new communications media such as the Internet, and the effect of AIDS on the gay community in the late 1980s.

NIPPLE CLAMP: Any clamp or clamp-like device designed to be clamped to a subject's nipples. May include a mechanism for adjusting or limiting the amount of pressure applied to the nipple. Clothespins make good (and cheap!) nipple clamps. *See related* **clover clamps, tweezer clamps**.

NOSE HOOK: A set of rigid, blunt hooks, about an inch long, connected to a length of rope, cord, or chain. The hooks are inserted in a person's nose and the rope is tied above or behind the person, forcing the head up. Sometimes used in **shibari**.

NOSTRIL STRAP: *See* **nose hook**.

NULLIFICATION: Sexual arousal from the act of amputation. *Commentary:* very, very, very rare.

OBJECTIFICATION: Sexual arousal from any act in which one person is dehumanized or dehumanizes another. **Animalism**, and some forms of **humiliation play** and **utility D/s**, involve objectification.

ODALISQUE: (Literally, Turkish *oda* chamber, room + *liq* woman) *Archaic* A female sex slave.

OLD LEATHER: Anything of or related to the gay male **BDSM** community which began in the United States and Canada after WWII and was most popular primarily between the 1960s and the late 1980s; characterized by a very rigid and structured hierarchy, elaborate codes of conduct, ritualized **protocol**, and a strong sense of community, duty, and loyalty. Often modeled on military traditions and practices, the old leather community was almost exclusively comprised of gay men and was suspicious of "outsiders." *Contrast* **new leather**; *See related* **hanky code**.

ONE-COLUMN TIE: In **bondage**, any form of tie which binds one of the body to something else; as, for example, any tie which binds a wrist to a fixed object such as a headboard. *See related* **two-column tie**.

ORGASM CONTROL; *also,* **ORGASM DENIAL:** The practice whereby one person is not permitted to reach sexual orgasm without the permission of another person, or for a set period of time, or sometimes at all, even though that person may be permitted (or required) to engage in sexual activity or sex.

ORIENTATION PLAY: Any activity in which a person is ordered or instructed to engage in sexual activity with another person whose sex is not appropriate for the first person's sexual orientation or identity, as for example instructing a straight female to engage in sexual activity with another woman.

OTK: (Acronym) *see* Over the knee.

OVER THE KNEE (OTK): A style of spanking in which the dominant or top is seated and turns the submissive or bottom over his or her knee so as to spank the buttocks.

OVERSEER'S WHIP: A type of singletail, usually about six feet long and having a braided lash but without a rigid handle, commonly used by slave traders and slave owners in United States history. Very similar to a bullwhip.

PADDLE: Any stiff, hard implement, often made of wood, used for striking a person, most commonly on the buttocks. *Also, verb* to strike with a paddle.

PAIN PLAY: Any activity in which one person inflicts pain on a consenting partner, for the pleasure of one or more of the people involved. Spanking, flogging, paddling, whipping, and so on are all forms of pain play. *See related* sadist, masochist.

PAIN SLUT: *Colloquial* A masochist who enjoys forms of pain play involving large amounts of pain.

PAINGASM: *Colloquial* An orgasm achieved through painful stimulation. *See related* contra-polar stimulation.

PANIC SNAP: A specific type of carabiner designed in such a way that the mechanism can be opened to release a rope or chain even if a full weight is bearing down on it.

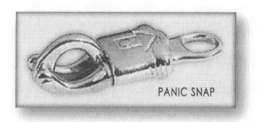

PANIC SNAP

PANSEXUAL: 1. Of or relating to all sexual orientations, sexes, and gender identities. 2. One who engages in sexual or erotic activities with partners of all sexes and orientations. **Pansexual event:** an event catering to people of any sexual orientation or identity. **Pansexual group:** any group open to membership by any person regardless of sex, sexual orientation, or sexual identity.

PARACHUTE: A small leather cone with a hole in its center, which is often used in CBT. The parachute is wrapped around the scrotum, and weights are suspended from it, pulling on the scrotum and compressing the testicles.

PERCUSSION: Any form of impact play involving striking with a blunt or fairly heavy implement, such as a buck hammer or Taylor hammer.

PERVERTIBLE: *Colloquial* Any object which serves an ordinary and prosaic function, but which also has a use in BDSM activities. For example, clothespins are often used as nipple clamps; saran wrap can be used for mummification; paint stirrers are sometimes used as paddles; and so on. *Etymology:* This term was coined by David Stein.

PILLORY: *Archaic; see* stock. *Also, verb, archaic:* to expose to scorn or ridicule.

PILLORY BED: A bed with a stock built into the headboard and/or footboard, such that a person lying on the bed may have the **stock** closed over his or her ankles, wrists, or wrists and head to restrain the person and prevent him or her from leaving the bed.

PLASTICUFF: *See* cable tie.

PLAY PARTY: 1. A social gathering in which people participate in BDSM activities, often in a space outfitted as a dungeon. Play parties may be public or private gatherings, and may or may not permit overt sexual activity. Play parties often offer the advantage of access to equipment and furniture that many people may not own. Play parties also offer the opportunity for people to engage in exhibitionism and voyeurism. 2. *See* **polyamory: play party**

PLAY PIERCING: A form of needle play in which the needles are placed through the skin or through parts of the body such as nipples. The piercings thus made may or may not have items such as rings placed through them. A defining element of **play piercing** is that the piercings are not intended to be permanent and the needles or other items are removed at the end of the session.

PONY PLAY: An activity in which the submissive takes on the role of a pony; for example, by walking on all fours, sometimes with a bit or bridle in the mouth; by pulling carts; by allowing the dominant to ride on his or her back; and so on. *See related* animalism, mouth bit.

POPPER: 1. *See* cracker (def. 1). 2. *Colloquial* A vial of amyl nitrate, butyl nitrate, cyclohexylnitrite, or any similar high-volatility organic nitrate or nitrite compound, whose vapors produce euphoria and sometimes heightened sexual sensation when inhaled.

POST: *See* whipping post.

POSTURE COLLAR: A specific type of high, rigid collar, often shaped to the wearer's neck, which prevents the wearer from moving his or her neck and forces the wearer to hold his or her head high. *See related* corset collar.

POWER EXCHANGE: Any situation where two or more people consensually and voluntarily agree to a power relationship in which one (or more) people assume authority and one (ore more) people yield authority. This relationship may be for a predetermined time, or indefinite. Relationships based on indefinite power exchange are often referred to as TPE relationships. The defining factor of power exchange is the conscious, deliberate construction of a power dynamic in which at least one person assumes psychological control to some agreed-upon extent over at least one other person.

PREDICAMENT BONDAGE: A type of bondage in which the intent is to place the **bound** person in an awkward, difficult, inconvenient, or uncomfortable situation, or to set out a challenge for the **bound** person to overcome. For example, a person might be **bound** in such a way that his or her hands and feet are largely but not completely immobilized, then asked to perform a task (such as to serve the **dominant** partner a drink) which is made difficult by the **bondage**; or, a person might be bound and told to hold a weight in his or her teeth attached to a line connected to nipple clamps in such a way that if he or she drops the weight, it will suddenly yank off the **nipple clamps**, then be spanked or tickled in an attempt to get him or her to drop the weight.

PRISON STRAP: *See* hog slapper.

PRODOMME: A female dominant who earns money by dominating her clients. *Commentary:* Men who earn a living in a similar way seem so rare as to be virtually nonexistant.

PROSTATE MILKING: *See* milking (def. 1).

PROTOCOL: Any defined, enforced code of behavior which a submissive is expected to abide by. A **protocol** often imposes constraints and limits on the **submissive's** behavior, particularly in social settings; for example, a **protocol** may specify that a submissive is not to speak to another person without the dominant's permission, may not speak unless spoken to, and so on.

PSYCHOLAGNY: *Psychology* Orgasm without physical stimulation. *Commentary:* In some D/s relationships, the dominant partner will train the submissive partner to orgasm on command, with a word or a gesture, but without being touched physically.

PSYCHOLOGICAL BONDAGE: Bondage without the use of ropes or other restraints, in which the submissive is simply commanded not to move.

PUMP GAG: A type of gag consisting of a blunt, rounded, or penis-shaped rubber bladder which is placed in the mouth and can then be inflated with air by means of a hand pump. The gag increases in size, filling the mouth, when inflated. *Commentary:* Some inflatable gags can be quite dangerous, as they can enlarge until they press against the back of the throat, cutting off breathing and causing suffocation. Some pump gags have breathing tubes through them to mitigate this danger. Some forms of pump gags may not legally be sold in the United States.

PUNISHMENT TIE: Any form of bondage done in such a way that the bound person's pose or the bondage itself is painful or uncomfortable, or any kind of **bondage** done with the intent of causing pain or discomfort to the bound person. Some forms of shibari include punishment ties. *See related* pain play.

PUPPY PLAY: An activity in which the submissive takes on the role of a puppy, as by barking, walking on all fours, and in some cases even sleeping in a doghouse or cage. *See related* animalism, kennel play.

QUEENING: A practice whereby a dominant, usually but not always female, sits on the face of a submissive, who is often restrained, forcing the **submissive** to perform oral sex and/or anilingus. Sometimes may also include breath control. *See related* queening stool.

QUEENING STOOL: A low stool, typically only about six inches high, with a large round opening in the bottom, used for queening. The **queening stool** is placed over the face of a prone submissive, allowing a female dominant seated on the stool to receive oral sex from the **submissive.**

QUIRT: A type of whip with two or (occasionally) three short lashes affixed to a long, thin handle.

RACE PLAY: A form of <u>role play</u> in which the participants assume the roles of people of different races, often in a setting in which the participant's race is relevant to the power dynamic (as, for example, a form of role play in which one person assumes the role of a Southern plantation owner and one person assumes the role of an African slave).

RACK: (Acronym) *see* <u>risk aware consensual kink</u>.

RACK: (Non-Acronym) Any type of <u>bondage</u> furniture consisting of a framework or platform to which a person may be bound; often derived from a Medieval implement consisting of a platform and a wheeled mechanism designed to stretch or pull the person bound to it.

RAPE PLAY, *also* **RAPE FANTASY:** A form of <u>role play</u> in which one person stages a mock "rape" for the purpose of gratification of all the people involved. *See related* <u>consensual non-consent</u>, <u>resistance play</u>. *Commentary:* A surprisingly common form of BDSM play, often staged so as to fulfill a woman's sexual fantasies of rape or coerced sex in a safe and controlled way.

RESISTANCE PLAY: Any mutually <u>consensual</u> activity in which one person struggles against another and is subdued by "force." May involve <u>rape play</u>; some forms of <u>bondage</u> include resistance as well. *See related* <u>consensual non-consent</u>.

RETIFISM: *Psychology; see* <u>shoe fetishism</u>.

RIGGER: *Colloquial* A person who specializes in tying up others, often using elaborate techniques such as <u>shibari</u>, primarily as an art form rather than for sexual gratification. *Commentary:* Talented riggers can earn a living by selling photographs of their work to magazines or Web sites which cater to <u>bondage</u> enthusiasts, writing books on the subject, working for **bondage**-related Web sites, and so on.

RIDING CROP: *See* <u>crop</u>.

RIMMING: *Colloquial* <u>Anilingus</u>.

RING GAG: A specific type of <u>gag</u> consisting of a metal ring, often padded with leather, which has a strap attached to it. The ring is placed in the mouth in such a way as to hold the mouth open, and the strap secures it in place.

RISK AWARE CONSENSUAL KINK (RACK): A loosely defined code of conduct in the <u>BDSM</u> community which holds that a given activity is ethically acceptable between adults so long as everyone involved is aware of the risks involved, if any, and gives informed <u>consent</u> to that activity. The idea behind "risk aware consensual kink" is an acknowledgement of the fact that some BDSM activities may involve risk of injury, and that as long as all the participants are aware of any risk and consent to the activity, the activity is ethical. *See related* <u>SSC</u>, <u>edge play</u> (def. 1).

ROD: *Archaic; see* <u>cane</u>.

ROLE PLAY: Any activity in which the people involved assume roles or identities different from their own and act out a scenario. For example, one extremely common form of role-play has one of the participants assume the role of a teacher or other authority figure, and the other assume the role of a student or other character in a position of less authority, and the people act out a scenario in which the character in the position of authority somehow takes advantage of that authority, often in a sexual way.

ROPE CUFF: Any form of tie which binds the wrists or ankles together.

ROPE DRESS: *See* karada.

ROPE GAG: A type of gag made by tying a rope around or through the mouth. Occasionally, a rope can be made to serve two functions by tying it around a person's head so that it passes through the mouth and around a fixed object; this both restrains the head and prevents speech.

S&M: *See* sadomasochism.

SADIST: One who is aroused, excited, or receives sexual gratification from inflicting pain on another. *Contrast* masochist. *Commentary:* A sadist does not necessarily take pleasure in inflicting pain indiscriminately; for most sadists, the pleasure relies on knowing that the subject is also enjoying the experience.

SADOMASOCHISM: Any activity or practice involving the inflicting or receiving of pain; pain play.

SAFE CALL: A practice sometimes used as a safety measure when meeting a new partner for the first time. The safe call is a prearranged telephone call made to a trusted friend at a specific time to let that friend know that everything is okay; may involve the use of special code words to indicate whether or not the person making the safe call is in danger or distress.

SAFE, SANE, AND CONSENSUAL (SSC): A code of conduct which holds that any activity between adults is acceptable as long as it is safe, sane, and consensual. Often held up as a test to whether or not a particular activity is ethical. *See related* RACK. *Commentary:* Many people see a flaw in the idea of "safe, sane, and consensual" because whether or not an activity is "safe" and "sane" is subjective, and because people may choose to engage in activities which might not always be "safe," as in some forms of edge play (def. 1). (This is true even outside the BDSM community; consider skydiving, for example). Because of this, SSC has given way to the code of conduct called "RACK" (risk-aware consensual kink) in some places.

SAFEWORD: A predefined "code word" which a submissive can use to stop an ongoing activity if it becomes too much. *Commentary:* Safewords are often used in situations such as resistance play, where the **submissive** may be expected to struggle or resist and where the word "no" might not actually mean no. In such cases, for safety's sake it's often helpful to have some word that *does* mean "no," and is a word unlikely to come up otherwise.

SA'FORA: *See* kajira.

SCARFING: *Colloquial* Breath control by means of using a scarf or scarf-like object as a ligature around the neck. *Usage:* A relatively uncommon term; appears to have originated in the United States.

SCARIFICATION: A form of <u>body modification</u> involving cutting the skin, often in intricate or elaborate patterns, in such a way that the healing process leaves behind a permanent scar.

SCAT; *also* **SCAT PLAY:** Any activity involving feces. *Commentary:* Very likely to elicit a <u>squick</u> reaction from most people.

SCENE: 1. A specific period of <u>BDSM</u> activity; as in, *We had a scene lasting about two hours last night.* 2. *Colloquial* The BDSM community as a whole. 3. *In the scene:* participating in the organized BDSM community.

SCOLD'S BRIDLE: A lockable metal cage which encloses the head, with an integrated metal protrusion which goes into the wearer's mouth, preventing speech. Also called a "brank" or sometimes "branks." *Commentary:* A rare piece of <u>BDSM</u> equipment modeled after a similar device used in Medieval times to punish gossipy or "troublesome" women.

SCOLD'S BRIDLE

SCOURGE: A specific type of <u>flogger</u> which usually has two or three long, heavy lashes attached to a rigid handle.

SELF-BONDAGE: The act or practice of tying one's self up or otherwise restraining one's self, sometimes as a part of masturbation. Often includes some mechanism by which the person may be freed after a set amount of time, which may include a timer mechanism to release a key or otherwise release the person.

SENNET WHIP: A type of <u>singletail</u> consisting of a length of thin rope or pleated cord, usually about 18 to 24 inches in length, knotted on the striking end and then dipped in hot tar, tallow, or wax to increase its weight and stiffness.

SENSATION PLAY: Any <u>BDSM</u> activity involving creating unusual sensations on a person, who may be <u>blindfolded</u>, as with ice cubes, soft fur or cloth, coarse materials, and the like. Sensation play is much more mild than <u>pain play</u> and may or may not include an element of <u>power exchange</u>.

SENSORY DEPRIVATION: Any practice intended to reduce a person's ability to see, hear, or use his or her other senses, either to create a psychological state of arousal or fear or as part of sensation play. *See related* ball hood, blindfold, isolation hood.

SERPENT'S TONGUE: 1. *Colloquial; see* tawse. 2. An implement for striking consisting of a heavy, wide leather strap with a deep "V"-shaped cut in it, so that it tapers into two pointed triangular tails at the striking end.

SERVICE D/S: A specific type of D/s centered around the submissive serving the dominant in practical ways, as by bringing the dominant food or drink and so on. For people involved in service D/s, sexual submission may or may not be a part of the relationship. *Commentary:* For a submissive whose focus is service D/s, everyday acts that many people might take for granted become a powerful symbol of **submission**. Even something as simple as bringing the **dominant** a drink can be a token of the **submissive's** submission.

SESSION: *See* scene (def. 1). *Usage:* Most often used to indicate a **scene** with a prodomme.

SHIBARI: A type of bondage originating in Japan and characterized by extremely elaborate and intricate patterns of rope, often used both to restrain the subject and to stimulate the subject by binding or compressing the breasts and/or genitals. Shibari is an art form; the aesthetics of the bound person and the bondage itself are considered very important. Also sometimes called **kinbaku.** *See related* karada, shinju, kami, kotori, sukuranbo, takate-koto. *Usage:*Most technically, **shibari** is the act of tying, and **kinbaku** is artistic bondage. In general use, however, **shibari** and **kinbaku** are often used as synonyms.

SHINJU: A type of rope harness, originating in Japan, which goes around and over the breasts. A **shinju** does not restrict motion, and can be worn under clothing; as the subject moves, the ropes shift against the breasts, providing constant stimulation. Often used in shibari.

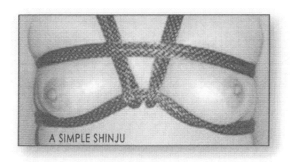

A SIMPLE SHINJU

SHOE FETISHISM: A type of sexual expression centered around a fixation on shoes, sometimes as part of submission. Submissive shoe fetishism may involve acts such as licking, kissing, or caring for the dominant partner's shoes.

SHREW'S FIDDLE: *Colloquial; see* fiddle.

SIGNAL WHIP: A type of small singletail, usually three to four feet in length.

SINGLE-GLOVE: *See* armbinder.

SINGLETAIL: Any of a class of whips having a single lash; most commonly applied to bullwhips and similar implements. *Commentary:* Most varieties of singletail whips can inflict great injury and can be dangerous in the hands of an inexperienced user. Singletail whips require skill and training to use properly, and are not easy to master. Use of a singletail is sometimes considered edge play(def. 1).

SISSY: A male submissive subject to feminization, as by being made to wear women's clothing, act like a woman in social settings, and so on.

SISSIFICATION: *see* feminization.

SLAVE: A submissive, usually in a TPE relationship. Contrast master. *Commentary:* People who self-identify as "master" or "slave" often see dominance or submission as a cornerstone of their identity, an essential part of who they are as people; this self-identify may affect and inform almost every aspect of their lives.

SJAMBOK: A specific type of heavy, short whip-like implement used for striking, formerly made of tightly rolled rhinoceros hide but today often made of plastic or rigid rubber. The **sjambok** is typically about an inch wide at the handle end, half an inch wide or less at the striking end, and three to five feet in length.

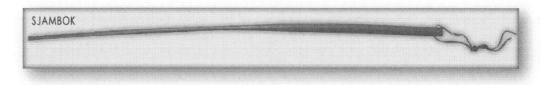

SJAMBOK

SLAVE AUCTION: An event sometimes held at play parties, conventions catering to BDSM participants, and the like, in which **submissives** are auctioned off for the use by the highest bidder in some context or for a set period of time. Slave auctions are sometimes held at **BDSM**-related events to raise money for charity.

SLAPHAPPY: *See* slapper. *Usage:* Becoming archaic.

SLAPPER: An implement used for striking a person, consisting of two thick leather paddles bound together at the handle, such that when the person is struck the two paddles hit one another, creating a loud sound.

SLEEPSACK; *also,* **SLEEP SACK:** *See* body bag.

SLING: An item of furniture, usually made of leather, canvas, or nylon webbing, suspended by chains or cables from the ceiling. A person may sit in the sling and arranged for easy availability to such activities as sexual intercourse, fisting, and the like. Slings may include additional mechanisms to restrain the person within the sling or to keep the legs spread apart. *See also* fisting sling.

SMOTHERBOX: A lockable box, often padded with leather, designed to be locked over the head of a submissive and used for queening. The **smotherbox** contains a large opening which exposes the **submissive's** face, allowing the dominant to straddle or sit on the box. May include a mechanism for affixing the box to the floor or to an item of furniture such as a bed or bench, so that the **submissive** cannot move.

SNAKE: A type of flexible singletail which lacks a rigid handle.

SOFT LIMIT: A limit which is not necessarily be set in stone, but which may be flexible or may change over time. *Contrast* hard limit. *See related* edge play(def. 2). *Commentary:* One of the most powerful aspects of BDSM is that it offers a way for people to challenge their soft limits, testing themselves against their own boundaries in a safe and controlled way.

SOMNOPHILIA: *Psychology* A Sexual arousal from having sex with a sleeping person.

SOUND: A thin, solid metal rod designed to be inserted in the urethra, often as a part of a medical role play.

SPANK: To strike on the buttocks, either with an open hand or with a paddle.

SPANKING BENCH: A low bench, often padded and often equipped with restraints or tie-down points, over which a person can be bent or tied and spanked or flogged.

SPANKING GLOVE: A glove, often made of leather or heavy rubber and frequently (though not always) fingerless, designed to protect the wearer's palm as the wearer spanks another person.

SPECULUM: A medical instrument commonly consisting of two or occasionally three probes designed to be inserted into the vagina or (less commonly) the anus, together with a mechanism intended to spread the probes apart, opening the vagina or anus. Sometimes used in medical role play scenarios.

SPENCER PADDLE: A specific type of oblong wooden paddle, allegedly invented by an American schoolteacher named Harold Spencer in the 1930s, that has a rounded end, is generally about fifteen to twenty inches long, and has a number of holes drilled in the striking surface. The holes are intended to prevent the formation of a cushion of air between the **paddle** and the person being paddled, which Spencer reasoned might soften the blow. *Commentary:* Paddles of this design were used in American schools until very recently; as a result, this style of **paddle** is popular among people who enjoy paddling as part of student/teacher role play.

SPIDER GAG: A specific type of ring gag featuring a central ring to which short rods or metal extensions are fitted, so as to hold the mouth open and keep the lips open as well.

SPREADEAGLE: A posture in which a person is bound or restrained with the legs spread apart and the arms spread wide with the hands over the person's head.

SPREADER BAR: An implement consisting of a rigid bar or rod, often with attachment points for restraints built into it at each end, designed to be attached to a person's feet or ankles so as to hold the person's legs spread apart. May be adjustable in length.

SPREADER BAR

SQUICK: *Colloquial* A feeling of disgust, repulsion, or similar negative emotional reaction to the idea of an activity which does not appeal to someone. *Also, verb* to feel disgust or revulsion at an idea; *Water sports make Lisa squick. Etymology:* The word "squick" has an interesting history. It was coined by a regular user of the old Usenet newsgroup alt.sex.bondage to describe a sudden and unexpected revulsion experienced by her partner when a group of very young kittens tried to nurse on him. It was originally intended to mean a strong negative response that was both surprising and unexpected. Since then, it has commonly been used to describe an emotional reaction of disgust in general, in spite of the original intent.

SSC: *See* <u>safe, sane, and consensual</u>.

ST. ANDREW'S CROSS: A popular type of bondage furniture consisting of an X-shaped cross, commonly made of wood but occasionally made of metal or other materials, to which a person can be bound and <u>flogged</u>, <u>whipped</u>, and so on.

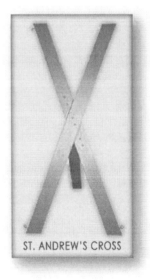
ST. ANDREW'S CROSS

STEEL BONDAGE: *Colloquial* Any form of <u>bondage</u> involving metal restraints or equipment, as <u>handcuffs</u>, <u>leg irons</u>, and the like.

STING: A sensation of quick, sharp pain. *Usage:* The feeling caused by being struck by a <u>flogger</u> is usually described in terms of <u>thud</u> or **sting**. *Commentary:* All other things being equal, a **flogger** with a large number of <u>lashes</u> (def. 2) produces a sensation with less **sting** and more **thud** than a similar **flogger** with fewer **lashes**; a **flogger** with narrow **lashes** produces a sensation that is more **sting** and less **thud** than a similar **flogger** with wide **lashes**; a **flogger** with soft **lashes** (as with a **flogger** made with **lashes** of suede or deerskin) produces more **thud** and less **sting** than a similar **flogger** made with stiff **lashes;** and a **flogger** with braided or knotted **lashes** produces more **sting** than a similar **flogger** whose **lashes** are not braided or knotted.

STOCK: A device used for bondage consisting of a vertical wooden post or a wooden frame atop which is set two heavy wood planks which close around a person's neck and wrists.

STOCK WHIP: 1. *See* signal whip. 2. Any of a class of singletail whips having a relatively long, rigid handle, often made of wood, which is outside the braidings of the whip's lash (as opposed to **singletails** such as a bullwhip, where the handle is enclosed in the end of the lash)..

STRAITJACKET: A heavy jacket, often made of canvas, whose sleeves end in long straps, which are wrapped around the jacket and buckled in place. A person confined in a straitjacket has very little freedom of motion; freeing one's self from a straitjacket is virtually impossible.

STRAP: An implement used for striking a person, consisting of a long, flat piece of heavy leather. *Also, verb* to strike with a strap.

STRAP-IN: A dildo designed to penetrate a person either vaginally or anally and then be held in place by a strap or harness, sometimes equipped with a lock to prevent it from being removed.

STRAP-ON: A dildo attached to straps, a harness, or some other mechanism designed to be worn around the waist.

STRAPPADO BONDAGE: A specific bondage technique in which a person's hands are tied behind his or her back, then a rope is tied to the wrists and attached to an overhead fixture or pulley tightly enough so that the bound person is forced to bend over with his or her arms in the air. *Commentary:* This is a physically demanding form of **bondage** which exerts strain on the arms and shoulders and may be dangerous if done by people who are not experienced and knowledgeable.

SUB FRENZY: *Colloquial* A very strong, sometimes overwhelming, desire to find a dominant partner or to become immersed in BDSM-related activities, sometimes seen in people who identify strongly as submissive, particularly people who have either just newly discovered their **submissive** side or who have not partaken in BDSM-related activities for a long time. People in the grip of **sub frenzy** may sometimes make unwise or unsafe choices.

SUBMISSIVE: One who assumes a role of <u>submission</u> in a <u>power exchange</u> relationship. A submissive is a person who seeks a position of or occupies a role of intentional, consensual powerlessness, allowing another person to take control over him or her. *Contrast* <u>dominant</u>; *see related* <u>bottom</u>, <u>switch</u>.

SUBSPACE: A specific state of mind that a <u>submissive</u> may enter, particularly after intense activities and/or (depending on the person) intense pain play, characterized by euphoria, bliss, a strong feeling of well-being, or even a state similar to intoxication. Thought to be related to the release of <u>endorphins</u> in the brain. The euphoria associated with **subspace** may last for hours or sometimes even days after the activity ceases.

SUBMIT: To give up power or control. A person who gives up power or psychological control to another is said to submit to that person. **Submission**: the act of giving up control.

SUKARANBO; *also,* **SUKURANBO:** In <u>shibari</u>, a type of rope harness which wraps around the buttocks and upper thighs and passes between the legs and over the genitals, passing between the labial lips of a female wearer. The rope may feature a knot at the place where it touches the clitoris. A **sukuranbo** does not restrict motion, and may even be worn under or over clothing; as the wearer walks or moves, the ropes slide over the genitals, causing sexual stimulation.

SUSPENSION: Any form of <u>bondage</u> in which the person bound is suspended partially or completely off the floor, often by ropes affixed to an overhead point (as with a <u>kotori</u> in <u>shibari</u>), or by means of a rigid bar with attached <u>suspension cuffs</u>.

SUSPENSION BAR: A short bar, often made of metal and which may be straight or slightly curved, with a mounting point in the center and additional mounting points designed for rope, chain, or <u>suspension cuffs</u> on each end. A person is bound to the suspension bar, which is hung from an overhead point by means of a cable or chain connected to its central mounting point. May often be used in conjunction with a lift, winch, or pulley system such that a person may be bound to the suspension bar and the bar may then be raised or lowered.

SUSPENSION CUFFS: Any restraints designed to encircle the wrists, ankles, hands, or feet and designed in such a way as to distribute the wearer's weight so that the wearer may be partially or completely suspended from the cuffs. Some suspension cuffs contain an integrated <u>panic snap</u>.

SUSPENSION FRAME: Any frame, rack, or similar structure designed for the purpose of <u>suspension</u>. Common configurations of suspension frames include an open "box" with mounting points along its upper edges, in which a person can be suspended so that the person hangs horizontally within the box; a rectangular upright frame, from which a person may be suspended with rope or suspension cuffs; and a long wood or metal pole, supported by two legs on each end, from which a person may be suspended by ropes.

SUSPENSION RACK: *See* suspension frame.

SUTURING; *also,* **SUTURE PLAY:** The practice of temporarily suturing or sewing parts of the body, particularly the genitals, for sexual gratification. Forms of suturing include sewing the labia closed and sewing the foreskin of the flaccid penis to the scrotum *See related* needle play, lacing (def. 2). *Commentary:* An unusual practice that may not safe unless done by a skilled and knowledgeable person.

SWITCH: 1. One who can change roles, being either dominant or submissive (or, less frequently, sadistic or masochistic) at different times or with different partners. 2. A thin, flexible rod, often made from a green branch of a tree such as a willow tree, used for striking people; similar to a cane. 3. *See* **polyamory:** switch. *Also, verb* 1. To change roles, as from a **dominant** role to a **submissive** role. 2. *(infrequent)* To strike with a switch (def. 2).

SWINGER: *See* **polyamory:** swinger.

SYBIAN: One popular variety of commercially-available fucking machine consisting of a dildo affixed to a dome-shaped saddle which the user sits on. *Commentary:* The Sybian has been described by a friend of mine as "a machine that rips orgasms out of women." After my experiences watching people use these machines, I have to agree.

TAKATE-KOTO: A type of rope harness, originating in Japan, which goes around the torso and holds the arms behind the back. Often used in shibari.

TAYLOR HAMMER: A common medical instrument consisting of a triangular rubber hammer attached to a metal handle, used for testing reflexes by tapping just beneath the knee. Sometimes used for percussion in the BDSM community.

TAWSE: An instrument used for striking or whipping a person, consisting of a thick, heavy leather strap which splits into two or three parallel tails at the striking end.

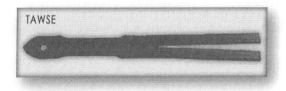

TAWSE

TELEDILDONICS: *Colloquial* Of or relating to any form of sex toy or fucking machine designed to be operated remotely, as by radio, over a computer network, and so on.

TENS UNIT: An electrical device which applies electrical signals through pads affixed to the skin, commonly used in the medical community to relieve pain by blocking the transmission of pain impulses through the nerves. Stands for "transcutaneous electrical nerve stimulation." Used in BDSM as a form of electrical play. *See related* violet wand. *Commentary:* A **TENS unit** can have an effect ranging from a mild tingle to a very strong sensation, depending on how it is used. It can also cause involuntary muscle contractions. Some **TENS units** used in **BDSM** play include electrodes designed to be inserted in the vagina or anus; some people find that the vaginal contractions induced by a vaginal TENS probe can cause intense, long-lasting orgasms.

THUD: A sensation of heavy, dull impact. *Usage:* The feeling caused by being struck by a flogger is usually described in terms of **thud** or sting. *Commentary:* All other things being equal, a **flogger** with a large number of lashes (def. 2) produces a sensation with less **sting** and more **thud** than a similar **flogger** with fewer **lashes**; a **flogger** with narrow **lashes** produces a sensation that is more **sting** and less **thud** than a similar **flogger** with wide **lashes**; a **flogger** with soft **lashes** (as with a **flogger** made with **lashes** of suede or deerskin) produces more **thud** and less **sting** than a similar **flogger** made with stiff **lashes;** and a flogger with braided or knotted **lashes** produces more **sting** than a similar **flogger** whose **lashes** are not braided or knotted.

TOMCAT: A specific type of whip consisting of a non-rigid handle similar to the handle of a bullwhip or snake whip which ends with a number of narrow lashes similar to a flogger.

TOP: One who administers some form of stimulation, such as spankings, floggings, or some other kind of stimulation on another person but does not have psychological control or power over that person. Contrast bottom; see related dominant.

TIGHTLACER: *Colloquial* One who practices lacing (Def.1).

TOP DROP: *Colloquial* A sudden, abrupt feeling of depression, unhappiness, or similar negative emotion in a dominant which may occasionally occur immediately after a period of **BDSM** activity. May include feelings of guilt, especially if the **dominant** believes he or she has made an error, or has traditional ideas about relationship or socially appropriate behavior.

TOTAL POWER EXCHANGE (TPE): A relationship in which one person surrenders control to another person for an indefinite duration, and in which the relationship is defined by the fact that one person is always dominant and the other is always submissive. One of the more extreme forms of power exchange. Sometimes referred to as **lifestyle D/s**. *See related* master, slave.

TPE: *see* Total Power Exchange.

TRAINING COLLAR: A collar given to a submissive in the early stages of a **BDSM** relationship (particularly a **TPE** relationship) when the **submissive** and the dominant are still exploring the possibility of a committed relationship. Similar in some ways to an engagement ring in a wedding.

TRAMPLING: A practice in which one person lies prone and is stepped or walked on by another.

TRANSVESTITE: One who engages in cross-dressing.

TRIPLE WEAVE: A flashy flogging technique involving the use of a flogger in each hand. The floggers are swung in an alternating overhand/underhand pattern; each **flogger** moves in a circle on each side of the weilder's body. *See related* florentine.

TWEEZER CLAMPS: A type of <u>nipple clamp</u> consisting of long, thin, tweezer-like clamps made of flexible spring steel, with a ring which can be used to adjust their tightness. *Commentary:* Among the mildest of all forms of nipple clamps, typically causing little or no pain.

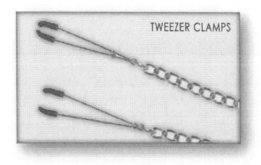

TWO-COLUMN TIE: In <u>bondage</u>, any form of tie which binds two parts of the body together; as, for example, any tie which ties the wrists together, or ties a wrist to an ankle. *See related* <u>one-column tie</u>.

UGOL'S LAW: A law first stated by Harry Ugol in the Usenet newsgroup alt.sex.bondage which holds that if there's some kink you have or something turns you on, no matter how strange or bizarre it may be, you're not the only one who has that kink. *Commentary:* I receive a great deal of email from these pages; much of it along the lines of "I didn't realize other people had the same fantasies and ideas that I do!" The nice thing about living in a world of six billion people is that, no matter how weird or bizarre your turn ons may be, yes, there are other people like you.

UNIFORM PLAY: Any of a wide variety of different forms of <u>role play</u> in which the wearing of uniforms, such as military uniforms, is a significant part of the **role play**. *Commentary:* Many people find uniforms, particularly uniforms that convey rank or indicate hierarchy or authority (such as police or military uniforms) arousing.

UTILITY D/S: A specific type of <u>D/s</u> centered around using the <u>submissive</u> in utilitarian capacities; for example; the submissive may kneel and act as a table for the <u>dominant</u> to eat from, and so on. For people involved in utility D/s, sexual submission may or may not be a part of the relationship.

UTILITY GAG: A specific type of <u>gag</u> which has a special attachment point for various types of accessories, such as feather dusters, drink serving trays, ash trays, and so on. Used as a part of <u>forniphilia</u> or <u>humiliation play</u>, or to make the wearer into a tool during <u>utility D/s</u>.

VAGINAL HOOK: A smooth metal hook, usually about an inch thick and six to eight inches long, designed to be inserted into the vagina. The other end typically is bent into a loop into which a rope can be tied. *See related* <u>anal hook</u>.

VAMPIRE GLOVES: Gloves used for <u>sensation play</u> which have a large number of short spikes or needles protruding from the palms and/or fingers.

VANILLA: *Colloquial* Not interested in or involved with <u>BDSM</u> or activities related to BDSM; as, *a vanilla person. Usage:* Sometimes considered condescending or insulting.

VETO: *See* **polyamory:** <u>veto</u>.

VIOLET WAND: A device used for <u>electrical play</u> consisting of a handle, which contains a high-voltage coil called an "Oudin coil," and several interchangeable electrodes, most commonly made of glass and filled with a gas which glows a brilliant purple in the presence of an electrical field. *Commentary:* One of the most common and safest of electrical play devices, the violet wand works by creating a strong static electrical field on the electrode. The violet wand feels nothing like you might expect, and almost everyone I know, including people who believe they would hate anything related to electricity, wants one once they've felt it. Violet wands are often referred to as Tesla coils, though this is technically not quite accurate; an Oudin coil operates on similar principles, but the primary and secondary windings of an Oudin coil share a common core, while a Tesla coil is air cored.

VIPER: An instrument used for striking a person, consisting of a rigid handle and a small number of narrow, flat lashes made of thin rubber, each of which tapers to a point at the striking end.

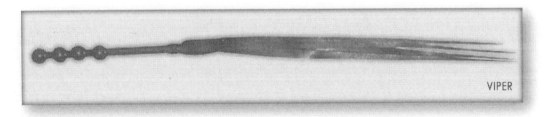

VOYEUR: One who is excited or aroused by watching others, particularly in a sexual context or while engaged in sexual activity.

VOYEURISM: The act of engaging in <u>voyeuristic</u> behavior. *See related* **polyamory:** <u>candaulism</u>.

WARTENBERG WHEEL: A small implement consisting of a short handle to which is affixed a small wheel with a number of sharp needle-like projections around its outer edge. Used by neurologists to test nerve function in the skin and by people in the <u>BDSM</u> community for <u>sensation play</u>.

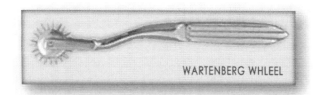
WARTENBERG WHLEEL

WANNABE: *Colloquial* A disparaging term for a person, usually a self-identified <u>dominant</u>, who is inexperienced yet assumes knowledge or experience far exceeding his or her actual degree of expertise. *Usage:* An insulting term which indicates disrespect or contempt on the part of the speaker for the person so named. *Commentary:* Such people, because of their lack of experience, may be dangerous.

WATER SPORTS: Any of a class of activities involving urination, often urination on a person. *See also* <u>golden shower</u>. *Commentary:* Often elicits a <u>squick</u> reaction from most people, including most people in the BDSM community.

WAXING: 1. The practice of dripping hot wax onto a person, as from a paraffin candle or from molten paraffin wax prepared in a double boiler, for the purpose of <u>sensation play</u> or <u>pain play</u>. 2. The practice of removing hair from the body by spreading a thick waxy substance on the body, allowing it to cool and harden, and then ripping it off suddenly, pulling out the hair by the roots.

WHIP: An implement used for striking people, consisting of one or more lashes (often made of leather or of some stiff material wrapped or braided in leather) affixed to a handle. 2. Any of a class of knots made by wrapping one part of a rope repeatedly around itself or around another rope. *Also, verb* 1. To strike with a **whip**, <u>flogger</u>, or similar object. 2. To strike repeatedly and rapidly. 3.*Uncommon:* To tie using a whip knot. 4. To trim the end of a rope by means of a whip knot, to prevent the rope from fraying. *See also* <u>singletail</u>, <u>bullwhip</u>, <u>signal whip</u>, <u>tomcat</u>, <u>quirt</u>, <u>lunge whip</u>.

WHIPPING POST: A fixed upright post, often made of wood and secured at the base so as to be immobile, to which a person may be <u>bound</u> and then <u>whipped</u> or <u>flogged</u>.

WIITWD: *Colloquial* An acronym meaning "what it is that we do"--a shorthand for the entire spectrum of <u>BDSM</u>-related activities.

WOODEN HORSE: An implement consisting of a wooden plank supported edgewise between two upright fixed posts, or of two sheets of wood coming together at a sharp angle with the edge facing up, to which a female <u>submissive</u> is bound with her legs off the floor. The **submissive** is bound in such a way she straddles plank or the point of the triangle, causing her entire body weight to rest on her clitoris. Some **wooden horses** include an integrated dildo which penetrates the person affixed to it. *Commentary:* Extremely painful. May cause nerve damage in the clitoris if not done carefully.

WOODEN PONY: An implement consisting of a wooden plank supported edgewise between two upright fixed posts, which a female <u>submissive</u> straddles and is bound in place. The plank is at such a height that the **submissive's** weight is not borne by the plank so long as she remains standing on tiptoes; as her legs tire, she will eventually have no choice but to lower herself onto the edge of the plank, which is extremely painful.

X-FRAME: *See* St. Andrew's Cross.

YOKE: A restraint device consisting of a metal bar or wooden plank, often about three feet long, with a locking cuff for the wrist on each end and a locking collar in the middle.

ZIE: *See* **polyamory:** zie.

ZIR: *See* **polyamory:** zir.

ZIP STRIP; *also,* **ZIPPER:** An arrangement of clothespins tied along a length of cord or twine, which can be placed on the body and then yanked off one by one or all at once.

ZIP TIE: *See* cable tie.

Glossary Of Polyamory Terms

This glossary is intended as a guide to many of the terms you might hear in the polyamorous community. Some of the terms used in the polyamorous community have definitions which are not clearly established or universally accepted, particularly with regards to terms used to describe various relationship styles. Where possible, I have tried to define such terms in ways that reflect all these different usages. Many of the terms in this glossary are terms used primarily in swinging; it should not be inferred from this that polyamory and swinging are the same thing. Rather, there is enough crossover between the poly and swinging community that knowledge of some swinging terms is often helpful.

The definitions given here, particularly of colloquialisms, reflect the usage I am most familiar with. Some terms contain commentary; anything following the word *Commentary* indicates my own experiences, interpretations, or views on a particular subject, and should not be assumed to be part of the formal definition of the word.

Comments or additions? Email Franklin at: mailto:mtacitr@aol.com.

Terms

ABUNDANT LOVE: The belief or philosophy that it is possible to love more than one person at the same time.

ADELPHOGAMY; *also,* **FRATERNAL POLYANDRY, LEVIRATIC POLYANDRY:** (Literally, *adelphos* brother + *gamos* marriage) A specific form of polyandry, practiced historically and occasionally still practiced in some portions of Tibet and Nepal, in which a set of brothers is married to the same woman.

ADULT BUFFET: *Colloquial* A specific type of group sex in which a group of consenting adults gets together for the purpose of sex, and each person in the group is free to have sex with any of the other members of the group he or she chooses. *Usage:* Originated with the swinging community; uncommon outside it.

AGAMY: (Literally, *a* no + *gamos* marriage) 1. A state or condition of not engaging in marriage, or more generally not engaging in marriage or reproduction. 2. *Sociology* Of or relating to a society with no recognized rules or prescriptions on marriage, or which does not recognize marriage at all.

ALT.POLYCON (APC): A long-running annual convention of <u>polyamorous</u> people and people interested in **polyamory,** organized by the members of the UseNet newsgroup alt.polyamory and featuring a series of workshops, lectures, and so forth.

AMBIGUSWEETIE: *Colloquial* A partner with whom one's relationship is ambiguous or not clearly defined, often intentionally; as, *We are not <u>primary partners</u> or <u>secondary partners</u> or simply friends, but rather ambigusweeties. Etymology:* This term was coined by Chris Dunphy, from "ambiguous sweetie."

APC (acronym): *See* <u>alt.polycon.</u>

BIGAMY: (Literally, *bi* two + *gamos* marriage) 1. A relationship in which one person is <u>married</u> to two spouses, regardless of the sex of those spouses. 2. *Legal* In most Western countries, the crime of entering in one **marriage** while still legally **married** to another person; **marriage** fraud. *Contrast* <u>monogamy</u>; *See related* <u>polygamy</u>, <u>polygyny</u>, <u>polyandry</u>. *See related* <u>Enoch Arden Act</u>.

BIPOLY: *Colloquial* Of or related to a person who is both <u>bisexual</u> and <u>polyamorous</u>.

BI POLY SWITCH: *Colloquial; sometimes humorous* Of or related to a person who is <u>bisexual</u> and <u>polyamorous</u> and who is a BDSM <u>switch</u>, capable of taking on a <u>dominant</u> or <u>submissive</u> role in sex. *Commentary:* A popular T-shirt reads "I'm a bi poly switch and I still won't sleep with you."

BISEXUAL: Of or related to sexual attraction to or sexual activity with both men and women; as, a **bisexual person**: a person who is sexually attracted to or sexually active with partners of both sexes. *See related* <u>hot bi babe.</u>

BODY FLUID MONOGAMY: The practice of limiting any activity which involves the exchange of bodily fluids, including such activities as unprotected sexual intercourse, to only one partner. *See also* <u>fluid bonding</u>, <u>condom contract.</u> *Usage:* Originated in the BDSM community; becoming increasingly uncommon in the BDSM and poly communities.

BOSTON MARRIAGE: *Archaic* A term used primarily in the 19th century for a household of two unmarried women who were financially and romantically independent. Today, it is generally presumed that many such arrangements were lesbian relationships.

CANDAULISM: Sexual arousal from watching one's <u>spouse</u> have sex with or engage in sexual activity with another person. *See related* **BDSM:** <u>voyeurism</u>

CELLULAR FAMILY: A family of three or more adults (and optionally children) who live together or near one another, share responsibility for joint finances and/or domestic responsibilities, and consider themselves to be part of a single family. *See related* <u>group marriage</u>. *Etymology:* The term was coined by Deboah Anapol.

CHEATING: In a relationship, any activity which violates the rules or agreements of that relationship, whether tacit or explicit. *Commentary:* In traditional monogamous relationships, any sexual activity with anyone outside that relationship is generally viewed as **cheating.** In a polyamorous or swinging relationship, sexual activity with people outside the relationship may or may not be seen as **cheating,** depending on the context of that sexual activity and whether or not it violates the agreements of the people in that relationship. Even in such relationships, most commonly sexual activity without the knowledge and explicit consent of the other members of the relationship is likely to be viewed as **cheating.**

CHOICE FAMILY; *also* **CHOSEN FAMILY:** *See* intentional family.

CLOSED MARRIAGE: Any marriages where there is no emotional intimacy or sexuality outside the marriage; monogamous marriage. *Contrast* open marriage. *Commentary:* This is the most common form of marriage in most Western countries.

CLOSED GROUP MARRIAGE: A polyfidelitous relationship in which all the members consider themselves to be married. *See related* group marriage.

CLOSED-GROUP SWINGING: A form of swinging in which people will have multiple sexual partners within a specific group (as, for example, two couples who will swap partners), but will not have sex with people outside the group. A **closed-group swinging** relationship can look very similar to a polyfidelitous relationship from the outside; the primary difference between them often being the focus of the relationship (sexual vs. romantic) rather than the form of the relationship. *See also* friends-first swinging.

CLOSED RELATIONSHIP: Any romantic relationship, such as a conventional monogamous relationship or a polyfidelitous relationship, which specifically excludes the possibility of sexual or romantic connections outside that relationship.

CLOSED SWINGING: A practice in which a group of swingers will exchange partners and then have sex separately, usually in separate rooms; **swinging** without group sex. *Contrast* open swinging. *Usage:* Common in the **swinging** community; uncommon outside it.

CLUSTER MARRIAGE: A polyamorous relationship in which two or more married couples cohabitate and exchange partners. *See* group marriage; *See related* intentional family, co-spouse, co-husband, co-wife.

CROSS-COUPLE: Of or relating to activities between a member of one couple and a member of another couple; as, for example, **cross-couple relationship,** a relationship between one person who is part a couple and a second person who is part of another couple.

COMPERSION: A feeling of joy when a partner invests in and takes pleasure from another romantic or sexual relationship. *Commentary:* **Compersion** can be thought of as the opposite of "jealousy;" it is a positive emotional reaction to a lover's other relationship. The term was coined by the Kerista Commune.

COMPLEX MARRIAGE: A doctrine which holds that all the male members of a particular group or community are, upon joining the group, married to all the female members, and all the female members are, upon joining the group, **married** to all the male members. This doctrine was established as part of the <u>Oneida Community.</u>

CONDOM CONTRACT; *also* **CONDOM COMPACT, CONDOM COMMITMENT:** A formal agreement within a relationship to confine exchange of bodily fluids and barrier-free sexual contact to the people in that relationship, each of whom has previously been screened for sexually transmitted diseases. **Condom contracts** may specify under what conditions a member of that group may exchange body fluids or have sexual contact without barriers with a new partner, or may specify that such contact is not permissible with any new partner.

CO-HABITATE; *also,* **COHABITATE:** To live together. **Cohabitating:** the state or practice of living together.

CO-HUSBAND: A man in a <u>group marriage</u> who shares a <u>spouse</u> in common with at least one other man in that **group marriage.** *See also* <u>co-wife</u>, <u>co-spouse.</u>

CO-PRIMARY: A person who is one of two or more <u>primary</u> partners in a <u>polyamorous</u> relationship, as *Bob and Joe are my co-primaries. See also* <u>primary/secondary</u>; *See related* <u>secondary</u>, <u>tertiary.</u>

CORPORATE MARRIAGE: A <u>group marriage</u> whose members register the union as a legal corporation, the terms of which spell out the financial entanglements and obligations of all the members.

CO-SPOUSE: A person in a <u>group marriage</u> who shares a <u>spouse</u> in common with another person in that **group marriage.** *See also* <u>co-husband</u>, <u>co-wife.</u>

CO-WIFE: A woman in a <u>group marriage</u> who shares a <u>spouse</u> in common with at least one other woman in that **group marriage.** *See also* <u>co-husband</u>, <u>co-spouse.</u>

COVENANT MARRIAGE: *Legal* A <u>marriage</u> which includes a legally-binding clause in the **marriage** contract specifying that the couple can not divorce, or can not divorce easily. *Commentary:* Only a handful of states in the United States recognize **covenant marriage** provisions.

COWBOY: *Colloquial* A <u>monogamous</u> man who engages in a relationship with a <u>polyamorous</u> woman with the intention of separating her from any other partners and bringing her into a **monogamous** relationship.

CUDDLE PARTY: *Trademark* A social gathering of adults which encourages consensual physical affection, such as cuddling, massage, and other forms of physical expression, but which forbids overt sexual activity or sexual stimulation. *Commentary:* The term "Cuddle Party" has been trademarked by Reid Mihalko, who owns a business organizing such parties in many cities, which are pay-for-attendance events.

CUPCAKE PARTY: *Colloquial* A gathering, usually involving only women and most often in a private residence, in which a group of people gather to explore their sexuality, discuss sex, experiment with sex toys, and so on. *Etymology:* The hostess of a **cupcake party** often provides refreshments, hence the name.

CYCLIC MONOGAMY: 1. *Colloquial* A relationship in which a person has several partners, and spends a set period of time with each partner, during which time he is sexually involved only with that partner. 2. *Sociology* Serial monogamy. *Commentary:* In the case of Def. 1, there have been several recorded cases in which a person, usually a man, has a job or life which requires regular travel, and maintains romantic partners in separate cities. Generally speaking, these partners do not know about one another, and each believes that the relationship is monogamous, though this is not always so; in some cases, some or all of the partners know of the existence of the other partners.

DADT (acronym): *See* don't ask, don't tell.

DEMOCRATIC FAMILY: *Colloquial* A family, typically a family practicing group marriage, in which all the adult partners are considered equal.

DOMESTIC GROUP: *Sociology* A group of people, often but not always related by birth or marriage, who live together and practice joint control over the household and group property.

DON'T ASK, DON'T TELL (DADT): A relationship structure in which a person who is partnered is permitted to have additional sexual or romantic relationships on the condition that his or her partner does not know anything about those additional relationships and does not meet any of those other people. *Commentary:* Many people in the polyamorous community frown on **don't ask, don't tell** relationships, and choose not to become involved in such relationships. There are many dangers in such relationships, including the idea that a person who claims to be involved in such a relationship may simply be **cheating** (as the relationship often provides no mechanism by which that person's partner may be contacted to confirm that the relationship permits other relationships); the fact that many people choose **DADT** relationships as a way of avoiding and not dealing with emotional issues such as jealousy; and the fact that **DADT** relationships are built on a foundation of lack of communication within the existing relationship.

DYAD: A relationship involving exactly two people. The most accepted form of romantic relationship in most Western countries is a monogamous **dyad.** *Contrast* triad, quad; *See related* serial monogamy.

ÉGOTISME À DEUX: (literally, French, egotism for two): A term used by members of the Oneida community for monogamy.

ELECTIVE AFFINITY: *Sociology* A social system whereby people choose their own mates or spouses, as opposed to a society which practices arranged marriage.

EMOTIONAL FIDELITY: A belief or practice that emotional intimacy or love must be kept exclusive to a particular relationship, though sexual activity or other forms of physical intimacy may occur outside that relationship. *Commentary:* Some swingers practice **emotional fidelity.**

ENDOGAMY: A state or practice whereby individuals are permitted to marry only within a specific group, such as a religious or social group.

ENOCH ARDEN ACT; *also,* **ENOCH ARDEN LAW:** *Legal* Any law or statute permitting remarriage in a case where a person's spouse is missing and presumed dead, and exempting such a person from charges of bigamy should it later turn out that the missing spouse is still alive. *Etymology:* Enoch Arden was a character in a poem by Alfred Tennyson.

ETHICAL SLUT: *Colloquial* A person who openly chooses to have multiple simultaneous sexual relationships in an ethical and responsible way, and who openly revels in that decision. *See related* responsible non-monogamy. *Commentary:* The term comes from the book The Ethical Slut, which advocates reclaiming the word "slut" from its derogatory meaning of a promiscuous woman.

ETHICAL SLUT, THE: A book (Dossie Easton and Catherine A. Liszt, Greenery Press, 1998, ISBN 1890159018) which outlines a framework for responsible non-monogamy and champions taking joy in ethical, safe promiscuity. *Commentary:* **The Ethical Slut** is not a book about polyamory *per se;* the primary focus is on creating relationships which are not sexually monogamous and are positive and healthy, but it does not focus exclusively on loving or emotional intimate relationships, and does not create frameworks for managing the emotional or romantic component of such relationships. Nevertheless, it is very popular in the **polyamory** community, and is very useful to many **polyamorous** people. The ideas described in **The Ethical Slut** are pertinent to and valuable in swinging relationships as well.

EXCLUSION JEALOUSY: *Psychology* A fear, which may be irrational, of being neglected or abandoned by a lover, particularly if that lover takes another partner or expresses sexual or romantic interest in another. *Commentary:* The term **exclusion jealousy** was coined by Ronald Mazer in the book *The New Intimacy: Open-Ended Marriage and Alternative Lifestyles* (Beacon Press, 1973, ISBN 0595001025).

EXCLUSIVE RELATIONSHIP: 1. A monogamous relationship. 2. Any relationship which does not permit its partners to seek other romantic or sexual partners at will; as, for example, a polyfidelitous relationship.

EXOGAMY: Marriage to a partner outside of one's particular group, such as a religious or social group.

EXPANDED FAMILY: *See* intentional family.

FISHING FLEET: *Colloquial* Originally, the wives of sailors at sea, who would socialize together and look for prospective lovers together. More generally, a group of women who will get together and seek out new sexual partners, typically without their partners' knowledge, while their partners are unavailable or away.

FLUID BONDING: Of or related to practices which involve the exchange of bodily fluids, such as barrier-free sexual intercourse and **BDSM:** blood play. *See related* condom contract.

FOUR-CORNERED MARRIAGE: A group marriage with exactly four adult members; usually but not always a **group marriage** with two men and two women. *See related* quad. *Etymology:* The term "four-cornered marriage" is often attributed to Robert Heinlein.

FRATERNAL POLYANDRY: *See* adelphogamy.

FREE AGENT: *Colloquial* A person who practices **polyamory** in a way that tends to separate or isolate all of his or her romantic relationships from one another, treating each as a separate entity. A **free agent** often presents himself or herself as "single" or behaves in ways which are typically associated with the behavior of a single person even when he or she has romantic partners, and often does not consider the potential impact of new relationships upon existing relationships when deciding whether or not to pursue those new relationships.

FREE LOVE: The belief that sexual relationships should be unrestricted and disassociated from ideas of love, commitment, marriage, or obligation. *Commentary:* Many advocates of **free love** object to the concept of **marriage** altogether, as they see it as a way to impose constraints and obligation on sexuality. *Etymology:* The term **free love** is generally attributed to John Humphrey Noyes, founder of the Oneida Community, who later abandoned it in favor of complex marriage.

FREEMATE: A non-married partner in a group relationship. *See related* metamour, group marriage.

FRICTION PARTY: *Colloquial; see* cuddle party. *Commentary:* The term "friction party" is not trademarked; the term **cuddle party** is. Friction parties, unlike cuddle parties, are informal social gatherings that aren't typically run as a business, may not be open to general admission (that is, they may be private), and may or may not charge for access.

FRIENDS-FIRST SWINGING: A form of swinging in which the people involved do not engage in sexual activities with anonymous or random partners, but instead have sex outside an existing relationship only with other people who are already close friends. In this form of **swinging**, emotionally intimate bonds can and often do form between all the people involved; this kind of **swinging** can often look very similar to polyamory, the primary difference between them often being the focus of the relationship (sexual vs. romantic) rather than the form of the relationship. *See also* closed-group swinging. *Commentary:* Hollywood images of swing clubs and anonymous sex aside, **friends-first swinging** is arguably one of the most common forms of **swinging.**

FRIENDS WITH BENEFITS (FWB): A relationship in which two (or more) people establish a friendship which includes sex or sexual activity, but without romantic love and typically without the same type or degree of expectations or other practical or emotional entanglements that typically accompany romantic relationships.

FRUBBLE: A pleasant emotion of happiness arising from seeing one's partner with another partner. *Contrast* wibble; *See also* compersion. *Usage:* Primarily British; less common outside the United Kingdom.

FUCKBUDDY: *Colloquial; vulgar See* friends with benefits.

FWB (ACRONYM): *See* friends with benefits.

GEOGRAPHICAL NON-MONOGAMY: Any relationship or arrangement whose partners permit one another to have other sexual partners while they are physically apart, as for example a relationship in which one person takes a temporary position in another town ir is assigned overseas for a time. Usually carries an implicit understanding tat when the couple is physically together again, the relationship will become monogamous. *See related* hundred-mile rule.

GROUP MARRIAGE: A relationship in which three or more people consider themselves married to one another; in the polyamory community, most often a relationship involving more than one man and more than one woman, who may live together, share finances, raise children together, and otherwise share those responsibilities normally associated with **marriage. A group marriage** is not recognized by and has no legal standing within most Western countries, but may have symbolic or have emotional value to the people involved. Many people who believe in **group marriage** may create civil contracts and other legally binding business arrangements which specify the type and extent of financial commitments within the **marriage**, or even form a legal corporation which defines the **marriage**. *See related* corporate marriage, cluster marriage, polygamy, polyandry, polygyny, troika.

HANDFASTING: A Pagan or Wiccan ceremony similar to marriage in the sense that it unites two people in a common bond, but dissimilar to a traditional Western **marriage** in that it does not necessarily convey sexual exclusivity and may not be intended to be permanent (some **handfasting** ceremonies last "for a year and a day," others for "as long as the love shall last"). A **handfasting** is not legally recognized as a **marriage** unless the person performing the **handfasting** is authorized to perform marriages in a particular jurisdiction (requirements for such authorization vary from place to place) and the other legal requirements of **marriage** are met. *Commentary:* **Handfasting** ceremonies are not directly related to polyamory; however, some people, particularly those involved with Wiccan or neo-Pagan spirituality or beliefs, may combine the two. While not all Pagans are **polyamorous** and not all **polyamorous** people are Pagan, there is enough overlap between the communities that some **polyamorous** people practice **handfasting** as an emotional or spiritual symbol of their relationships and commitment.

HARD SWINGER: A swinger who has sexual intercourse or engages in other sexual activity with other swingers outside of his or her existing relationship. *Usage:* Common in the **swinging** community, but uncommon in the polyamorous community. *Contrast* soft swinger.

HBB (Acronym): *Colloquial; see* hot bi babe.

HEINLEIN, ROBERT A. (1907-1988): An American science fiction author well-known in the polyamory community as an early advocate and outspoken champion of **polyamory**. Many of his novels, most notably the Hugo-award-winning *Stranger in a Strange Land* (Ace, 1961, ISBN 0441790348), feature **polyamorous** characters and relationships.

HINGE: *Colloquial; see* pivot.

HOT BI BABE (HBB): *Colloquial; often derogatory, condescending, or ironic* A bisexual person, usually though not always female, who is willing to join an existing couple, often with the presumption that this person will date and become sexually involved with both members of that couple, and not demand anything or do anything which might cause problems or inconvenience to that couple. The term is often used to be dismissive of a couple seen to be only superficially polyamorous, as *They're just looking for a hot bi babe.* Such a person may be referred to as a "mythical hot bi babe." Some members of the polyamory community self-identify as **hot bi babes** as a form of tongue-in-cheek intentional irony.

HOTWIFE; also, HOT WIFE: *Colloquial* A married woman who takes male lovers outside the marriage, often in the context of <u>swinging</u> or **BDSM:** <u>cuckoldry</u>

HUNDRED-MILE RULE: *Colloquial* An arrangement within a nominally <u>monogamous</u> <u>marriage</u> or relationship, particularly a **marriage** in which one of the partners travels a great deal or is often away from home for extended periods of time, which says that sexual dalliances which occur during the course of these travels or over a certain distance from the home don't "really" count and hence aren't <u>cheating</u>. *See related* <u>don't ask, don't tell</u>.

INTENTIONAL COMMUNITY: A residential community made up of people who share a common set of ideas, principles, or goals, and deliberately set out to create a planned community which reflects those ideas and goals. **Intentional communities** need not be <u>polyamorous</u>; there are **intentional communities** built around common religious, philosophical, or economic ideas, for example. Some **polyamorous** families create **intentional communities** with the idea of deliberately constructing a community built around non-<u>monogamous</u> relationship structures.

INTENTIONAL FAMILY: A family made up of people who have consciously and deliberately chosen to consider one another as a single family, as opposed to family that is the result of birth or <u>marriage</u> (i.e., family in law). *See related* <u>cluster marriage</u>, <u>polyamory</u>, <u>group marriage</u>. *Usage:* Most often used to describe a family of three or more adults.

INTIMATE NETWORK: *Colloquial* The sum total of a person's partners, those partners' partners, and so on. *Usage:* The term "intimate network" is most often used to describe the set of romantic and sexual relationships and friendships involved in a <u>polyamorous</u> relationship structure that is not closed; that is, the term **intimate network** is not often used to describe a <u>polyfidelitous</u> relationship or a <u>closed group marriage</u>, though it can be. The term is also sometimes used in a way that includes people who are close friends, but are not necessarily romantically or sexually involved, with a person or that person's partners.

KERISTA COMMUNE: An experiment in <u>polyamorous</u> living in San Francisco, which was founded in 1971 and broke up in 1991. The **Kerista Commune** was founded on the ideas of <u>group marriage</u>, shared economic resources, and <u>intentional community</u>. The commune was organized into "clusters," each of which was typically made up of between four and fifteen people and each of which functioned as a single <u>polyfidelitous</u> group. The **Kerista Commune** championed group control of individual responsibility, even going so far in some cases as to make group decisions about individual members' vocations, and assigning members to sleeping partners on a rotating schedule. The commune disbanded following very serious internal rifts in the early 1990s. *Commentary:* The **Kerista Commune** was an early advocate of **polyamory**, coining terms now common in the polyamorous community such as <u>compersion</u> and **polyfidelity**. The group eventually failed for a number of reasons, among them personality conflicts within the group, problems with financial management, an emphasis on fixed and inflexible sleeping schedules, and hostile attitudes toward bisexuality and homosexuality on the part of some members.

KEY CLUB: *Colloquial; see* <u>swing club</u> (Def. 2).

KEY PARTY: A specific type of <u>play party</u> (Def. 1), usually attended by couples, in which each male deposits his keys into a container as he arrives. As the guests leave, each female draws a set of keys at random from the container, then goes home with the male to which they belong that night. *Usage:* A **key party** is typically a <u>swinger</u> event.

LANGDON CHART: A chart which indicates a person's current and past sexual partners, and all their current and past sexual partners, and so on. *Etymology:* Coined by Kevin Langdon in the mid-1960s.

LDR (acronym): *See* <u>long-distance relationship</u>.

LESBIAN SHEEPITUDE: *Colloquial* A term used to describe a situation where one person has a romantic or sexual interest in another person, which may be reciprocated, but neither of them indicates this interest or makes the first move. *Etymology:* The colloquialism comes from the behavior of sheep; a female ewe indicates sexual interest and receptiveness by standing still, so two hypothetical lesbian sheep would indicate their sexual receptivity by each standing still, and no mating would take place. *Commentary:* This expression is often heard on the UseNet newsgroup alt.polyamory.

LEVIRATIC MARRIAGE: *Sociology* A system by which when a man dies, his brother marries his widow.

LEVIRATIC POLYANDRY: *Sociology* <u>Adelphogamy</u>.

LIFE PARTNER: A partner, usually a romantic and sexual partner, with whom one has the intent of a long-lasted and intertwined committed relationship. *Commentary:* A **life partner** need not necessarily be a <u>spouse</u>, though most often a **spouse** is a **life partner**. In some cases, someone may consider a partner's partner to be a **life partner** even though there is no direct sexual or romantic relationship with that person.

LIMERENCE: A strong desire for, longing for, or preoccupation with another person, accompanied by a sometimes overwhelming desire for reciprocation. **Limerence** may be accompanied by idealization of the person so desired. *Etymology:* The term **limerence** was coined by Dr. Dorothy Tennov, who described it in her book *Love and Limerence: The Experience of Being in Love* (Scarborough House, 1979, ISBN 0812862864). *Commentary:* **Limerence** is distinct from <u>new relationship energy</u> in that it is more akin to what people commonly call a "crush," and may not be associated with a relationship at all. Some researchers have linked **limerence** to quantifiable physiological processes in the brain, particularly to depressed levels of the neurotransmitter serotonin. Some people in the <u>polyamory</u> community use the word **limerence** as a synonym for **new relationship energy**, though this usage is not technically correct.

LINE MARRIAGE: A specific form of <u>group marriage</u> in which younger partners are added to the relationship as older partners age; in theory, such a relationship would eventually reach equilibrium, adding new partners as existing partners die. *Etymology:* The term (and the idea behind it) was coined by science fiction writer <u>Robert Heinlein</u>.

LONG-DISTANCE RELATIONSHIP (LDR): A relationship in which the people involved do not live together, and are separated by great distances; as, for example partners who live in different cities, in different states, or even in different countries.

LOVER-IN-LAW: *Colloquial* 1. A partner of one's partner; metamour. 2. The biological family of one's partner. *Commentary:* In the sense of Def. 1, most often applied to a **metamour** with whom one has a close relationship.

LOVE TRIANGLE: 1. *See* triad. 2. In contemporary American vernacular outside of the poly community, a relationship in which two people both love a third; in this usage, the assumption is that each of the two is competing for the undivided affections of the third, and that the third is being placed in a position where he or she is expected to choose one of the two competing partners.

LOVE QUADRANGLE: *See* quad.

LOVESTYLE: *See* relationship orientation. *Usage:* Most common in New Age or tantra communities.

LOVING MORE: A magazine (PEP Publishing; ISSN 1523-5858) and organization dedicated to polyamory. The organization which publishes **Loving More** also sponsors a series of annual conventions by the same name.

MARIAGE Á TROIS: (Literally, French, marriage of three) A marriage involving exactly three people, in which one person is married to two partners. *See related* triad, vee. *Usage:* Most commonly used of situations in which one man is **married** to two women.

MARRIAGE: A relationship, most commonly between one man and one woman in Western countries, which is sanctioned by the State and/or by a religious institution and which confers upon its members certain social and economic conditions, typically including rights of joint property ownership, rights of inheritance and of decision-making in legal and medical matters, and certain legal rights and responsibilities concerning mutual child rearing. These rights and responsibilities have varied over time and today vary from place to place, but common to all of them is the expectation that people who are married are in a legally recognized, financially entwined, committed relationship which is not trivial to separate. Traditionally, marriages in most Western countries carry with them expectations of sexual and emotional monogamy. *See related* closed marriage, open marriage, group marriage, polygamy, polygyny, polyandry. *Commentary:* Increasingly, Western countries are being forced to grapple with the issue of same-sex partnerships being officially recognized as **marriages**, both because gays and lesbians want the social status conferred by **marriage** and because gays and lesbians want the legal rights so conferred, particularly with regard to economic matters such as inheritance and joint property ownership, practical matters such as insurance and the right to make medical decisions on behalf of an incapacitated partner, and so on. Many people also feel that these legal rights and responsibilities do not have to be limited to exactly two people, and that partnerships involving more than two people are entitled to equal treatment under the law as well.

MÈNAGE Á TROIS: (Literally, French, house of three) 1. Sexual activity involving three people. 2. *See* triad. *Commentary:* In the sense of Def. 2, usually applied to a **triad** in which all three people involved live together.

METAMOUR: (Literally, *meta* with; about + *amor* love): The partner of one's partner, with whom one does not share a direct sexual or loving relationship. *See related* vee.

MONOAMORY; *also* **MONAMORY:** (Literally, *mono* one + *amor* love): The state or practice of loving only one person at a time. *Contrast* polyamory; *See also* monogamy. *Commentary:* The word **monoamory** was coined as a response to the fact that the word **monogamy** literally means "one marriage;" technically speaking, a **monogamous** person, according to the word's roots, should be a person with only one spouse, regardless of the number of other romantic or sexual partners that person has. In practice, it means essentially the same thing as **monogamy,** though it is sometimes applied to a person who self-identifies as **monogamous** but is involved in a romantic relationship with a person who self-defines as **polyamorous.**

MONOGAMY: (Literally, *mono* one + *gamos* marriage) Formally, the state or practice of having only one wedded spouse. Informally, the state or practice of having only one wedded **spouse** at a time, or more generally, having only one sexual partner or only one romantic relationship at a time. **Monogamous:** of or related to the practice of **monogamy,** as in *monogamous relationship:* a relationship permitting one and only one romantic or sexual partner. *Contrast* polyamory, polygamy, polygyny, polyandry; *See related* closed marriage, serial monogamy.

MONO/POLY: *Colloquial; see* poly/mono.

MULTILATERAL MARRIAGE: *See* group marriage.

MULTILATERAL SEXUALITY: *See* responsible non-monogamy. *Usage:* Most common in the swinging community.

N: *Colloquial* A polyamorous relationship involving four people, generally two couples where one member of one couple is also involved sexually and/or romantically with one member of the other couple. *See also* quad; *See related* triad, vee.

NEW RELATIONSHIP ENERGY (NRE): A strong, almost giddy feeling of excitement and infatuation common in the beginning of any new romantic relationship. While similar in some ways to limerence, **new relationship energy** is distinct in that it often follows the beginning of a relationship (as opposed to desire for a relationship), and can last as long as several years. *Contrast* old relationship energy. *Commentary:* Some researchers believe that **new relationship energy** is the result of the hormones oxytocin and vasopressin, which are released by the brain during the start of a new relationship and after a mother gives birth and are believed to have a role in emotional bonding and in the feelings of happiness and well-being that often accompany the start of a new relationship.

NONEXCLUSIVE MONOGAMY: Of or related to any marriage involving exactly two people, whereby each of the two is permitted to have sex with others outside the relationship but may not marry (or in some cases conduct emotionally intimate relationships) outside the relationship. *Contrast* group marriage. *Commentary:* the word monogamy in **nonexclusive monogamy** is used in the formal sense of "one **marriage,**" rather than in the general sense of "one sexual partner."

NRE (acronym): *See* new relationship energy.

NRE JUNKIE: *Colloquial; usually derogatory* A term sometimes applied, often dismissively, to a person who starts many new relationships in rapid succession but does not seem to maintain relationships for very long. Such a person may appear to seek out the euphoria and intense emotion associated with new relationship energy over the maintenance of a long-term relationship. *Commentary:* Some psychologists and psychiatrists believe that the intensity and euphoria associated with **new relationship energy** can be psychologically addictive; in the psychiatric community, the term "love addiction" is sometimes used to describe this behavior.

NUCLEAR FAMILY: A family consisting of one man and one woman, married to one another, and their children. In some religious and social groups, this structure is idealized as the only "right" form of family, though historically it has never been the dominant family structure in Western history.

OLD RELATIONSHIP ENERGY (ORE): The feeling of comfort, security, and stability often associated with a long-standing romantic relationship. *Contrast* new relationship energy.

OMNIGAMY: 1. Group marriage. 2. Of or relating to having multiple spouses of both sexes. 3. Complex marriage. In the sense of Def. 2, *See related* bisexual.

OMNISEXUAL: (literally, all sexes) bisexual. *Usage:* In some communities, particularly some parts of the lesbian and gay community, antipathy toward or hostility to people who self-identify as **bisexual** has become common. The term **omnisexual** has started to become popular as a synonym for **bisexual** but without the negative connotations of the word.

ONEIDA COMMUNITY: A religious intentional community founded in New York in 1848 by John Humphrey Noyes. Noyes founded a branch of Christianity called "Christian Perfectionism," a doctrine which holds that it is possible for a Christian to reach a state of sinlessness and moral perfection before God. The Oneida Community was created as a deliberately and intentionally Christian group, led by Noyes and championing this doctrine of Christian Perfectionism. One of the more notable features of the Oneida Community was the idea that all male members of the community were married to all female members of the community, and vice-versa, an arrangement Noyes termed complex marriage. Another interesting feature of the **Oneida Community** was its belief that men should learn to control the process of ejaculation during sexual intercourse; this practice was used as a method of birth control within the community. The **Oneida Community** disbanded in 1881, by which time it had grown to 306 members.

OPEN MARRIAGE: Any marriage whose structures or arrangements permit one or both of the members involved to have outside sexual relationships, outside romantic relationships, or both. The term **open marriage** is a catchall for marriages which are not emotionally or sexually monogamous; and may include such activities as polyamory or swinging. *Contrast* closed marriage; *See related* group marriage. *Commentary:* The term "open marriage" is sometimes used as a synonym for **polyamory**, though this is not necessarily the case; some relationships may be open but not **polyamorous** (as in some **swinging** relationships which explicitly ban emotional entanglement with anyone outside the relationship), and some relationships may be **polyamorous** but not open (as in polyfidelitious relationships).

OPEN SWINGING: A practice in which a group of swingers will exchange partners and then have sex together in the same room; sometimes but not always assumes group sex. *Contrast* closed swinging. *Usage:* Common in the **swinging** community; uncommon outside it.

ORE (acronym): *See* old relationship energy.

OTHER SIGNIFICANT OTHER (OSO): 1. A partner's other partner; <u>metamour</u>. 2. A person's partner, sometimes but not always a non-<u>primary</u> or non-<u>spouse</u> partner; as, *Bob is my husband, and Joe is my **other significant other.***

OSO (acronym): *See* <u>other significant other</u>.

OXYTOCIN: A naturally-occuring hormone produced in the hypothalamus and secreted from the pituitary gland. **Oxytocin** is produced both by men and women, and in women is known to play a role in uterine contraction during childbirth and in milk production. Production of this hormone increases during the early stages of a new relationship and during sex, and it is believed to be partly responsible for mediating the processes involved in emotional intimacy. <u>New relationship energy</u> is thought to be a result in part of **oxytocin** production. *See related* <u>vasopressin</u>.

PANAMOROY: Of or relating to romantic or sexual love with partners of many sexes, sexual orientations, gender identities, and/or <u>relationship orientations</u>. ***Panamorous,*** of or relating to one who identifies as a person capable of romantic or sexual love with many kinds of partners regardless of their sex, sexual orientation, or gender identity.

PARALLEL PLAY: *Colloquial* Of or related to two (or more) couples or groups having sex in the same room, without members from one couple or group having sexual contact with members of another couple or group. *Usage:* Most commonly used in the <u>swinging</u> community.

PARAMOUR: (literally, *par* way + *amor* love; *by way of love*) 1. A married person's outside lover. 2. A mistress--the unmarried female lover of a married man. 3. A nonmarried member of a <u>polyamorous</u> relationship. *See related* <u>other significant other</u>.

PIVOT: *Colloquial* In a <u>vee</u> relationship, the person who has two partners.

PLATONIC RELATIONSHIP: A close, emotionally intimate relationship in which there is no sex or physical intimacy.

PLAY PARTY: 1. In the <u>swinger</u> community, a party, often hosted at a <u>swing club</u> but sometimes hosted at a private residence, at which **swingers** get together for the purpose of recreational sex. 2. A party with emphasis on shared sexual activity or experience. 3. *See* **BDSM:** <u>play party</u>. *See related* <u>key party</u>.

PLURAL MARRIAGE: *See* <u>polygamy</u>.

POLY: *Colloquial* Of or related to <u>polyamory</u>; as, *a poly relationship, a poly person.*

POLYAMORY: (Literally, *poly* many + *amor* love) The state or practice of maintaining multiple sexual and/or romantic relationships simultaneously, with the full knowledge and consent of all the people involved. **Polyamorous:** of or related to the practice of **polyamory,** as in *polyamorous relationship:* a relationship involving more than two people, or open to involvement by more than two people; *polyamorous person:* a person who prefers or is open to romantic relationships with more than one partner simultaneously. *Contrast* <u>monogamy</u>; *See related* <u>polyfidelity</u>, <u>triad</u>, <u>quad</u>, <u>vee</u>, <u>N</u>, <u>polygamy</u>, <u>polygyny</u>, <u>polyandry</u>, <u>swinging</u>, <u>responsible non-monogamy</u>. *Commentary:* There is some debate over the origin of the word. The Oxford English Dictionary attributes the word to Jennifer Wesp, who founded the newsgroup alt.polyamory in

1992. The term **polyamorous** is often attributed to Morning Glory Zell, who used it to describe situations in which a person engages in multiple loving, committed relationships simultaneously in the essay "A Boquet of Lovers." It appears that both people coined the term independently and simultaneously. **Polyamory** is not necessarily related directly to marriage or to polygamy; a person may have no spouse or only one **spouse** and still be **polyamorous**. Many people use the term "polyamory" to describe only those relationships in which a person has multiple loving partners; some people have extended the term to include relationships in which a person has multiple sexual partners regardless of the emotional component or degree of commitment between them, though this meaning was not a part of Morning Glory Zell's original intent for the word. In 1992, when the editors of the Oxford English Dictionary contacted Morning Glory Zell to ask for a formal definition and background of the word; part of her response was *"The two essential ingredients of the concept of "polyamory" are "more than one" and "loving." That is, it is expected that the people in such relationships have a loving emotional bond, are involved in each other's lives multi-dimensionally, and care for each other. This term is not intended to apply to merely casual recreational sex, anonymous orgies, one-night stands, pick-ups, prostitution, "cheating," serial monogamy, or the popular definition of swinging as "mate-swapping" parties."*

POLYANDRY: (Literally, *poly* many + *andros* man) The state or practice of having multiple wedded husbands at the same time. *Contrast* monogamy; *see related* polygamy, polygyny, bigamy.

POLYFAMILY: *Colloquial* 1. A set of polyamorous people who live together and identify as part of the same family. 2. A **polyamorous** group whos members consider one another to be family, regardless of whether or not they share a home.

POLYFI: *Colloquial; see* polyfidelity.

POLYFIDELITY: (Literally, *poly* many + *fidelitas* faithfulness) A romantic or sexual relationship which involves more than two people, but which does not permit the members of that relationship to seek additional partners outside the relationship, at least without the approval and consent of all the existing members. Some **polyfidelitous** relationships may have a mechanism which permits adding new members to the relationship with mutual agreement and consent of the existing members; others may not permit any new members under any circumstances. *Etymology:* The term **polyfidelity** was coined by the Kerista Commune.

POLYFUCKERY: *Colloquial; vulgar; often derogatory* A coarse term sometimes used to describe people who call themselves "polyamorous" while engaging in a large number of sexual relationships which are short-lived or not emotionally intimate; as *Bob practices polyfuckery.* Almost always indicates derision of the activity or person so named. *Usage:* Almost always used only of people who self-describe as 'polyamorous;' not used to describe, for example, people who identify as swingers. *See related* polysexual.

POLYGAMY: (Literally, *poly* many + *gamos* marriage) The state or practice of having multiple wedded spouses at the same time, regardless of the sex of those **spouses**. *Contrast* monogamy; *See related* polyandry, polygyny, bigamy. *Commentary:* **Polygyny** is the most common form of **polygamy** in most societies which permit multiple **spouses**. For that reason, many people confuse the two. Some objections to the practice of **polyamory**--for example, objections based on the perception that **polyamorous** relationships are inherently disempowering to women--arise from the misperception that **polyamory** or **polygamy** are the same thing as **polygyny.**

POLYGYNY: (Literally, *poly* many + *gynos* woman) The state or practice of having multiple wedded wives at the same time. *Contrast* monogamy; *See related* polygamy, polyandry, bigamy. *Commentary:* According to some sociologists, **polygynous** societies represent the most common form of society, with 850 of the 1170 societies recorded in *Murdock's Ethnographic Atlas* being **polygynous.** Modern Muslim societies are **polygynous,** and certain religious traditions, including Fundamentalist Mormonism (FLDS) in the United States, advocate **polygyny.**

POLYKOITY: (Literally, *poly* many + *koitus, coitus* sex) *Anthropology* The state or practice of having more than one sexual partner, either at the same time or over the course of one's lifetime, without regard to the relationship with those partners or their relationships with each other.

POLY MIXED RELATIONSHIP: *Colloquial* A poly/mono relationship.

POLY/MONO; *also,* **MONO/POLY:** *Colloquial* Of or relating to a relationship between a person who self-identifies as polyamorous and a person who self-identifies as monogamous.

POLYSATURATED: *Colloquial* Polyamorous, but not currenlty open to new relationships or new partners because of the number of existing partners, or because of time constraints which might make new relationships difficult. *Contrast* polyunsaturated. *Usage:* Often considered humorous or slightly silly. Seems to be most common primarily in the western United States.

POLYSEXUAL: *Colloquial* Of or related to relationships which are sexually non-monogamous but which are not emotionally intimate. *Usage:* Sometimes condescending or derogatory; as *Bill is not really polyamorous, but only polysexual.* May indicate dismissal or derision of the relationship so named. *See related* swinging.

POLYTROTHISM: The state or practice of maintaining multiple egalitarian relationships, each of which is equal with respect to decision-making and other practical matters. *Contrast* primary/secondary; *See related* democratic family.

POLYUNSATURATED: *Colloquial* Polyamorous, and currently seeking or open to new partners. *Contrast* polysaturated. *Usage:* Often considered humorous or slightly silly. Seems to be most common primarily in the western United States.

POLYWOG: *Colloquial, often humorous* A child in a polyamororous household.

PRIMARY/SECONDARY: A polyamorous relationship structure in which a person has multiple partners who are not equal to one another in terms of interconnection, emotional intensity, intertwinement in practical or financial matters, or power within the relationship. A person in a **primary/secondary** relationship may have one (or occasionally, more than one) primary partner and one or more additional secondary or tertiary partners. A **primary/secondary** relationship may be "prescriptive" (that is, a **primary** couple consciously and deliberately creates a set of rules whereby any additional partners are **secondary,** often because this is seen as a mechanism which will protect the existing relationship from harm caused by additional relationships) or it may be "descriptive," and emerge from the nature and the situation of the relationship. *See related* tertiary, veto. *Commentary:* In practice, prescriptive **prima-**

ry/secondary relationships may create an environment where the people in those additional relationships feel unappreciated or insignificant, which is why some experienced **polyamorous** people do not construct their relationships along enforced **primary/secondary** lines.

PRIMARY: In a primary/secondary relationship, the person (or persons) in the relationship with the highest degree of involvement or entanglement, or sometimes the person accorded the most importance. A person may be **primary** either as a natural consequence of the circumstance and nature of the relationship (because that person has the greatest degree of financial entanglement, for example), or as a deliberate consequence of the relationship structure and agreements (as in the case of an existing couple who set out to add additional partners only on the condition that those existing partners are seen as "less important" than the couple). *See also* co-primary; *Contrast* secondary, tertiary. *Commentary:* People who deliberately seek to construct a relationship along prescriptive **primary/secondary** lines typically designate one and only one relationship as the **primary** relationship. People who do not seek to construct a relationship along prescriptive primary/secondary lines may have more than one **primary** relationship; a relationship becomes **primary** when it reaches a certain point of emotional commitment, practical entanglement, or both.

PUPPY-PILE POLY: *Colloquial* Polyamorous relationships in which all the people involved are to some degree physically and/or romantically involved with one another, with the implication that the people involved may share sex and/or sleeping space (hence, "all in one puppy pile").

QUAD: A polyamorous relationship involving four people, each of whom may or may not be sexually and emotionally involved with all the other members. *See related* N. *Commentary:* One of the most common ways for a **quad** to form is when two **polyamorous** couples begin romantic relationships cross-couple.

QUADOSHKA: *See* tantra.

RELATIONSHIP ORIENTATION: A preference for sexual or loving relationships of a particular form; as, for example, a preference for relationships which are monogamous, for relationships which are polyfidelitous, for relationships which are polyamorous, and so forth. *See related* switch (Def. 1). *Commentary:* Just as some people feel that their sexual orientation is fluid and a matter of choice where other people feel that their sexual orientation is fixed and not subject to choice, so do some people feel that their **relationship orientation** is subject to choice whereas others feel their **relationship orientation** is not a matter of choice. It has been my observation that some people seem to be inherently **monogamous,** and can't be happy any other way; some people seem to be inherently **polyamorous,** and can't be happy any other way; and some people seem to be able, under the right circumstances and with the right partners, to be happy in a **monogamous** or a **polyamorous** relationship.

RESPONSIBLE NON-MONOGAMY: Any relationship which is not sexually and/or emotionally exclusive by the explicit agreement and with the full knowledge of all the parties involved. **Responsible non-monogamy** can take several forms, the two most common of which are polyamory and swinging, and is distinct from cheating in that everyone involved knows about and agrees to the activity. **Responsible non-monogamy** often explicitly spells out the conditions under which it is permissible for one person to take on additional partners, and often includes some form of safer-sex agreement such as a condom contract as well. *Contrast* monogamy, closed marriage.

SACRED SEXUALITY: *See* tantra.

SAFE-SEX CIRCLE: *See* condom contract.

SECONDARY: In a primary/secondary relationship, the person (or persons) in the relationship who, either by intent or by circumstance, have a relationship which is given less in terms of time, energy and priority in a person's life than a primary relationship, and usually involves fewer ongoing commitments such as plans or financial/legal involvements. A **secondary** relationship may be secondary as a result of a conscious decision on the part of the **primary** partners, or simply as a result of circumstance or the natural development of the relationship. *See related* tertiary.

SECONDARY SIGNIFICANT OTHER: *Colloquial* A romantic partner other than one's primary partner or spouse. *Usage:* Used almost completely within the context of primary/secondary relationships.

SERIAL MONOGAMY: A relationship pattern in which a person has only one sexual or romantic partner at a time, but has multiple sexual or romantic partners in a lifetime, and may change partners frequently. Arguably the most common form of relationship in the United States, **serial monogamy** is predicated on the idea that a person can love more than one other person romantically in a lifetime, but not at the same time. *Contrast* polyamory, polygamy, swinging; *See related* monogamy.

SIGNIFICANT OTHER: *Colloquial* A romantic partner. *Usage:* The term **significant other** is intended to be free of assumptions about the gender of that partner. *See related* other significant other.

SOFT SWINGER: A swinger who has sexual intercourse or engages in other sexual activity only with his or her partner, but may do so at a **swing club,** or in the presence of other **swingers.** Occasionally, **soft swingers** may engage in some limited form of sexual activities, often stopping short of sexual intercourse, with partners outside the existing relationship. *Usage:* Common in the **swinging** community, but uncommon in the polyamorous community. *Contrast* hard swinger.

SPICE: *Colloquial* The plural of spouse. *Usage:* often considered humorous.

SPOUSE: A person's husband or wife.

SORORAL POLYGYNY: A form of polygyny where a man marries two or more women who are sisters.

SSO (acronym): *See* secondary significant other.

SWING CLUB: 1. A place where swingers meet to socialize or engage in recreational sex. 2. A social organization for **swingers.** *See related* friends-first swinging, closed-group swinging.

SWING PARTY: *See* play party (Def. 1).

SWINGER: A person who engages in swinging.

SWINGING: The practice of having multiple sexual partners outside of an existing romantic relationship, most often with the understanding that the focus of those relationships is primarily sexual rather than romantic or emotionally intimate. *See also* friends-first swinging, closed swinging, closed-group swinging, swing club. *Commentary:* The common perception of **swinging** is that those who engage in this behavior have sex outside of their existing relationship purely for recreation, and that emotional bonds or emotional intimacy are specifically excluded. This is true in some cases, and in fact some **swing clubs** specifically prohibit people from carrying on friendships or relationships outside the club. However, in practice **swinging** is much more nuanced, and people who self-identify as **swingers** can and sometimes do form close emotional relationships with their partners. Many people in both the swinging and **polyamorous** communities, though not all, see **swinging** and polyamory as two ends of a continuum, different in degree of intent, focus, and emphasis on romantic and emotional relationships rather than different in kind.

SWITCH: 1. *Colloquial* A person capable of being happy in either a monogamous or a polyamorous relationship. 2. *See* **BDSM:** switch.

TANTRA: (Literally, Sanskrit thread; loom; to weave) A form of sexual expression or activity which emphasizes spiritual connection, and holds that sex is a sacred act which can bring those who engage in it to a higher spiritual plane. *Commentary:* **Tantra** is not directly related to polyamory; however, some people, particularly those involved with New Age spirituality, often combine the two. The original practice of **tantra** stems from several Hindu and Buddhist religious traditions which emphasize rituals (including ritualized meditation and mantra) and mysticism, but do not necessarily teach or require sexual ritual. The New Age practice has discarded much of the original teaching, choosing instead to emphasize sexual ritual as a spiritual act.

TERTIARY: A person (or persons) in a relationship which is generally quite casual, expects little in the way of emotional or practical support, or is very limited with respect to time, energy, or priority in the lives of the people involved. *Contrast* primary; *See related* primary/secondary, secondary. *Commentary:* A **tertiary** relationship may be very limited in scope or priority for many reasons, one of the most common of which is often distance.

TOCOTOX (acronym): *Colloquial* Too Complicated To Explain. Often used as a form of shorthand, particularly in online conversations, when the various interrelationships between the people in a polyamorous relationship can't be described easily.

TRIAD: 1. A polyamorous relationship composed of three people. 2. A union or group of three. *Usage:* In the sense of Def. 1, generally, the word **triad** is most often applied to a relationship in which each of the three people is sexually and emotionally involved with all the other members of the **triad**, as may be the case in a **triad** consisting of one man and two bisexual women or one woman and two **bisexual** men; however, it is sometimes also applied to vee relationships.

TROIKA: A group marriage involving exctly three people. *See related* triad.

TROILISM: Sexual activity involving exactly three people; either in the form of three people simultaneously engaging in sexual activity, or in the form of one person watching while two others have sex. *See related* ménage à trois (Def. 1).

VASOPRESSIN: A hormone produced by the hypothalamus and released by the pituitary gland. Vasopressin is known to be involved in the regulation of blood pressure and the uptake of water by the kidneys, and is also believed to be involved in mediating such responses as aggression and mating. Levels of **vasopressin** in the body rise sharply immediately after sex; it is believed that this may play a role in **new relationship energy**. *See related* oxytocin.

VEE: *Colloquial* A polyamorous relationship involving three people, in which one person is romantically or sexually involved with two partners who are not romantically or sexually involved with each other. *See also* triad, pivot; *See related* quad, N.

VETO: A relationship agreement, most common in prescriptive primary/secondary relationships, which gives one person the power to end another person's additional relationships, or in some cases to disallow some specific activity, such as some specific sexual or BDSM-related activity. A **veto** may be absolute, in which one partner may reject another partner's additional relationships unconditionally, or may be conditional and used more as a way to indicate a serious problem in a relationship. *Commentary:* Not all polyamorous recognize or permit **veto** power. **Veto** is most common in **primary/secondary** relationship configurations, particularly in relationship configurations where an established couple is seeking additional partners. **Veto** is typically limited only to the primary partners, and a relationship which grants a **veto** power to a secondary partner is rare in the extreme.

WIBBLE: A feeling of insecurity, typically temporary or fleeting, when seeing a partner being affectionate with someone else. **Wibbley:** of or related to **wibble,** as *Seeing those two together makes me feel wibbley. Contrast* compersion, frubble. *Usage:* Primarily British; less common outside the United Kingdom.

ZIE: *Colloquial* A proposed gender-neutral pronoun meaning "he" or "she."

ZIR: *Colloquial* A proposed gender-neutral pronoun meaning "him" or "her."

Appendix

Appendix 1: Ideal Partner Profile
Appendix 2: BDSM Worksheet
Appendix 3: Role Play Worksheet
Appendix 4: Spanking Partner Worksheet
Appendix 5: Humiliation Activities Worksheet
Appendix 6: Fetish Consent Worksheet

Ideal Partner Profile

The ideal partner profile allows you to envision the kind of person you would like to meet and date. Clarifying what you find attractive will help you to be more selective when meeting people. It also provides you with topics of conversation—being careful not to treat the interaction as an interview "for the job."

For detailed instructions see the chapter *Choose A Playmate*.

1. **Physical Features/Age Range.** *Describe what really attracts you physically to a person.*

2. **Personality.** *Describe what kind of personality is compatible with yours: friendly, sarcastic, artistic, conservative, etc.*

3. **Sexuality.** *Describe the basic sexual tastes, orientation, and requirements of your ideal partner.*

Ideal Partner Profile (cont.)

4. **Intellect.** *Describe your intellectual ideal. Decide if an intellectual peer is essential or if appearance and personality matter more.*

5. **Social Status.** *Describe the social status of your ideal partner. Will you expect this person to be at home at the opera or rock concerts?*

6. **Religious Beliefs/Spirituality.** *Describe the religious or spiritual background you would like your ideal partner to have.*

7. **Deal Breakers.** *Describe any non-starters. For some people this is smoking, having kids, being divorced, etc.*

Ideal Partner Profile (cont.)

Now let yourself be wildly creative and draw a picture of your ideal partner. It doesn't matter if you're a great artist or not, just give yourself a few visual indicators that will remind you of what you look for. It could be appearance, personality, energy, or whatever matters to you.

This will reinforce your ideal image in your conscious mind. Try it!

BDSM Worksheet

[The following worksheets are adapted from http://tngc.org courtesy of The Next Generation Chicago.] This worksheet facilitates self-awareness and shared communication with a play partner regarding BDSM activities.

For each activity, first say whether you have done the activity (**Yes / No**). Then rate how much you enjoy the activity if you have tried it, or how much you want to try it if you have not.

Rate your interest from 1 to 5 with **1=complete turn-off** and **5=wild turn-on**.

SEX	Experienced		Interest Level				
Anal Sex (get)	Yes	No	1	2	3	4	5
Armpit Sex (get)	Yes	No	1	2	3	4	5
Ass Cheek Sex (get)	Yes	No	1	2	3	4	5
Butt Plugs (get)	Yes	No	1	2	3	4	5
Dildo - Anal (get)	Yes	No	1	2	3	4	5
Dildo - Oral (get)	Yes	No	1	2	3	4	5
Finger Sex (get)	Yes	No	1	2	3	4	5
Genital Intercourse	Yes	No	1	2	3	4	5
Hand Job (give)	Yes	No	1	2	3	4	5
Including Others	Yes	No	1	2	3	4	5
Licking (get)	Yes	No	1	2	3	4	5
Licking (give)	Yes	No	1	2	3	4	5
Massage (give)	Yes	No	1	2	3	4	5
Oral Sex (give)	Yes	No	1	2	3	4	5
Phone Sex	Yes	No	1	2	3	4	5
Sex In Public	Yes	No	1	2	3	4	5
Sex Outdoors	Yes	No	1	2	3	4	5
Swinging	Yes	No	1	2	3	4	5
Teasing (get)	Yes	No	1	2	3	4	5
Vibrators (get)	Yes	No	1	2	3	4	5

BONDAGE	Experienced		Interest Level				
Blindfolds (get)	Yes	No	1	2	3	4	5
Body Bags (get)	Yes	No	1	2	3	4	5
Bondage - full body (get)	Yes	No	1	2	3	4	5
Bondage - Intricate Rope (get)	Yes	No	1	2	3	4	5
Bondage - Mental (get)	Yes	No	1	2	3	4	5
Bondage - Outdoors (get)	Yes	No	1	2	3	4	5
Bondage - Private (get)	Yes	No	1	2	3	4	5
Bondage - Public (get)	Yes	No	1	2	3	4	5
Boxing / Closeting (get)	Yes	No	1	2	3	4	5
Caging (get)	Yes	No	1	2	3	4	5
Cock Bondage (get)	Yes	No	1	2	3	4	5
Crucifixion (get)	Yes	No	1	2	3	4	5

	Experienced		Interest Level				
Cuffs Leather (get)	Yes	No	1	2	3	4	5
Cuffs Metal (get)	Yes	No	1	2	3	4	5
Duct Tape (get)	Yes	No	1	2	3	4	5
Full Head Hoods (get)	Yes	No	1	2	3	4	5
Gags - Ball Type (get)	Yes	No	1	2	3	4	5
Gags - Bits (get)	Yes	No	1	2	3	4	5
Gags - Cloth (get)	Yes	No	1	2	3	4	5
Gags - Inflatable (get)	Yes	No	1	2	3	4	5
Gags - Phallic (get)	Yes	No	1	2	3	4	5
Gags - Tape (get)	Yes	No	1	2	3	4	5
Gas Masks (get)	Yes	No	1	2	3	4	5
Gates of Hell (get)	Yes	No	1	2	3	4	5
Harnessing - Leather(get)	Yes	No	1	2	3	4	5
Harnessing - Rope(get)	Yes	No	1	2	3	4	5
Headphone/Earplugs (get)	Yes	No	1	2	3	4	5
Masks (wear)	Yes	No	1	2	3	4	5
Mummification (get)	Yes	No	1	2	3	4	5
Padlocks (get)	Yes	No	1	2	3	4	5
Plastic Wrap (get)	Yes	No	1	2	3	4	5
Restraint Duration 1-3hrs (get)	Yes	No	1	2	3	4	5
Restraint Duration 3+ hrs (get)	Yes	No	1	2	3	4	5
Restraint Duration Multiple Days (get)	Yes	No	1	2	3	4	5
Restraint Duration Overnight Or Full Day (get)	Yes	No	1	2	3	4	5
Restraint In Public - Under Clothes (get)	Yes	No	1	2	3	4	5
Restraints - Ankle (get)	Yes	No	1	2	3	4	5
Restraints - Arm leg sleeves (get)	Yes	No	1	2	3	4	5
Restraints - Hand Cuffs (get)	Yes	No	1	2	3	4	5
Restraints - Leather (get)	Yes	No	1	2	3	4	5
Restraints - Metal (get)	Yes	No	1	2	3	4	5
Restraints - Rope (get)	Yes	No	1	2	3	4	5
Restraints - Thumb Cuffs (get)	Yes	No	1	2	3	4	5
Restraints - Wrist (get)	Yes	No	1	2	3	4	5
Restraints - Wrist To Ankle/Neck/Waist (get)	Yes	No	1	2	3	4	5
Silk Scarves (get)	Yes	No	1	2	3	4	5
Sleepsacks (get)	Yes	No	1	2	3	4	5
Slings/Swings (get)	Yes	No	1	2	3	4	5
Spreader bars (get)	Yes	No	1	2	3	4	5
St. Andrews Cross	Yes	No	1	2	3	4	5
Stethescope (get)	Yes	No	1	2	3	4	5
Stocks (get)	Yes	No	1	2	3	4	5
Straight Jackets (get)	Yes	No	1	2	3	4	5
Suspension - Horizontal (get)	Yes	No	1	2	3	4	5
Suspension - Inverted (get)	Yes	No	1	2	3	4	5
Suspension (get)	Yes	No	1	2	3	4	5

S&M	Experienced		Interest Level				
Abrasion (get)	Yes	No	1	2	3	4	5
Anal Dilation (get)	Yes	No	1	2	3	4	5
Anal Fisting (get)	Yes	No	1	2	3	4	5
Asphyxiation (get)	Yes	No	1	2	3	4	5
Bastinado (get)	Yes	No	1	2	3	4	5
Beating - Hard (get)	Yes	No	1	2	3	4	5
Beating - Soft (get)	Yes	No	1	2	3	4	5
Belt/Strap (get)	Yes	No	1	2	3	4	5
Biting (get)	Yes	No	1	2	3	4	5
Caning (get)	Yes	No	1	2	3	4	5
Choking (get)	Yes	No	1	2	3	4	5
Clothespins (get)	Yes	No	1	2	3	4	5
Cock and Ball Torture (get)	Yes	No	1	2	3	4	5
Cupping/Suction (get)	Yes	No	1	2	3	4	5
Cutting (get)	Yes	No	1	2	3	4	5
Electricity - Tens Unit (get)	Yes	No	1	2	3	4	5
Electricity - Violet Wand (get)	Yes	No	1	2	3	4	5
Face Slapping (get)	Yes	No	1	2	3	4	5
Fireplay (get)	Yes	No	1	2	3	4	5
Flogging (get)	Yes	No	1	2	3	4	5
Hair pulling (get)	Yes	No	1	2	3	4	5
Hairbrushes (get)	Yes	No	1	2	3	4	5
Hot Oils (get)	Yes	No	1	2	3	4	5
Ice Cubes (get)	Yes	No	1	2	3	4	5
Injections (get)	Yes	No	1	2	3	4	5
Nipple Clamps (get)	Yes	No	1	2	3	4	5
Nipple Torture (get)	Yes	No	1	2	3	4	5
Nipple Weights (get)	Yes	No	1	2	3	4	5
Paddling (get)	Yes	No	1	2	3	4	5
Piercing - Temporary (get)	Yes	No	1	2	3	4	5
Pinching (get)	Yes	No	1	2	3	4	5
Punching (get)	Yes	No	1	2	3	4	5
Riding Crops (get)	Yes	No	1	2	3	4	5
Scratching (get)	Yes	No	1	2	3	4	5
Spanking - On All Fours (get)	Yes	No	1	2	3	4	5
Spanking - Over Knee (get)	Yes	No	1	2	3	4	5
Spanking Hard (get)	Yes	No	1	2	3	4	5
Spanking Soft (get)	Yes	No	1	2	3	4	5
Strapping - Full Body (get)	Yes	No	1	2	3	4	5
Urethral Sounds (get)	Yes	No	1	2	3	4	5
Whipping - Buggywhip (get)	Yes	No	1	2	3	4	5
Whipping - Bullwhip (get)	Yes	No	1	2	3	4	5
Whipping - Cat (get)	Yes	No	1	2	3	4	5
Whipping - Genitals (get)	Yes	No	1	2	3	4	5
Whipping - Knotted Whip (get)	Yes	No	1	2	3	4	5
Whipping - Quirt (get)	Yes	No	1	2	3	4	5
Whipping - Signal Whip (get)	Yes	No	1	2	3	4	5
Whipping - Switch (get)	Yes	No	1	2	3	4	5
Whipping - Taws (get)	Yes	No	1	2	3	4	5

FETISH	Experienced		Interest Level				
Abandonment (get)	Yes	No	1	2	3	4	5
Acrophilia	Yes	No	1	2	3	4	5
Acrotomophilia	Yes	No	1	2	3	4	5
Agalmatophilia	Yes	No	1	2	3	4	5
Barosmia	Yes	No	1	2	3	4	5
Being Recorded	Yes	No	1	2	3	4	5
Bestiality (others)	Yes	No	1	2	3	4	5
Bestiality (you)	Yes	No	1	2	3	4	5
Body Worship (give)	Yes	No	1	2	3	4	5
Boot Worship (get)	Yes	No	1	2	3	4	5
Branding (sub)	Yes	No	1	2	3	4	5
Brown Showers (get)	Yes	No	1	2	3	4	5
Brown Showers (give)	Yes	No	1	2	3	4	5
Castration Fantasy	Yes	No	1	2	3	4	5
Catheterization (get)	Yes	No	1	2	3	4	5
Chamber Pots (use)	Yes	No	1	2	3	4	5
Cock Rings (others)	Yes	No	1	2	3	4	5
Cock Rings (you)	Yes	No	1	2	3	4	5
Corsets (others)	Yes	No	1	2	3	4	5
Corsets (you)	Yes	No	1	2	3	4	5
Cross-Dressing (others)	Yes	No	1	2	3	4	5
Cross-Dressing (you)	Yes	No	1	2	3	4	5
Diapers (you)	Yes	No	1	2	3	4	5
Dirty Sex	Yes	No	1	2	3	4	5
Douching (get)	Yes	No	1	2	3	4	5
Enemas (get)	Yes	No	1	2	3	4	5
Erotic Dancing (sub)	Yes	No	1	2	3	4	5
Exhibitionism	Yes	No	1	2	3	4	5
Fear	Yes	No	1	2	3	4	5
Feathers/Fur (others)	Yes	No	1	2	3	4	5
Feathers/Fur (you)	Yes	No	1	2	3	4	5
Foot Worship (get)	Yes	No	1	2	3	4	5
Golden Showers (get)	Yes	No	1	2	3	4	5
Gun Play	Yes	No	1	2	3	4	5
High Heel Worship (get)	Yes	No	1	2	3	4	5
Humiliation (get)	Yes	No	1	2	3	4	5
Infantilism (others)	Yes	No	1	2	3	4	5
Latex (others)	Yes	No	1	2	3	4	5
Latex (you)	Yes	No	1	2	3	4	5
Leather (others)	Yes	No	1	2	3	4	5
Leather (you)	Yes	No	1	2	3	4	5
Lingerie (others)	Yes	No	1	2	3	4	5
Lingerie (you)	Yes	No	1	2	3	4	5
Medical Instruments	Yes	No	1	2	3	4	5
Needles	Yes	No	1	2	3	4	5
Oral/Anal Play (get)	Yes	No	1	2	3	4	5
Pain	Yes	No	1	2	3	4	5
Piercing (Permanent) (get)	Yes	No	1	2	3	4	5
Posing for Erotic Photos	Yes	No	1	2	3	4	5
Prostitution (real)	Yes	No	1	2	3	4	5
Public Exposure	Yes	No	1	2	3	4	5
PVC (others)	Yes	No	1	2	3	4	5
PVC (you)	Yes	No	1	2	3	4	5

RITUALS	Experienced		Interest Level				
Sensory Deprivation (get)	Yes	No	1	2	3	4	5
Shaving (get)	Yes	No	1	2	3	4	5
Skinny-Dipping	Yes	No	1	2	3	4	5
Spandex (others)	Yes	No	1	2	3	4	5
Spandex (you)	Yes	No	1	2	3	4	5
Speculums (anal)	Yes	No	1	2	3	4	5
Spitting	Yes	No	1	2	3	4	5
Supplying Victims	Yes	No	1	2	3	4	5
Swallowing Semen	Yes	No	1	2	3	4	5
Taking Erotic Photos	Yes	No	1	2	3	4	5
Tasting Yourself	Yes	No	1	2	3	4	5
Tattoo (others)	Yes	No	1	2	3	4	5
Tattoos (you)	Yes	No	1	2	3	4	5
Tickling (get)	Yes	No	1	2	3	4	5
Uniforms (others)	Yes	No	1	2	3	4	5
Uniforms (you)	Yes	No	1	2	3	4	5
Voyeurism	Yes	No	1	2	3	4	5
Wearing Fluids	Yes	No	1	2	3	4	5
Wrestling	Yes	No	1	2	3	4	5

ROLE PLAY	Experienced		Interest Level				
Chauffeuring (sub)	Yes	No	1	2	3	4	5
Fantasy Gang Rape (get)	Yes	No	1	2	3	4	5
Fantasy Rape (get)	Yes	No	1	2	3	4	5
Initiation Rites (sub)	Yes	No	1	2	3	4	5
Interrogations (sub)	Yes	No	1	2	3	4	5
Kidnapping (sub)	Yes	No	1	2	3	4	5
Medical Scenes (sub)	Yes	No	1	2	3	4	5
Other Animal Play (sub)	Yes	No	1	2	3	4	5
Physical Examinations (sub)	Yes	No	1	2	3	4	5
Pony Play (sub)	Yes	No	1	2	3	4	5
Prison Scenes	Yes	No	1	2	3	4	5
Prostitution (pretend)	Yes	No	1	2	3	4	5
Punishment Scene (sub)	Yes	No	1	2	3	4	5
Puppy Play (sub)	Yes	No	1	2	3	4	5
Religious Scenes (sub)	Yes	No	1	2	3	4	5
Schoolroom Scenes (sub)	Yes	No	1	2	3	4	5
Serving as Art (sub)	Yes	No	1	2	3	4	5
Serving as Ashtray (sub)	Yes	No	1	2	3	4	5
Serving as Furniture (sub)	Yes	No	1	2	3	4	5
Serving as Maid (sub)	Yes	No	1	2	3	4	5
Strap on Dildos (sub)	Yes	No	1	2	3	4	5

POWER PLAY	Experienced		Interest Level				
Bathroom Use Control (sub)	Yes	No	1	2	3	4	5
Begging (sub)	Yes	No	1	2	3	4	5
Behavior Restrictive Rules (sub)	Yes	No	1	2	3	4	5
Butt Plugs - Public (sub)	Yes	No	1	2	3	4	5
Chastity Belts (sub)	Yes	No	1	2	3	4	5
Clothing Choice (sub)	Yes	No	1	2	3	4	5
Cock Worship (sub)	Yes	No	1	2	3	4	5
Collar and Leash (sub)	Yes	No	1	2	3	4	5
Collars (sub)	Yes	No	1	2	3	4	5
Competition (sub)	Yes	No	1	2	3	4	5
Crawling (sub)	Yes	No	1	2	3	4	5
Eye Contact Restriction (sub)	Yes	No	1	2	3	4	5
Following Orders	Yes	No	1	2	3	4	5
Food Choice/Directed Eating (sub)	Yes	No	1	2	3	4	5
Forced Dressing (sub)	Yes	No	1	2	3	4	5
Forced Exercise (sub)	Yes	No	1	2	3	4	5
Forced Homosexuality (sub)	Yes	No	1	2	3	4	5
Forced Masturbation (sub)	Yes	No	1	2	3	4	5
Forced Nudity (sub)	Yes	No	1	2	3	4	5
Forced Servitude (sub)	Yes	No	1	2	3	4	5
Given Away	Yes	No	1	2	3	4	5
Hot or Sensual Waxing (sub)	Yes	No	1	2	3	4	5
Housework (sub)	Yes	No	1	2	3	4	5
Humiliation - Private (sub)	Yes	No	1	2	3	4	5
Humiliation - Public (sub)	Yes	No	1	2	3	4	5
Humiliation - Verbal (sub)	Yes	No	1	2	3	4	5
Kneeling (sub)	Yes	No	1	2	3	4	5
Lecturing (sub)	Yes	No	1	2	3	4	5
Manicures (get)	Yes	No	1	2	3	4	5
Manicures (give)	Yes	No	1	2	3	4	5
Name Change (sub)	Yes	No	1	2	3	4	5
Orgasm Control (sub)	Yes	No	1	2	3	4	5
Orgasm Denial (sub)	Yes	No	1	2	3	4	5
Personality Modification (sub)	Yes	No	1	2	3	4	5
Pussy Worship (sub)	Yes	No	1	2	3	4	5
Serving Orally (sub)	Yes	No	1	2	3	4	5
Sexual Deprivation (sub)	Yes	No	1	2	3	4	5
Sleep Deprivation (sub)	Yes	No	1	2	3	4	5
Speech Restrictions (sub)	Yes	No	1	2	3	4	5
Standing in Corner (sub)	Yes	No	1	2	3	4	5
Struggling (sub)	Yes	No	1	2	3	4	5
Symbolic Jewelry (sub)	Yes	No	1	2	3	4	5
Weight Gain/Loss (sub)	Yes	No	1	2	3	4	5

Role Play Worksheet

This worksheet allows you to identify your main interests as well as those things you're uncomfortable with, including activities that are off-limits. These questions are intended to be answered by a bottom (sub) but a top (dom) can use it by imagining themselves on the giving side of the scenario.

For each activity, first say whether you have done the activity (**Yes / No**). Then rate how much you enjoy the activity if you have tried it, or how much you want to try it if you have not.

Rate your interest from 1 to 5 with **1=complete turn-off** and **5=wild turn-on**.

These specific types of people turn me on

	Experienced		Interest Level				
Airmen, Pilots	Yes	No	1	2	3	4	5
Business People, Yuppies, Managers	Yes	No	1	2	3	4	5
Cowboys, Farm Boys	Yes	No	1	2	3	4	5
Daddy, Uncle	Yes	No	1	2	3	4	5
Executioners	Yes	No	1	2	3	4	5
Firemen	Yes	No	1	2	3	4	5
Gentlemen, Nobility	Yes	No	1	2	3	4	5
Hunters	Yes	No	1	2	3	4	5
Motorcycle People, Hells Angels	Yes	No	1	2	3	4	5
Nurses, Doctors	Yes	No	1	2	3	4	5
Policemen, Security People	Yes	No	1	2	3	4	5
Prostitutes, Tramps	Yes	No	1	2	3	4	5
Sailors, Coast Guard, Merchant Marine	Yes	No	1	2	3	4	5
Servants	Yes	No	1	2	3	4	5
Soldiers, Marines, Paratroopers	Yes	No	1	2	3	4	5
Surfers, Life Guards	Yes	No	1	2	3	4	5
Teachers	Yes	No	1	2	3	4	5
Truck Drivers	Yes	No	1	2	3	4	5
Wrestlers	Yes	No	1	2	3	4	5
Other: _____	Yes	No	1	2	3	4	5

These articles of clothing or fabrics turn me on

	Experienced		Interest Level				
Boots	Yes	No	1	2	3	4	5
Denim	Yes	No	1	2	3	4	5
High Heels	Yes	No	1	2	3	4	5
Leather	Yes	No	1	2	3	4	5
Masks	Yes	No	1	2	3	4	5
Patent Leather, PVC	Yes	No	1	2	3	4	5
Rubber, Latex	Yes	No	1	2	3	4	5
Servants Uniform	Yes	No	1	2	3	4	5
Sexy Lingerie	Yes	No	1	2	3	4	5
Uniforms	Yes	No	1	2	3	4	5
Wet Suits	Yes	No	1	2	3	4	5
Other: _____	Yes	No	1	2	3	4	5

These scenes turn me on | Experienced | Interest Level

Scene	Experienced	Interest Level
A stranger walks into my bedroom and finds me playing with myself	Yes No	1 2 3 4 5
Being in a public place and dominated in a subtle way	Yes No	1 2 3 4 5
Being locked up and left alone	Yes No	1 2 3 4 5
Being spanked in the traditional way	Yes No	1 2 3 4 5
Being taken out with collar and leash	Yes No	1 2 3 4 5
Being tied and tortured	Yes No	1 2 3 4 5
Being tied up and (in a sexual way) exposed	Yes No	1 2 3 4 5
Being tied up and (sexually) teased	Yes No	1 2 3 4 5
Being tied up and tickled	Yes No	1 2 3 4 5
Being tied up and whipped, flogged or caned	Yes No	1 2 3 4 5
Being tied up in a comfortable position	Yes No	1 2 3 4 5
Being tied up in discomfort	Yes No	1 2 3 4 5
Being tied up, caressed and loved	Yes No	1 2 3 4 5
Being tortured without being tied or cuffed	Yes No	1 2 3 4 5
Being used by more than one dominant	Yes No	1 2 3 4 5
Caned, flogged or whipped without being tied or cuffed	Yes No	1 2 3 4 5
Having a romantic dinner by candlelight	Yes No	1 2 3 4 5
I am a little schoolgirl	Yes No	1 2 3 4 5
I am a total slave every day of the week	Yes No	1 2 3 4 5
I am are sold on a slave market	Yes No	1 2 3 4 5
I am are tied and teased	Yes No	1 2 3 4 5
I am grabbed by the hair and dragged into the bedroom	Yes No	1 2 3 4 5
I am in the woods and suddenly this man comes from behind and grabs me	Yes No	1 2 3 4 5
I am ordered to please others	Yes No	1 2 3 4 5
I am sitting/kneeling at my Master's feet	Yes No	1 2 3 4 5
I am spanked because I have been a naughty girl	Yes No	1 2 3 4 5
I am tied, gagged and blindfolded and left alone	Yes No	1 2 3 4 5
I am tied, gagged, blindfolded and thoroughly whipped	Yes No	1 2 3 4 5
I am used as a dog, pony or pet	Yes No	1 2 3 4 5
I am used as a slave in private	Yes No	1 2 3 4 5
I am used as a slave in public	Yes No	1 2 3 4 5
I am verbally humiliated	Yes No	1 2 3 4 5
I have to sign a contract	Yes No	1 2 3 4 5
My mental limits are tested and stretched	Yes No	1 2 3 4 5
My partner and I are making love in a public place	Yes No	1 2 3 4 5
My physical limits are tested and stretched	Yes No	1 2 3 4 5
Not being tied up, but verbally commanded into certain positions and having to maintain these	Yes No	1 2 3 4 5
Playing in combination with other couples	Yes No	1 2 3 4 5
Rough sex/being "raped"	Yes No	1 2 3 4 5
Used as a servant	Yes No	1 2 3 4 5
Other: _____	Yes No	1 2 3 4 5

These environments or scenery turn me on

	Experienced		Interest Level				
A dungeon, castle	Yes	No	1	2	3	4	5
A school or a classroom	Yes	No	1	2	3	4	5
Abandoned construction sites	Yes	No	1	2	3	4	5
Back alleys	Yes	No	1	2	3	4	5
Barracks	Yes	No	1	2	3	4	5
BDSM-clubs	Yes	No	1	2	3	4	5
Boot camp	Yes	No	1	2	3	4	5
Churches and abbeys	Yes	No	1	2	3	4	5
Estates	Yes	No	1	2	3	4	5
Farms and stables	Yes	No	1	2	3	4	5
Hospital, dentist	Yes	No	1	2	3	4	5
Interrogation room	Yes	No	1	2	3	4	5
Jail, police station	Yes	No	1	2	3	4	5
Junkyards and car dumps	Yes	No	1	2	3	4	5
Medieval scenery	Yes	No	1	2	3	4	5
Nudist beaches	Yes	No	1	2	3	4	5
Parking spaces	Yes	No	1	2	3	4	5
The bath room	Yes	No	1	2	3	4	5
The red light district	Yes	No	1	2	3	4	5
The shrink's couch	Yes	No	1	2	3	4	5
Truck stops	Yes	No	1	2	3	4	5
Woods and forests	Yes	No	1	2	3	4	5
Your bedroom	Yes	No	1	2	3	4	5
Other: _____	Yes	No	1	2	3	4	5

I enjoy the following psychodramas

	Experienced		Interest Level				
Dialogue in adapted language ("Master" and "slave")	Yes	No	1	2	3	4	5
Dialogue in normal language	Yes	No	1	2	3	4	5
I like to be persuaded, rather than commanded	Yes	No	1	2	3	4	5
It is OK for the dominant to loose his temper	Yes	No	1	2	3	4	5
Make me feel cheap	Yes	No	1	2	3	4	5
Make me feel guilty	Yes	No	1	2	3	4	5
Make me feel owned	Yes	No	1	2	3	4	5
Make me feel used	Yes	No	1	2	3	4	5
Make me feel useless	Yes	No	1	2	3	4	5
Military/jail type commands	Yes	No	1	2	3	4	5
Obey rules or else	Yes	No	1	2	3	4	5
Objectify me	Yes	No	1	2	3	4	5
Obvious and explicit role play	Yes	No	1	2	3	4	5
Reasonable rules	Yes	No	1	2	3	4	5
Strict training	Yes	No	1	2	3	4	5
Subtle role play	Yes	No	1	2	3	4	5
Swearing and filthy talk	Yes	No	1	2	3	4	5
The dominant must have compassion	Yes	No	1	2	3	4	5
The dominant must have no compassion at all	Yes	No	1	2	3	4	5
The dominant must only have compassion after the scene	Yes	No	1	2	3	4	5
The dominant talks, the submissive is silent or speaks only when spoken to	Yes	No	1	2	3	4	5
Unreasonable rules	Yes	No	1	2	3	4	5
Other: _____	Yes	No	1	2	3	4	5

I prefer these sex and sexuality elements

	Experienced		Interest Level				
An orgasm is a must to end the scene	Yes	No	1	2	3	4	5
An orgasm must only be allowed as a reward	Yes	No	1	2	3	4	5
An orgasm turns me off	Yes	No	1	2	3	4	5
I like as many orgasms as I can get	Yes	No	1	2	3	4	5
I need to be sexually aroused before I enter into a scene	Yes	No	1	2	3	4	5
I need to be sexually aroused when in scene	Yes	No	1	2	3	4	5
I want my sexual abilities to be stretched	Yes	No	1	2	3	4	5
I want no sex during a scene	Yes	No	1	2	3	4	5
I want to beg for an orgasm first	Yes	No	1	2	3	4	5
I want/need sex during a scene	Yes	No	1	2	3	4	5
Orgasms are not important at all	Yes	No	1	2	3	4	5
Orgasms are not important, but nice	Yes	No	1	2	3	4	5
Sex should be used to relieve the tension	Yes	No	1	2	3	4	5
Other: _____	Yes	No	1	2	3	4	5

I love these toys and props

	Experienced		Interest Level				
Ball And Chain	Yes	No	1	2	3	4	5
Blindfold	Yes	No	1	2	3	4	5
Body Bag	Yes	No	1	2	3	4	5
Bondage Table	Yes	No	1	2	3	4	5
Cage	Yes	No	1	2	3	4	5
Canes	Yes	No	1	2	3	4	5
Cross, Rack	Yes	No	1	2	3	4	5
Gags	Yes	No	1	2	3	4	5
Leather Cuffs And Belts	Yes	No	1	2	3	4	5
Masks	Yes	No	1	2	3	4	5
Needles And Pins	Yes	No	1	2	3	4	5
Nipple Clamps And Clothespins	Yes	No	1	2	3	4	5
Riding Crops	Yes	No	1	2	3	4	5
Ropes	Yes	No	1	2	3	4	5
Sex Toys (Vibrators, Butt Plugs)	Yes	No	1	2	3	4	5
Silk To Be Tied With	Yes	No	1	2	3	4	5
Sling	Yes	No	1	2	3	4	5
Steel Cuffs And Chains	Yes	No	1	2	3	4	5
Whips	Yes	No	1	2	3	4	5
Other: _____	Yes	No	1	2	3	4	5

Safe words and signals

A scene should go on up to the point where I use a safe word or signal	Yes	No
All activity should stop immediately when I use a safe word or signal	Yes	No
I do not want to use any safe word at all and my signals should be ignored completely	Yes	No
I should be able to communicate in plain language	Yes	No
I want to be tested when I use a safe word or signal	Yes	No
The dominant should be able to read my body language	Yes	No
The dominant should establish one or more safe words	Yes	No
The use of safe words and signals should be avoided as much as possible	Yes	No
When I cry, the scene should stop	Yes	No
When I use a safe word or signal the dominant should establish if the scene can continue	Yes	No
Other: _____	Yes	No

To me erotic power exchange is

A lifestyle that I consider important and want to practice as much as possible	Yes	No
A lifestyle that should be present at all times	Yes	No
My way of life	Yes	No
Something I like incidentally, just as a kick	Yes	No
Something I like, but not too often	Yes	No
Something I want as much as possible	Yes	No
Something I want exercised at all times and no matter what the consequences are.	Yes	No
The most important thing I can think of	Yes	No
Other: _____	Yes	No

How To Start a Kinky Relationship

Spanking Partner Worksheet

This worksheet facilitates communication regarding Domestic Discipline (DD) lifestyles. The worksheet is completed by the spankee for the spanker's use. The list can also be filled out by the spanker for ideas and to indicate interest, then reviewed with the spankee.

For each activity, first say whether you have done the activity (**Yes / No**). Then rate how much you enjoy the activity if you have tried it, or how much you want to try it if you have not.

Rate your interest from 1 to 5 with **1=complete turn-off** and **5=wild turn-on**.

TYPE	Experienced		Interest Level				
Discipline	Yes	No	1	2	3	4	5
Erotic	Yes	No	1	2	3	4	5
Fun	Yes	No	1	2	3	4	5
Just Because	Yes	No	1	2	3	4	5
Sensual	Yes	No	1	2	3	4	5

CLOTHING	Experienced		Interest Level				
Bare Bottom	Yes	No	1	2	3	4	5
Completely Nude	Yes	No	1	2	3	4	5
Nightgown & Bare Bottom	Yes	No	1	2	3	4	5
Over Clothing	Yes	No	1	2	3	4	5
Over Panties	Yes	No	1	2	3	4	5
Over Panties Then To Bare	Yes	No	1	2	3	4	5
Tight Teddy Hiked Up Crack	Yes	No	1	2	3	4	5

POSITIONS	Experienced		Interest Level				
Bent Over Edge Of Bed	Yes	No	1	2	3	4	5
Bent Over Straight Back Chair	Yes	No	1	2	3	4	5
OTK / Spanker's Right Leg Over Spankee's Legs, Holding Wrists Behind Back (If Right Handed)	Yes	No	1	2	3	4	5
OTK/Spanker Sitting In Straight Back Chair	Yes	No	1	2	3	4	5
Over Arm Of Sofa/Chair	Yes	No	1	2	3	4	5
Over Back Of Sofa/Chair	Yes	No	1	2	3	4	5
Over Kitchen Table	Yes	No	1	2	3	4	5
Over Lap On Bed Or Sofa	Yes	No	1	2	3	4	5
Over Spanking Horse (For Enthusiasts)	Yes	No	1	2	3	4	5
Spankee Laying On Bed With Pillows To Raise The Bottom	Yes	No	1	2	3	4	5
Whipping Post	Yes	No	1	2	3	4	5

IMPLEMENTS	Experienced		Interest Level				
Bath Brush	Yes	No	1	2	3	4	5
Belt/Strap	Yes	No	1	2	3	4	5
Birch Rod Soaked In Brine	Yes	No	1	2	3	4	5
Cane	Yes	No	1	2	3	4	5
Flogger	Yes	No	1	2	3	4	5
Hairbrush	Yes	No	1	2	3	4	5
Hand	Yes	No	1	2	3	4	5
Leather Paddle	Yes	No	1	2	3	4	5
Oven Shovel	Yes	No	1	2	3	4	5
Paddle With Holes/Without	Yes	No	1	2	3	4	5
Paddle Wooden/Acrylic	Yes	No	1	2	3	4	5
Riding Crop	Yes	No	1	2	3	4	5
Rubber Hose	Yes	No	1	2	3	4	5
Rubber Spatula	Yes	No	1	2	3	4	5
Sandal/Slipper	Yes	No	1	2	3	4	5
Switch	Yes	No	1	2	3	4	5
Tawse	Yes	No	1	2	3	4	5
Wooden Ruler	Yes	No	1	2	3	4	5
Wooden Spoon	Yes	No	1	2	3	4	5
Yardstick	Yes	No	1	2	3	4	5

POST SPANKING / AFTERCARE	Experienced		Interest Level				
Corner Time	Yes	No	1	2	3	4	5
Hugs/Cuddling	Yes	No	1	2	3	4	5
Photograph Of Marks	Yes	No	1	2	3	4	5
Sex	Yes	No	1	2	3	4	5
Sitting On Lap	Yes	No	1	2	3	4	5
Spankee Feeling Guilt Free	Yes	No	1	2	3	4	5
Spankee Feeling Love, Cherished, Protected & Secure	Yes	No	1	2	3	4	5
Spankee Required To Thank Spanker	Yes	No	1	2	3	4	5

EXTRAS	Experienced		Interest Level				
Corner Time	Yes	No	1	2	3	4	5
Corner Time W/Hands On Head	Yes	No	1	2	3	4	5
Corner Time While Holding Implement	Yes	No	1	2	3	4	5
Counting Strokes	Yes	No	1	2	3	4	5
Fetching The Switch	Yes	No	1	2	3	4	5
Flurries	Yes	No	1	2	3	4	5
Following Orders	Yes	No	1	2	3	4	5
Following The Spanking But While Still Over Lap Having The Red And Tender Bottom Cheeks Coated With Ben-Gay To Reinforce The Sting.	Yes	No	1	2	3	4	5
Hands During Spanking: Behind Head / Back / On Floor	Yes	No	1	2	3	4	5
Lectures/Scolding	Yes	No	1	2	3	4	5
Mouth Washing	Yes	No	1	2	3	4	5
Mouth Washing Done In Middle Of If Used During Spanking	Yes	No	1	2	3	4	5
No Clothes For 24 Hours	Yes	No	1	2	3	4	5
Penalties [Extra Swats] (Not Following Orders / Missing Count / Covering Up / Moving Out Of Position)	Yes	No	1	2	3	4	5
Phone Call Earlier In Day........Telling What Is To Come	Yes	No	1	2	3	4	5
Phrases Used	Yes	No	1	2	3	4	5
Required To Address The Spanker As Sir/Or Other Name	Yes	No	1	2	3	4	5
Restraints	Yes	No	1	2	3	4	5
Rubbing Bottom	Yes	No	1	2	3	4	5
Safe Word	Yes	No	1	2	3	4	5
Scolding Before/During	Yes	No	1	2	3	4	5
Sent To Bed Early	Yes	No	1	2	3	4	5
Shop For Implements Together	Yes	No	1	2	3	4	5
Spankee Explaining Why They Are Receiving Correction	Yes	No	1	2	3	4	5
Spankee Holds Implement During Hand Spanking And Then Hands Implement To Spanker	Yes	No	1	2	3	4	5
Spankee Ordered To Bare Bottom	Yes	No	1	2	3	4	5
Spankee Ordered To Retrieve Implement	Yes	No	1	2	3	4	5
Spankee Required To Ask For A Spanking	Yes	No	1	2	3	4	5
Spankee Required To Pay For Implements	Yes	No	1	2	3	4	5
Spankee Required To Show Spanker Condition Of Their Bottom By Dropping Panties (One Hour Afterwards Or Next Morning)	Yes	No	1	2	3	4	5
Spanker Baring Bottom	Yes	No	1	2	3	4	5
Stripped	Yes	No	1	2	3	4	5
Told What To Expect Ahead Of Time	Yes	No	1	2	3	4	5
Wearing A Sign "I Have Been Spanked For Being A Bad Girl/Boy."	Yes	No	1	2	3	4	5

Humiliation Activities Worksheet

This worksheet facilitates a conversation about what kind of humiliation activities a dom and a sub would like to participate in.

Note: Please avoid inflicting kinky values on people in the vanilla world. Avoid humiliation in settings such a restaurants or supermarkets if there is the possibility of a vanilla person seeing this.

Act as objects (furniture, etc.)
After orgasm, making sub drink his own cum
Age play
Always address you Sir, ma'am, etc.
Anal plugs
Baby pacifier tied around neck
Bathroom use control
Bathroom use in front of others
Become a human ashtray
Beg for cigarettes, drinks, etc.
Blindfolds
Boot worship at odd moments
Cage display
Cage display and ignore them
Carrying a doll or toy around
Cavity check in private
Cavity check in public
Clip on earrings that don't match
Crawl on all 4s
Cum or urinate into their food.
Curse words (Whore, Slut, Worthless, etc.)
Curtsy in public
Dancing/ stripped tease
Dom chooses cloths
Dom chooses food
Dom urinates into water, while sub is taking a bath
Eat from a pet dish
Eat from floor
Eat without utensils
Embarrassing positions
Enema
Eye contact restrictions
Feed submissive from hand
Feeding the food in restaurant (Remember: public discretion)
Feminine necklace exposed (for males)
Foot worship
Forced cross dressing
Forced bestiality (Not for everyone, this is a hard limit for most)
Forced dressing
Forced exercising
Forced masturbation in odd places
Forced nudity
Forced shopping for pantyhose: ask clerk "Would this fit me" (male)
Forced slave auction
Forced to be a slave
Forced to go to bathroom in front of others
Forced to sell lemonade in the street like a kid for .10 cents
Forced to wear a leash
Forced to wear a sign (slut, etc.)
Golden shower
Handcuffed to a shopping cart while shopping
Handcuffs in public

Harem--serving w/other(s)
Hood
Human garbage can
Immobilization
Lead on leash while having a rubber bone in the mouth
Leave bathroom door opened
Leave note with embracing instructions
Made to urinate in front of others into a cat liter box
Made to walk the streets in a Red Light District
Maid services
Make sub wear underwear that you've urinated on
Mask
Nipple clamps under see thru top
Orgasm control
Orgasm denial
Pantyhose work with shorts (male)
Pet play (forced sex w/pet)
Pet roles (act like a dog, cat, etc.)
Record real embarrassing sessions and make them watch it
Scat Play
Scolding
Send shopping with note and hand it to clerk.
Serve as toilet
Serve others (supervised)
Serve others (unsupervised)
Shave body hair
Shave head
Shave pubic hair
Slap face
Slave tattoos (temporary)
Spanking (public)
Speech restriction
Spell "Slave" with suntan lotion & get tan
Spitting in face
Stand in corner
Suck dildo in car, so others can see
Swallow urine
Take Pictures
Take Video
Undress in front of others
Verbal Abuse
Wear Collar everywhere
Wear Masters cum on your face without wiping
Wear T-shirt that says "I'm a sissy boy, I belong to Master", etc.
Wear a bra and get a tan (males)
Wear clothes that are ripped
Wear diapers
Wear no bra under see thru top
Wear no panties under see thru clothes
Wear unmatching clothes
Write on body (slut, sissy, etc.)

Fetish Consent Worksheet

This worksheet facilitates open communication regarding fetish activities between a top (master) and a bottom (slave). By consenting to participate in various fetish acts, both individuals can move forward in their sexual exploration with a clear idea of what each one expects. It's a tool to open discussion between partners and a chance for master and slave to create boundaries, establish limits. and generally feel comfortable in their chosen roles.

FETISH ACTIVITIES I AGREE TO

Yes	No	Maybe	Anal sex and/or rimming	Yes	No	Maybe	Light bondage using scarves, light rope, etc.
Yes	No	Maybe	Biting	Yes	No	Maybe	Massage
Yes	No	Maybe	Blindfolds	Yes	No	Maybe	Needle play
Yes	No	Maybe	Branding	Yes	No	Maybe	Nipple torture, clamps etc.
Yes	No	Maybe	Cock and ball torture, clamps, etc.	Yes	No	Maybe	Oral sex
Yes	No	Maybe	Collar/leash	Yes	No	Maybe	Pinching
Yes	No	Maybe	Confinement	Yes	No	Maybe	Pussy and/or cock worship
Yes	No	Maybe	Cross dressing	Yes	No	Maybe	Role playing
Yes	No	Maybe	Defilement: seeing a partner dirty or wet	Yes	No	Maybe	Scat
Yes	No	Maybe	Depilation/shaving	Yes	No	Maybe	Sensory deprivation
Yes	No	Maybe	Discipline	Yes	No	Maybe	Sensual waxing
Yes	No	Maybe	Enemas	Yes	No	Maybe	Sex during menstruation
Yes	No	Maybe	Exhibitionism/sex in public	Yes	No	Maybe	Spanking
Yes	No	Maybe	Feet worship	Yes	No	Maybe	Taking photographs for private use
Yes	No	Maybe	Filming for private use	Yes	No	Maybe	Talking dirty
Yes	No	Maybe	Fire play	Yes	No	Maybe	The rack/medieval devices
Yes	No	Maybe	Fisting	Yes	No	Maybe	Tickling
Yes	No	Maybe	Food play	Yes	No	Maybe	Toys such as anal beads or Ben Wa balls
Yes	No	Maybe	Heavy bondage: handcuffs, shackles, etc.	Yes	No	Maybe	Toys such as vibrators, dildos, or eggs
Yes	No	Maybe	High heels/boots	Yes	No	Maybe	Voyeurism
Yes	No	Maybe	Hot candle wax	Yes	No	Maybe	Water sports/urine
Yes	No	Maybe	Humiliation	Yes	No	Maybe	Whipping
Yes	No	Maybe	Infantilism/diapers	Yes	No	Maybe	OTHER: _____
Yes	No	Maybe	Knife play	Yes	No	Maybe	OTHER: _____
Yes	No	Maybe	Leather, fur or other texture stimulation	Yes	No	Maybe	OTHER: _____

MASTER'S CONDITIONS

_____
_____
_____
_____
_____

SLAVE'S CONDITIONS

_____
_____
_____
_____
_____

MASTER'S SIGNATURE
_____

SLAVE'S SIGNATURE
_____

35040099R00134

Made in the USA
Lexington, KY
28 August 2014